P9-CNH-184

UNKNOWN

VALOR

UNKNOWN

VALOR

★

A Story of Family, Courage, and Sacrifice
from Pearl Harbor to Iwo Jima

MARTHA MACCALLUM

with Ronald J. Drez

HARPER

NEW YORK · LONDON · TORONTO · SYDNEY

HARPER

Map on page ix of the Pacific and Adjacent Theaters, 1942, courtesy of the U.S. Army Center of Military History.

A hardcover edition of this book was published in 2020 by HarperCollins Publishers.

UNKNOWN VALOR. Copyright © 2020 by Martha MacCallum. All rights reserved. Printed in the United States of America. No part of this book may be used or reproduced in any manner whatsoever without written permission except in the case of brief quotations embodied in critical articles and reviews. For information, address HarperCollins Publishers, 195 Broadway, New York, NY 10007.

HarperCollins books may be purchased for educational, business, or sales promotional use. For information, please email the Special Markets Department at SPsales@harpercollins.com.

FIRST HARPER PAPERBACKS EDITION PUBLISHED 2021.

Designed by Elina Cohen

Library of Congress Control Number: 2020931372

ISBN 978-0-06-285386-8 (pbk.)

21 22 23 24 25 LSC 10 9 8 7 6 5 4 3 2 1

For Dan, Elizabeth, Reed, and Harry

Among the Americans who served on Iwo Island, uncommon valor was a common virtue.

—Admiral Chester W. Nimitz

"Greater love than this no man hath," said Our Savior, "that a man lay down his life for his friends." And the soldier who dies to save his brothers, and to defend the hearths and altars of his country, reaches this highest of all degrees of charity.

—Cardinal Mercier's Pastoral Letter, as quoted by G. B. Erskine, Major General Commanding, 3rd Marine Division

Contents

Contents

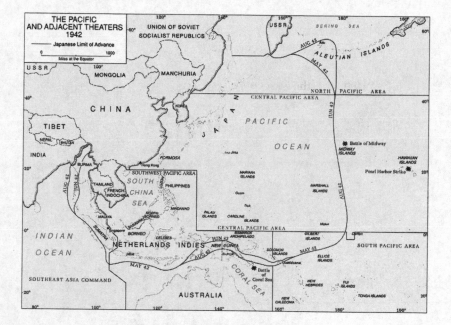

THE PACIFIC
AND ADJACENT THEATERS
1942

——— Japanese Limit of Advance

0   1800
Miles at the Equator

UNION OF SOVIET
SOCIALIST REPUBLICS

USSR

BERING SEA

ALEUTIAN ISLANDS

USSR

MONGOLIA   MANCHURIA

NORTH   PACIFIC   AREA

CHINA

CENTRAL PACIFIC AREA

TIBET

NEPAL BHUTAN

JAPAN

PACIFIC

INDIA

BURMA

FORMOSA

OCEAN

Battle of Midway
MIDWAY
ISLANDS

Iwo Jima

Hong Kong

Pearl Harbor Strike

HAWAIIAN
ISLANDS

SOUTHWEST PACIFIC AREA

THAILAND
FRENCH
INDOCHINA

SOUTH
CHINA
SEA

PHILIPPINES

MARIANA
ISLANDS

Guam

MARSHALL
ISLANDS

MALAYA

SUMATRA

Singapore

NORTH
BORNEO

SARAWAK

BORNEO

MINDANAO

PALAU
ISLANDS

CAROLINE   ISLANDS

Truk

Makin

CELEBES

CENTRAL PACIFIC AREA

GILBERT
ISLANDS

Canton

INDIAN

OCEAN

Java

NETHERLANDS INDIES

NEW GUINEA

BISMARCK
ARCHIPELAGO

SOLOMON
ISLANDS

SOUTH PACIFIC AREA

Buna

ELLICE
ISLANDS

SOUTHEAST ASIA COMMAND

CORAL
SEA

Battle
of
Coral Sea

Guadalcanal

NEW
HEBRIDES

FIJI
ISLANDS

AUSTRALIA

NEW
CALEDONIA

TONGA ISLANDS

Introduction

War Plan Orange

So long as the sun shall warm the earth, let no Christian be so bold as to come to Japan; and let all know that . . . if he violate this command, [he] shall pay for it with his head.[1]

—Imperial inscription at mass grave site of Christians

It's almost impossible to understate how little Americans knew about Japan before World War II.

In 1853, the empire of Japan was only known to the civilized world as a shadowy, mist-covered island kingdom somewhere east of China. There lived fierce warriors who brooked no intrusion from outside. Their quarantine was absolute. No one had pried open their door, although many had tried. Marco Polo had regaled his Venetian audiences with enchanting tales of a "great island to the east" of Cathay. It was 1295, and the explorer beguiled enraptured listeners with tales of that enigmatic, alluring place. They imagined the equivalent of the Lost Continent of Atlantis, the Fountain of Youth, or the Seven Cities of Cibola. Explorers and merchants sought to lift the veil on the Japanese kingdom, but all failed. Even the great armies of Kublai Khan, who had overrun the rest of Asia and terrorized Europe, had been hurled back in defeat when they had dared to storm the Japanese wall.[2]

Only faith had opened the door, and only a little. Jesuit, Dominican, and Franciscan missionaries had been allowed entry in the 1500s. They had baptized more than 200,000 Japanese as Christians.

But in 1639, the door had slammed shut. The imperial establishment deemed Christianity a threat, and the backlash was brutal. Crucifixions, beheadings, and burnings at the stake laid waste to what was seen as heresy against the rulers. When the last Christians had been murdered, the black curtain of absolute exclusion and secrecy again shrouded Japan.[3] The Dutch were permitted a small trading post as a reward for having participated in the persecution, using their enormous cannons to batter down the walls of their fellow Christians' strongholds.

In 1831, a Japanese vessel sailing the eastern Pacific Ocean was engulfed by the wind and waves of a great storm. The battered vessel did not sink but was blown way off course. The crippled ship made landfall near the Columbia River on the coast of the Washington Territory of the United States. Local British and American settlers saved seven desperate Japanese seamen, but a return to their homeland, seven thousand miles away, was hopeless. They lived in exile in North America for six years. In 1837, an opportunity arose: a trading voyage was sailing to a small island off the coast of China. The homesick Japanese seamen would be taken to their motherland, ferried there by humanitarian Americans. The US government believed that the gesture would help soften the Japanese intransigence and pave the way to trade.

The final run to Japan from the island off the Chinese coast would be made by the USS *Morrison*, specially outfitted for the mission. To ensure that there would be no misunderstanding on the part of the Japanese that it was a peaceful approach, all of *Morrison*'s guns were removed. As the ship sailed for Japan and slowly entered the forbidden waters of Tokyo Bay, a fleet of Japanese junks appeared as out of nowhere, swarming the ship like moths around a flame. Waves slapped the sides of the ship as the American crew eyed the men bobbing below on the exotic fleet of painted boats with accordion sails of maroon and ocher. They felt a thousand eyes on them from the shore as well. Silence hovered around them. As it became clear that *Morrison* was unarmed, Japanese batteries opened fire from the shore. *Morrison* hastily unfurled more sail, moving to another anchorage off the island of Kyushu, but the batteries, firing unrelentingly, found them there as well. Defenseless, the Americans turned tail, leaving the hostile waters behind like so many before them. The long-lost Japanese sailors were still on board, tainted by foreign soil and now considered worthless to their homeland.[4]

Nine years later, President James K. Polk would try his luck. In 1846, Polk sent Commodore James Biddle with two ships on a mission to open trade with Japan. This time, there was to be no peace offering. Biddle would enter Tokyo Bay on the ninety-gun *Columbus*, the corvette *Vincennes* by its side, in an impressive show of US force and firepower.

The ships' entrance into the bay was greeted by swarming primitive Japanese boats loaded with hostile warriors. *Vincennes* was promptly boarded and proclaimed a Japanese possession. Biddle's request to go ashore and meet with the imperial ministers was flatly denied. For ten days, Biddle would stay anchored, leaving his ship only to make repeated demands to see the proper authorities. For ten days the Japanese declined.

Defeated, Biddle prepared to depart. As he stepped from a Japanese junk onto his own captain's barge, a Japanese sailor shoved him, sending him sprawling to the bottom of his own boat. Japanese officers feigned shock at the disrespect but simply looked on.[5]

Two years later, the United States and Japan would meet again. In June 1848, sixteen American sailors on the whaler *Lagoda* jumped ship off the coast of Japan to escape the treatment of a cruel captain. Staggering ashore on Japanese soil, they quickly realized that they had jumped from the frying pan into the fire. The Japanese arrested and imprisoned them. Close confinement was their fate, and they were forced to humiliate themselves by desecrating a Christian cross and crucifixes.

Eight months later, Captain James Glynn mounted a rescue expedition to liberate the captives. On board his sixteen-gun sloop, USS *Preble*, Glynn sailed into Japanese waters and was greeted with the now-familiar unwelcoming party of warriors signaling him to turn and leave. Undaunted, *Preble* bowled through the Japanese boats like a rampaging bull and beat them to a more favorable anchorage near the shoreline.

When the outraged Japanese finally caught up to him, they disembarked and mounted the high ground overlooking the bay, which bristled with sixty cannons. As they trained the guns on *Preble*, Captain Glynn was unimpressed. He stood tall on his deck and with his booming voice demanded the release of the imprisoned Americans.

The Japanese scoffed and reminded Glynn of the humiliation they had inflicted on the proud Commodore Biddle. Glynn was not to be pushed around, and from his lofty perch, he hurled insults and invectives back at them. The bravado seemed to stun those within the sound of his voice. Seizing on their momentary disorientation, Glynn forcefully demanded the prisoners' release and proclaimed that the United States had not only the power to protect its citizens but the will to use it.

All beheld the stunning scene. The moments passed slowly, and then the prisoners, one by one, surrounded by their guards, made their way down the winding hill toward Glynn. The triumphant American captain postured on the deck of his sloop and sailed away homeward with his crew.[6]

Glynn's success turned the tide. He recommended to Commodore Matthew C. Perry to strike with a new mission while the iron was hot. President Millard Fillmore commissioned Perry to lead an expedition. Fillmore penned a personal letter to the Japanese emperor and entrusted its delivery to Perry.

After an eight-month voyage from Norfolk, Virginia, Perry's squadron, called the "Black Ships," bore into Japanese waters. The steam frigate *Mississippi*, belching smoke, churned the waters white in the wake of its powerful screws. The Japanese marveled at the smoking beast with no sails pushing through a nine-knot headwind and creating open water as the Japanese junks scrambled to get out of the way.

Mississippi's decks had been cleared and rigged for combat, its guns loaded. Marines and other armed sentries stood at the rails.[7]

For the next ten days, Perry frustrated every Japanese demand to leave. He refused to meet with anyone but the governor; no subaltern would be entertained. As if to further aggravate the Japanese, he ordered his crew to man small boats and conduct a complete survey and sounding of Tokyo harbor. It was too much for the Japanese to bear, but despite their vigorous objections, Perry pressed on. When the swarming boats edged closer, he scattered them with the threat of cannon fire.[8]

In the end, Perry won the day. He departed on July 17 with a promise from the governor to give an imperial answer concerning trade upon Perry's return in the spring of 1854.

Perry's report revealed the success of his mission: "It not only taught the Japanese the folly of attempting to sway the Americans by bravado and sham exhibitions of force, but has proved to the world, for the first time, the practicality of sailing even to the capital of Japan."[9]

When Perry returned, the Japanese agreed to a trade understanding. But they also got something else that would be transformative: before Perry departed Tokyo Bay, to prove his friendly intent, he invited Japanese officials to dine on his flagship. He amazed them as he led them to explore the inner workings of his steam-powered vessel. They were enthralled and took it all in, awestruck at American inventiveness and ingenuity. They saw what it would take to rival the US Navy.

It took them only forty years. In just that time, the swarming junks morphed into one of the most powerful navies in all the world. The reclusive island empire became a global sea power. In 1894, they put that power to work, crushing the Chinese fleet in the Battle of the Yellow Sea. Eleven years later it shocked the world by vanquishing the Russian fleet in the Battle of Tsushima.[10]

In 1898, the Americans won their own pivotal battle, the Spanish-American War. The fruits of victory were Guam and the Philippine

Islands, and with that, the United States' naval presence was now in Japan's backyard.

※

The two powerful navies war-gamed all possibilities. If ever a future conflict could be predicted, this was it. The United States' War Plan Orange became the military strategy to react to an attack by Japan against the United States and its tempting targets of Guam and the Philippines.

War Plan Orange was an offensive plan to wage war once the "inevitable" attack on those far-flung outposts of US power took place. It anticipated an attack on those US possessions by any nation and was color-coded depending upon the adversary: Black was Germany, Red was Great Britain, Green was Mexico, and Orange was Japan. But after World War I, the only possible adversary was Japan, so the reaction plan became Orange, officially adopted in 1924. After its adoption, it became dogma at the US Naval War College.

As the historian Ronald H. Spector noted in *Eagle Against the Sun*, "A generation of officers debated, tested, and refined, War with Orange. One hundred twenty-seven times—in chart maneuvers and board games—the American fleet crossed the Pacific to do battle with its Japanese opponents."[11] It was axiomatic: the Blue (US) Navy would cross the vast expanse of seven thousand miles of Pacific Ocean for a showdown, or climactic battle, with the Orange (Japanese) Navy somewhere in the western Pacific in a winner-take-all confrontation. The fact that the US Navy had never fought such a battle was not a consideration. Nor was the fact that most planners reluctantly recognized that Guam and the Philippines would be lost in the opening hostilities of a war with Japan.

The only debate was how to bring about the "all-out attack and absolute victory."[12] Some thought it would be a mad dash across the Pacific to smite the Orange Navy with superior numbers. Others "proposed to march across the central Pacific step by step, securing small islands in succession, each step supported by the previous one."[13]

It embodied the concept of sea power defeating land power. It would be a systematic drive, an irresistible force pressing forward to isolate Japan and bring about her defeat through siege and final bombardment. From the beginning, there was no thought of an invasion of the Japanese homeland. All agreed that would be a strategy that would bring about a mutual bloodbath. "The siege would continue relentlessly until Japan was utterly exhausted and sued for peace."[14]

War Plan Orange evolved over many years, from 1906 until December 6, 1941. But during all of the additions and modifications made by several generations of war planners, it had occurred to almost no one that there was a possible scenario that had never been explored: that there would be no Blue Navy to cross the Pacific after the first day of war.

It had, however, occurred to General William "Billy" Mitchell, the Army aviator, who since fighting in World War I had rattled cages up and down the chain of command. He wrote extensive papers and carried out bombing exercises to prove that the future of war was airpower. He had been exiled to a post in Hawaii after his exhortations got him in trouble with the White House and most of his superiors. Mitchell traveled to Europe and Asia to study aviation advances and in 1924 wrote a prophetic document. Mitchell believed that Japan was preparing to do battle with the United States. He predicted that air attacks would be made by the Japanese on Pearl Harbor. The report was largely ignored.[15]

UNKNOWN

VALOR

Peekskill, 1971

Fifty-five Welcher Avenue in Peekskill, New York, is where my grandparents Frank and Helen Bowes lived. My mom was raised there, and my sisters and I went there all the time when we were growing up.

It was a compact house, with three floors, an attic that held hidden treasures, and a basement with Grandpa's workbench and an icebox. The day my parents were married in 1955, it was so hot, my grandmother said, she had to dress in front of the open icebox. The Bowes family's home was handsome and had a modest understated elegance, just as they did.

Frank and Helen Bowes had married a bit later than most, in their early thirties. They had one daughter, Elizabeth Jane Bowes, my mother, who as a little girl was known as "Betts." She was the light of their lives.

They were middle-class, educated, hardworking people whose lives were filled with friends and church and community. Grandpa was a handsome man with a shock of black hair. He wore a brimmed hat and an overcoat to work every day and attributed the full head of hair that he maintained well into his eighties to consistent hat wearing. In his lightly worn green velvet chair, each evening he would read the *New York Times* and *The Sun* or one of his books, such as *The Seven Storey Mountain* by Thomas Merton or the latest novel by Herman Wouk. The house smelled of his pipe, in a good way. He worked for Liberty Mutual Insurance Company in New York. Back during the war, he would take the train to Boston to see clients there and also visit his sister, Anne, and his niece and nephew, Nancy and Harry Gray.

Grandma was a gym teacher at a home for "wayward girls." As a kid, I wondered how exactly they'd lost their "way," but I knew there was no way they would put anything over on Grandma. She was kind but firm, and on Thanksgiving she could beat potatoes into perfect submission with a masher.

The Boweses delighted in taking my sisters and me on outings and buying us red wool coats with black buttons from Best & Co. They crossed the Atlantic on the *Queen Mary* and brought us little kilts from Scotland. In the winter, they would go to Florida with friends for a month and send us a crate of oranges and grapefruits. There was something about the arrival of that box in the middle of a New Jersey winter. You could smell the oranges right through the packaging, all citrusy and exotic with a smiling orange with long eyelashes on the outside.

But before those days, there was the war. It was that part of their story that I searched for in the attic. On Sunday afternoons at Welcher Avenue, I would slip away while the grown-ups talked in the living room about politics, color TV, and life.

My first stop was a spot near the top of the first staircase. Seated there, I could reach the box of Russell Stover chocolates that my aunt kept on top of the secretary desk below on the first floor. I would forage through it, gobble one or two, then replace the top and make my way to the second floor. There were four small square bedrooms: Grandma's, Grandpa's, Aunt Jane's, and Mom's old room in the corner at the back of the house, overlooking a magnolia tree and a small side lot. There was one shared bathroom in the hall with faded yellow and white tile. I was a nosy kid, and at one time or another, I'd looked through every nook and cranny, finding jewelry boxes with rings with big topazes and tourmalines brought home from a friend's stay in South America, Mom's pressed flowers from long-ago dances at West Point, matchbooks with friends' names written on them, and, on Grandpa's dresser, dishes with foreign coins and shirt stays mixed together.

To the right of Grandma's room, the staircase continued up. Behind the door were a rough unpainted staircase and banister, and as I ascended, a hint of cool mustiness and mothballs filled my nostrils, signaling an entry into the past. This place was separate and apart from the bustle downstairs.

Light streamed in through the one big window under the roof peak. Under the long rack of out-of-season clothing covered in plastic bags was a rectangular dry cleaning box with a sketched silhouette of a wedding dress on top. My sister, Lisa, would take me up there, and we would stare at it, knowing that one day, when one of us got engaged, we would get to open the box and try on the dress, but not until then.

On the other side of the room, past the Christmas decorations and boxes of slides and suitcases, was an old brown chest of drawers where the story was kept. On top of the chest was a handsome picture of Grandpa's nephew, Harry, in uniform, a jaunty smile across his face and sparkly eyes looking out from under his US Marine cover.

My grandfather's neatly stacked saved newspapers were preserved in plastic bags on top. I visited them over and over, carefully separating them, reading the screaming headlines: "Hitler Invades Poland." "Paris Falls." "Japan Wars on US, Britain; Makes Sudden Attack on Hawaii; Battles at Sea; Heavy Fighting at Sea Reported." "Great Britain at War; The King's Message to the Empire; Fighting to Save World from Bondage of Fear."

They told the story of the war that had consumed the family's lives from 1941 to 1945. Grandpa followed the movement of Adolf Hitler's march across Europe with pins on a map on his workshop wall. He, Helen, and their friends listened intently to the radio updates, sat rapt at newsreels at the movie theater, and argued with friends and neighbors about whether or not we should go to the aid of Great Britain; whether Hitler would storm down the Mall in front of Buckingham Palace or even Fifth Avenue in New York, as he had down the

Champs-Élysées, where Nazi flags flanked the thoroughfare in the nightmare that crept closer by the day.

In 1971, I discovered a long thin drawer at the top of the chest. In it was a dark green notebook with the gold-stamped Liberty Mutual Insurance Company logo. Inside were yellowed newspaper clippings, photos of Marines crawling up black beaches, and a photo with the headline "Wrecked and Abandoned Landing Craft Litter Beach." Toward the back there was a photo of Marines burying their dead in a cemetery. It was all a mystery to me; many of the words I could not read, but the images I could not forget. On the front was Grandpa's handwriting on a piece of paper slipped inside the plastic, the words in blue ballpoint pen: "The Story of Iwo Jima."

✖

Iwo Jima, March 2019

Forty-eight years later, Frank Bowes's granddaughter is making her own way across the ocean to Iwo Jima.

I spent hours at the Japanese Embassy in New York getting my visa. It struck me as odd that the bloody battle to secure Iwo Jima ended in its return to Japan and now I need permission to go there.

I fly fourteen hours to Tokyo and another three to Guam. As we fly into Guam, the night sky is midnight blue and a full moon hangs over the sea, lighting the Mariana Islands. Below lies Tinian, to which the USS *Indianapolis* brought the parts of the first atomic bomb to be assembled. B-29s flew over these waters on their way to Iwo Jima, Okinawa, and Japan.

Tucked into my books are copies of the letters Harry Gray wrote my grandfather. My mother shared them with me as a child, and now I have shared them with my children. Like that of so many Americans, our story is woven into the wars waged and won for our freedom. These letters set me on this journey years ago. Deeper in my bag is a plastic bottle, to carry back sand for my aunt Nancy.

The Japanese open the island to veterans and their families, history buffs, and journalists only one day each year, on the anniversary of the battle in March.

I wake early, too restless to sleep, have coffee, and board the bus to the airport at 5:30 a.m. The security line is ridiculously long, and I'm annoyed by the lack of efficiency until I notice a man in his nineties in navy blazer and blue veteran's cap. He waits patiently, looking forward, and so will I.

We board the "Reunion of Honor" United flight. There is a jovial mood in our collection of travelers, most destined for a once-in-a-lifetime experience. Some have been here before, though. Bob Clemons is ninety-five and is traveling with his son and grandson. He is small in stature and stares out the window before drifting off to sleep. It will be his first time back since he was nineteen years old. I spoke with him yesterday and asked him what he remembered about Iwo. He said they had told them to kill any Japanese they encountered and to keep pushing until they reached the other side of the island. He also remembered running and tripping over scattered arms and legs. Bob said he loved Harry Truman because he ended the war and saved him from going to Okinawa. He said there was no way he was going there; he would've gone A.W.O.L. before he did.

Ronald "Rondo" Scharfe is standing in the aisle, chatting. He's ninety-one but moves like a seventy-two-year-old. He faked a baptismal certificate he stole from his church to join the Navy. At the age of sixteen, he drove a Higgins boat in the first wave and hit an underwater obstacle. The steering wheel ripped open his chest and crushed his nose and teeth. His company lost fourteen men.

Bob and Rondo say they never expected to get off the island alive. Rondo tells me that he always feels guilty that he got to have a life and get married and have kids when so many of the other guys did not. "I have a dream sometimes where I see two of my buddies as clear as day. I tell them to come on, I'll trade places with them. But just for the weekend," he says, his eyes brimming with tears. "But then I want to come back." Both men say they still have nightmares, seventy-four years later.

As we approach Iwo Jima, the United pilot tells us that we will soon see it on the left. He will fly two low circles over the island so everyone can take pictures and get a good look. There is a buzz of excitement as the gaping volcano Mount Suribachi comes into view, looming over the southern tip of the island. Those in the interior of the plane are passing their phones to the folks at the windows, craning their necks for a glimpse. Bob and Rondo stare down at the monster volcano in silence.

Once on the island, we walk the two-mile dirt road to Suribachi and climb it in the heat. The Japanese memorial stands large in the center. The American one is to the left. Next to it, the sawed-off end of the flagpole, on the spot where the famous flag-raising photo was taken, is in the ground, surrounded by a small patch of cement. People take turns taking photos; some have carried US flags to the spot, and they hold them up for the picture.

I look down at the stretches of black beaches below.

This is where Harry, Dom, Warren, Jay, George, Herman, and Charlie landed, among the sixty thousand boys of unimaginable courage from towns all across the United States, seven thousand miles away. Nearly seven thousand of them would die here on the eight-mile-square patch of nothing in the middle of nowhere in the costliest battle in the history of the US Marine Corps.

Admiral Chester W. Nimitz said after the war, "Among the Americans who served on Iwo Island, uncommon valor was a common virtue." For these young men and so many others whose tales of unknown valor lie only in their hearts, I tell their stories.

1

Arlington, Massachusetts, 1938

Frank Bowes heads up the hill, rifling in his overcoat pocket for the keys to his brother-in-law's house.

The always dapper Frank is a bit sweaty under the collar as he trudges north on Center Street. It is bitterly cold on this December night, and he pulls his coat tightly around. It has been a heck of a day. He barely made the train to Boston from Peekskill, then hustled through two meetings that morning: at a textile company north of Boston and the teachers' union, both his longtime clients at Liberty Mutual.

He walks and thinks, as the snow squeaks under the soles of his wing tips. Christmas wreaths are hung on the lampposts. Arlington is decked out. But it is going to be a rough Christmas. The red bows leave him unsettled, not merry.

Standing at the front door, he grips the key in his hand, separating it from his pocket change, his handkerchief, and his pipe. The worn black leather fob softened over time in another man's hand, in another man's pocket. On it are the worn words "Olmsted-Flint," where his brother-in-law, Harry Gray, Sr., worked. Olmsted made industrial belts for machinery, including the leather belts that powered the tallest wooden roller coaster at Revere Beach. Last summer, Harry Sr. went there to take the first test ride, to prove the belts would work.

"Better you than me," Frank joked. He wasn't much for rides, but

Harry Sr. loved anything fast and thrilling. As a boy in Long Island City, he spent his summers on the water on his fifteen-foot sailboat. He loved that boat, loved the water, remembers Frank.

Last winter, Harry Sr. made a model of it for young Harry. Frank could still smell the wood shavings, as the radio crackled and Harry Sr. hummed in the basement. It took him all of February to finish, but when it was done, Frank had to admit, it was a beauty.

She was two and a half feet long, with a tall mast and a little cabin with tiny benches inside. She had a wooden ship's wheel that turned and two perfectly scaled lifeboats with varnished seats. Harry Sr. made a polished stand, and Anne sewed three beautiful sails that hung on the mast, waiting for an imaginary wind. When Harry Sr. was done with it, he made a smaller one for little Nancy.

The two young families were as close as could be: four young parents with three little ones between them, starting their lives. The Great Depression was mostly over, and things were picking up. After years of angst and doubt, people were starting to feel pretty good about the future again.

Frank and his wife, Helen, and their four-year-old daughter, Betts, along with Harry Sr. and Anne and their two children, Harry Jr. and Nancy, often drove to Horseneck Beach to rent cabins for a week in the summer. Harry Sr. kept them laughing and singing, playing his mandolin in the kitchen after dinner. He was one of those guys, pretty good at most everything he tried. He played golf with his pals on Saturdays and Sundays, and with his family he was always the first one up, eagerly packing up the car. Then he'd scoop up Harry Jr. and Nancy from their beds, loudly announcing "Point of Pines or bust!"

There they'd run, laughing and shouting, on the paths until they all collapsed for lunch on a picnic blanket. Frank could still feel the mattress of thick pine needles under the wool plaid blanket. They were all in heaven under the umbrella of those heavily scented, towering trees.

They lay on their backs as the sun streamed down through the big bushy branches, and the world seemed just about perfect. When the day was over and they piled into the car, Harry would always have one more treat: "Who wants ice cream?" Sticky and drowsy, Harry Jr., Nancy, and Betts would fall asleep on one another's shoulders in the back seat on the way home. It was all as it should be, and they all just assumed it would be like that forever.

But it was not to be forever or anything close to it. Harry Sr. came home early from work on Saturday, December 3, not feeling right. He died in his bed that afternoon of heart failure.

Frank Bowes shakes the images from his head and turns the key at 17 Linwood, a house still in mourning. He opens the door, and they are all standing there to greet him: Anne takes his briefcase and hat as Harry Jr. and little eight-year-old Nancy look up at him.

"Well, ho, ho, ho!" he says, trying to lighten the mood. He hugs each one and musses Harry Jr.'s hair. Harry buries his face in his uncle's scratchy, manly coat. His senses fill with the sweet smell of pipe deep in the tweed, and he is relieved that Uncle Frank will sit at the head of the table tonight.

Anne Gray sits at the other end of the dinner table and smiles bravely to hold back her grief. She wants to try to forget her troubles for the moment, but she is still uneasy about the meeting she had that morning at Olmsted-Flint.

In her best dress and coat, the forty-year-old widow screwed up her courage and made her way to see her husband's former boss. He was very kind but explained that the new program known as Social Security would not cover her family because her husband's time at Olmsted fell just shy of the required three years to receive benefits. He was sorry but shrugged and said there was nothing they could do. Anne also went to the bank that morning. She and her husband had managed to put aside a little money, but there wasn't much; and after those savings ran out, she would be on her own.

Anne came from solid, hardworking stock, educated second-generation citizens of Massachusetts whose parents came from Ireland and England. Resourceful and proud, they lived within their means. No one complained. Like the rest of the family, she and Harry weathered the Great Depression, and they dreamed of owning their own home in the bustling town of Arlington. But that dream was from another life now. She gazes at her children, eating their dinner and laughing with Uncle Frank.

It will be first things first. She has to feed them and keep a roof over their heads. She has her mother to help, and she has her faith. She is smart and capable. She knows she will figure things out one way or the other. She's glad that Frank comes to Boston often for work. He will be the closest thing to a dad for young Harry—her pride-and-joy boy.

Young Harry is sharp as a tack, a bit of a prankster and a bit of an artist, too. He has a smile that melts everyone. Even the old man who runs the new roller rink in town has a soft spot for Harry when he and his chums roll through the door on Friday nights. Nancy is loving and chatty and admires everything about her big brother. But she has been quiet since losing her dad. Anne hopes that Nancy is young enough that she will forget all of this one day and just remember her adoring dad.

After dinner, Frank and Anne head upstairs and watch the kids brush their teeth and say their prayers. Frank lingers in young Harry's room, taking time to fold the boy's shirt and pants and lay them on the chair by the bed, just in case Harry feels like talking. He sits on the edge of the bed as Harry stares at the ceiling, and Uncle Frank rests his hand on the boy's forehead, gently brushing back his hair.

He unlocks a door with that touch, and tears well up in the twelve-year-old's eyes. On the nightstand is a picture of Harry, or "Junior," as they all call him, with his dad, fishing poles ready, smiles from ear to ear, both looking as though they are about to crack up. Frank kisses the boy on his forehead, and Harry closes his eyes and slowly, slowly drifts off to sleep. Frank sits motionless for a few minutes to be sure. Then he quietly stands, moves to the door, turns out the light. He goes downstairs to smoke his pipe and listen to the radio.

Anne is already downstairs, sitting in her chair.

The radio voices are deep and laced with static, bringing reports from across the ocean; from a world in flames. The war that President Franklin D. Roosevelt assures Americans is "not our fight." In London, Edward R. Murrow reports that Prime Minister Neville Chamberlain has spoken at a Jubilee Dinner for the Foreign Press Association. The prime minister said that British rearmament would continue unabated despite his commitment to the Munich Agreement and his belief that the British and German people are determined "never to go to war with one another again, and to settle any difference that might arise between us by the method of consultation."

Murrow says that at the press dinner there were empty seats. The German reporters had boycotted the evening. They had read an advance copy of Chamberlain's speech, and in it, the prime minister had chided them for the tone of their reporting and for rarely showing "any sign of a desire to understand our point of view."[1]

Anne and Frank listen as Murrow says that Jews have been ordered to stay off the streets of Germany during Nationalism Day. Hitler has declared that Jewish people have no role in German society. Their right to own real estate has been abolished, and business contracts with Jews are now considered void.

The news from the other side of the world continues. In Imperial Japan, Prime Minister Fumimaro Konoe has given a speech proclaiming a New Order of East Asia, encompassing Japan, Manchukuo, and China.[2] Where Manchukuo is, Frank and Anne don't know or particularly care. It all seems so far away from Arlington and all the quiet living rooms across the United States, where nearly all agree with their president that it is not their fight.

Anne is tired and has heard enough. She rises and walks toward the stairs. Her brother sees her sadness. "Hey, why the long face?" he chirps after her, just as he did when they were growing up in Worcester and his sister needed cheering up.

"How about we all go to the Capitol tomorrow night?" he says, looking at an ad in the paper. They made Dickens's *Christmas Carol* into a movie." Anne smiles a little and walks back to his chair.

"That would be wonderful, Frank. We'd like that. Good night."

She kisses him on the head and goes up to her room, to the bed that is now too big and empty. By Thursday, Frank will be back in Peekskill with Helen and Betts, and Anne will face the daunting prospect of Christmas without her husband, without the dad of those two precious children sleeping across the hall.

2

Infamy

On Saturday, December 6, 1941, Americans enjoy their last day of peace and isolation. Wars rage in Europe and Asia, but Americans have little interest. Of course, they watch the newsreels in the local theater. They shake their heads with pity when Edward R. Murrow recounts the unfathomable bombings in London. Great Britain is fighting for its very existence.

The Battle of Britain raged over the English Channel on July 10, 1940. Luftwaffe bombers roared overhead, rumbling the ground and striking terror into all below, battling to beat the British into submission. By September, it was an all-out assault against the civilian population of London to break the will of the people. Night after night, German raiders flew over the proud, historic city, pummeling its majestic buildings and streets with incendiary bombs. The Brits dug in during "the Blitz"; some huddled in wire cages made to fit under their beds, others fled to homemade bunkers in their small courtyards. As they weathered the onslaught by air, they watched the ocean for the expected invasion by sea.

On December 29, the 114th night of the Blitz, Murrow reported the unthinkable. In his deep staccato voice, he announced to the world that Saint Paul's Cathedral, with Christopher Wren's glorious dome, was engulfed in flames.

The queen mother continually encouraged her subjects to "keep calm and carry on" as parents huddled with their children in the Underground or loaded them onto trains to live with strangers outside the city. Their parents stayed behind, enduring the nightly raids by German bombers, not knowing if they would ever see their children again.

Americans shook their heads and talked about the war. In barbershops and corner stores, they shared their fears of what was to come, but when talk turned to US involvement, they drew the line. They were dead set against bailing out Europe as they had done in 1917.

They had seen it all in the catastrophic "war to end all wars," World War I: the anguish of the destroyed families of the 117,000 soldiers buried in the fields of France and of the 200,000 more who returned carrying the scars of that war and memories of which they could not speak.

Now European countries were fighting among themselves again. Did they not remember the gruesome war, the flesh and bone ripped apart by quick-fire machine guns in charges across no-man's-lands? The war that had driven so many of them to leave the continent behind for a new start. No, if the rest of the Western world was intent on destroying itself every few years, the United States would watch from the sidelines. Americans had other pursuits, such as the happiness promised by the framers of the Constitution. In reality, that happiness was still just out of their grasp. It was somewhere on the other side of war, the Depression, the Dust Bowl, bank foreclosures, and relentless unemployment.

According to Gallup, 81 percent of Americans were opposed to getting involved in Europe's war, and the president stood with them. Franklin Roosevelt was so adamant in his stance that anxious British officials, facing the full fury of the Germans, concluded that there wasn't the slightest chance of the United States entering the war unless the country itself was attacked.

Saturday nights, with the workweek behind them, Americans swayed to the sultry sounds of the big bands. It was a uniquely 1940s rhythm, a hip mover that made you want to dance or at least lean on the bar and tap your toe while sipping a martini. Glenn Miller, Sammy Kaye, and Jimmy Dorsey were an easy choice over war, setting the place hopping with "Chattanooga Choo Choo," "Daddy," and "Green Eyes." The Andrews Sisters softly crooned "I'll be with you in apple blossom time."

However, the bubble of peace in a world torn by war had not been easy to preserve. There had been enemy provocations. That fall, a German U-boat had torpedoed the US destroyer *Reuben James* off the coast of Iceland; 100 of the 144-man crew had perished at sea. Americans were outraged, and Woody Guthrie sang:

> *Now tonight there are lights in our country so bright*
> *in the farms and in the cities, they're telling of the fight.*
> *And now our mighty battleships will steam the bounding main*
> *and remember the name of that good Reuben James.*

President Roosevelt remembered the fallen with a black armband while assuring the nation that this attack would not alter German-American relations or escalate to war.

So young men went about their lives, finding jobs after the grim years of the Depression. They were enjoying life, and in 1941, that meant baseball! The New York Yankees' "Joltin' Joe" DiMaggio was on the path to a fifty-six-game hitting streak, and the Boston Red Sox slugger Ted Williams was sporting a rarified .400 batting average.

That spring, Harry Gray, now a freshman in high school, went roller-skating and to see *Gone with the Wind* at the Capitol Theatre in downtown Arlington.[1] It had been three years since his father died, and little by little, the Grays' life was finding a new normal. Anne had gone to typing school at night and landed herself a good job at Liberty Mutual, where her brother, Frank, worked. She was providing for her family and making ends meet. It was something she had never imagined having to do, but she was succeeding and was proud of it.

Fifteen hundred miles away in Gulfport, Mississippi, the Legion

Theatre had recently opened on 27th Avenue. It seated twelve hundred people, and, best of all, it had a balcony. Seventeen-year-old Jay Rebstock had been sent by his dad to the Gulf Coast Military Academy to get some "discipline" into his life. But on Saturday night, well, it was Saturday night and time to let off a little steam. Rebstock and his fellow cadets put on their best shirts and headed to town to catch Humphrey Bogart in *The Maltese Falcon*[2] and perhaps meet some girls on line to join them in the balcony seats.

The two young men, like so many others across the United States, had no idea what lay ahead, and they were, as they should be, blissfully lost in teenage life in their small towns in America. Adolf Hitler, Benito Mussolini, Emperor Hirohito, and Hideki Tojo were just names in the newspaper, monster characters in a faraway tragedy. Let Russia's and Germany's murderous empires devour each other. If they were bent on mutual destruction, so be it.

Still, the devil-may-care mood of the boys was not possible for their parents, who watched and worried as the Nazi black in the newsreel animations spilled farther and farther across Europe and Africa.

Young Harry Gray's uncle Frank feared that the United States could look away for only so long. When Helen and Betts were in bed, he would go down to his basement workshop. On the wall was his map with colored pins following the course of the war.

A year earlier, Germany, Italy, and Japan had signed the Tripartite Pact. In response, the United States and its European allies had banned steel and oil exports to Japan. Eventually, the Dutch colonial government in Jakarta hit Japan where it hurt most, freezing Japanese assets in Indonesia. Without Dutch petroleum, Japan's vast military machine would, in a short time, be gasping for air, unless they fought back.

Japan, an island nation, had few resources of its own and had absconded with China's bounty to scrape its way into the upper echelons of world power. Luckily, the Japanese were protected by huge expanses of sea and archipelagos barely worth colonization. Germany, nearly landlocked, had become an air power to subjugate its neighbors and rob their lands. Both seemed nearly impossible to stop, short of well-negotiated treaties.

)(

Frank takes another look at the map and wonders where it is all headed. He reaches up and pulls the cord that turns off the lightbulb over his workbench. As he walks upstairs, his thoughts go to Harry Jr. His memories of the boys fighting in the wretched trenches of World War I are still fresh; he hopes Harry can escape the madness, and stay safe at home in Arlington.

On that last peaceful evening, December 6, 1941, night falls on the continental forty-eight states. But far to the west, in the territory of Hawaii, it is still light. The last rays of the setting sun on the island of Oahu paint the sky orange and purple. It is Saturday night, liberty call has sounded, and grinning sailors in their pressed whites stroll out of the gates at Naval Station Pearl Harbor, a fresh pack of cigarettes and money in their pockets. They are off for a night on the town in Honolulu.

But not everyone is leaving. In fact, at the other entrance to the base, sailors and their girls buzz with excitement and squeeze through the crowded doorways of the Bloch Recreation Center for what is billed as the entertainment event of the year: the first annual "Battle of Music."[3]

Everybody has his or her favorite, and tonight is the semifinals of the big band–style competition that has been going since September. The crowd shuffles noisily for seats in the packed auditorium, laughing above the cacophony of the bands warming up. Tonight's semifinalists are the twenty-one-piece Navy bands from the battleships USS *Pennsylvania* and *Tennessee* and from the Navy fleet tender USS *Argonne*. A fourth band from the cruiser *Detroit* has made it to the semis but is missing because its ship has just left Pearl Harbor.

The band members from battleship *Arizona* line the wall behind the seats, watching the scene intently. They have already secured their spot in the next round and are there to size up the competition for the finals on December 20. They have a soft spot for the band from *Tennessee*, since they attended the Navy School of Music in Washington, DC, together.[4]

As the crowd settles down, the rules are simply spelled out: "Each band competes with a swing number, a ballad and a specialty tune, and performs for a jitterbug contest."[5]

It is the jitterbug contest that has the young sailors and Marines and their girlfriends sitting up in their seats. They are champing at the bit to get out there and start rocking, swinging, and flipping their dates. It is a perfect American night in that December of 1941. The kids are bursting with energy and ready to dance the night away.

Pennsylvania's band kicks off the program with a swing number, "There'll Be Some Changes Made," then moves into a sweet version of "Georgia on My Mind." But it is a roof-raising "Jingle Bells" for the jitterbug that gets everyone on their feet and starts the floor vibrating.[6]

Then the *Tennessee* and *Argonne* bands take their turns wowing the crowd, but in the end, it is *Pennsylvania*'s band that is whooping and hollering as the winner of the night. They advance to the finals, just two short weeks away. The band from USS *Nevada* packs up and leaves early. They need to be up to play morning colors at 8:00 a.m., out on "Battleship Row," where nine ships of the Pacific Fleet are lined up, two abreast, off Ford Island. The rest of the bands play long into the evening. It is a warm night and palm fronds rustle in the breeze over the harbor, but Christmas is in the air as the dancing goes on and on. Finally, after too many cocktails and too-swollen feet, the last dancers sway to one final song, singing "God bless America, land that I love . . ." Tuckered-out band members loosen their ties, pack up their instruments, and head back to the ships. Girls stroll down the walkways in bare feet, swinging their high heels in their hands. The men shuffle back on board and fall into their bunks, swaying to the gentle movement of the water below, sound asleep in no time.

Several hundred miles to the north of the sleeping sailors, the massive Japanese fleet churns the waters of this quiet night, ever closer with each passing minute. At exactly 6:00 a.m., the aircraft carriers halt and turn their bows into the wind. One after another, in practiced syncopation, 353 Japanese fighter pilots strap on their helmets and start their engines, then roar thunderously off the decks. By 7:30 a.m., in the distance they begin to make out the airfields they have studied, finally coming into view: Wheeler, Bellows, Ewa, and Hickam. Starting their descent through light cloud cover, they pierce the quiet air above the sleepy palm-lined harbor. US aircraft are lined up wingtip to wingtip on the airstrips, ready to be picked off. Anchored just off Ford Island, swaying on their chains at sunrise, are the ships of the US Pacific Fleet: *California*, *Maryland*, *Tennessee*, *Oklahoma*, *West Virginia*, *Nevada*, and *Arizona*, as well as *Utah*, which has been retired after thirty-three years. The battleship *Pennsylvania* is manned in dry dock. Eighty-six other Navy vessels jam the harbor.

The ships are full of slumbering young sailors, stacked three and four high in their racks. A few are already awake and up. They head into the galley for hot coffee, swap stories about shore leave and jitterbugging young ladies. Others are already at it, swabbing the decks and rubbing the brass to make it shine.

The Japanese squadron commander Mitsuo Fuchida, now over the target, determines that they have indeed caught the US Navy unawares. He shouts the signal to indicate it: "Tora! Tora! Tora!"

The morning calm is pierced by the guttural roar of propellers and screeching whistles of bombs rotating down in spirals to targets below. Dynamite rips through the ships' hulls, exploding their decks, slowly twisting the metal and then snapping the enormous masts. Oil and thick black smoke billow as the fighter planes sweep low across the water, dropping waves of bombs over and over. In all, 347 US warplanes and 18 warships, including all of the battleships, melt and twist into macabre hunks of metal, sinking in a stench of oil and fire. The Japanese lose just 29 planes. But 3,581 Americans are dead; more than half of them lie at the bottom of the shallow harbor, entombed in the *Arizona*. The killing blow to *Arizona* hit in between the first and second gun turrets. It is an armor-piercing round that goes through the decks and explodes in the powder magazine; this terrific explosion pancakes the front of the ship from the superstructure to the bow, instantly incinerating those inside. The ship goes down so quickly that in some parts, men are trapped under five feet of water. There is no way to get them out. For days after the attack, banging is heard from the men inside the ship, as they run out of oxygen. Among the dead are twenty-three sets of brothers, including the Beckers, the Dohertys, and the Murdocks, who had three brothers each on board; in each family, only one brother survived.[7]

Ж

History in ev'ry century
Records an act that lives forevermore.
We'll recall, as into line we fall,
The thing that happened on Hawaii's shore.

—Don Reid and Sammy Kaye, "Remember Pearl Harbor" (1941)

In Peekskill, New York, Frank Bowes decides it's a Howard Johnson's day, but he hasn't told anyone yet. He and his family walk down the steps of the Church of the Assumption after Sunday Mass. His daughter Betts and her best friend, Alice, skip down the stairs, hoping the grown-ups will head left at the bottom. That would mean they are going out for breakfast. Left it is! Betts and Alice run around the corner and pull open the big, heavy door. Coffee, toast, eggs, and chatter fill the air. They unbutton their church coats, and Frank hangs them on the hook built into the booth dividers. Betts and Alice swing their saddle-shoed feet and smile at each other. Helen's voice is loud and clear. "Hello, Joan," she says to the waitress. "Coffee, please, and two hot cocoas for the girls." Betts's and Alice's moms teach together, as does Helen's sister, Jane. They carefully pull off their church gloves and settle into chatter about school and husbands and Christmas lists, which the girls listen to intently to see what they can pick up, as seven-year-old girls will do. Frank and Larry settle in at a small table for two across from the booth and pull off their coats. Betts's eyes light up as Joan, who always piles on the whipped cream, slips the cups under their noses.

"It's hot, Betts, let it cool off." So Betts stares at the HoJo logo of the little boy and his dog, and the chef leaning down to show them the pancakes on his plate. Bing Crosby is on the radio singing "Silent Night" as she spins her spoon in the cup, blowing softly into it as the chocolate and cream swirl together.

Then she hears a grown-up gasp. She looks up.

Then, grown-up by grown-up, in a rising buzz, more gasps, then the words: Japanese. Bomb. Hawaii. What does it mean? She does not know, but suddenly everyone is shuffling, standing, chairs scraping across the linoleum floors. The parents start pulling on their coats. "What next?" they murmur. They forage in their pockets, leaving money on top of checks on the table, not waiting for change. "C'mon, girls, we have to go. We have to go." Mom grabs Betts by the hand, her hot cocoa still swirling in the cup. So terrible to leave it behind, she thinks.

At home, Helen and Aunt Jane sit down on the kitchen chairs, still in their coats. "What now?"

"We will enter the war, I imagine."

Betts has heard them all talk about "the war." They always told her not to worry, it is very far away. The maps down above the workbench in the basement are a different world.

Frank Bowes is down there already. Betts wanders over to the basement steps. She can smell his pipe. She holds the railing, goes down the wooden-slat steps, and sits on the last one. Frank rises from the step stool chair by the tool wall. He sweeps her up in his arms, leaving behind his maps and stacked newspapers, which show the movements of Hitler and Mussolini in Europe, and in the Pacific, the invasion of China by Emperor Hirohito and General Tojo. Frank had never imagined that the pushpins and arrows would sweep across the Pacific Ocean to the United States. He stares at the Hawaiian Islands in disbelief.

Later that night, Betts lies in bed, listening to the talk downstairs. A little girl in a house full of adults, she is used to staring up at the ceiling from her bed, hearing their chatter below, but tonight it is quieter, the words spaced farther apart. There are long gaps of silence that make her uneasy.

At noon the next day, Frank turns on the radio. Betts sits on the ottoman in front of his chair. Every American is doing the same thing, wherever they are. Everything has stopped. It is beginning to sink in: the United States is under attack. Where will they be hit next? What they dreaded and tried to push away has now landed on the back doorstep.[8]

The broadcast by the president from the House of Representatives in Washington, DC, is about to begin. They hear the raucousness inside the chamber as the rattled members of Congress settle into their chairs. President Roosevelt clears his throat and speaks.

Mr. Vice President, and Mr. Speaker, and Members of the Senate and House of Representatives:

Yesterday, December 7, 1941—a date which will live in infamy— the United States of America was suddenly and deliberately attacked by naval and air forces of the Empire of Japan.

The United States was at peace with that Nation and, at the solicitation of Japan, was still in conversation with its Government and its Emperor looking toward the maintenance of peace in the Pacific. Indeed, one hour after Japanese air squadrons had commenced bombing in the American Island of Oahu, the Japanese Ambassador to the United States and his colleague delivered to our Secretary of State a formal reply to a recent American message. And while this reply stated that it seemed useless to continue the existing diplomatic negotiations, it contained no threat or hint of war or of armed attack.

President Roosevelt's next sentences hammer at the perfidy of the enemy: the attack was "deliberately planned many days or even weeks ago," and the Japanese government "deliberately sought to deceive."

> I regret to tell you that very many American lives have been lost. In addition, American ships have been reported torpedoed on the high seas between San Francisco and Honolulu.

Frank and Betts listen, spellbound, as the president goes on. There is much more.

> Yesterday the Japanese Government also launched an attack against Malaya.
> Last night Japanese forces attacked Hong Kong.
> Last night Japanese forces attacked Guam.
> Last night Japanese forces attacked the Philippine Islands.
> Last night the Japanese attacked Wake Island.
> And this morning the Japanese attacked Midway Island.

The president's voice rises in fury at the unprovoked aggressions. His words, like hammer blows, land with incensed determination. He continues:

> But always will our whole Nation remember the character of the onslaught against us. No matter how long it may take us to over-come this premeditated invasion, the American people in their righteous might will win through to absolute victory.
> I believe that I interpret the will of the Congress and of the people when I assert that we will not only defend ourselves to the uttermost but will make it very certain that this form of treachery shall never again endanger us.
> Hostilities exist. There is no blinking at the fact that our people, our territory, and our interests are in grave danger.
> With confidence in our armed forces—with the unbounding

determination of our people—we will gain the inevitable triumph so help us God.

His words hang in the air in the silence of the chamber, and in living rooms across America. In Roosevelt's strong, resolute voice, he concludes:

I ask that the Congress declare that since the unprovoked and dastardly attack by Japan on Sunday, December 7, 1941, a state of war has existed between the United States and the Japanese Empire.[9]

3

Outrage

Every valley shall be exalted, and every mountain and hill made low; and the crooked shall be made straight, and the rough places plain.

—Isaiah 40:4

In Gulfport, Mississippi, on the second Sunday of Advent, Reverend James N. Brown reads the words of Isaiah: fathers, mothers, and children bow their heads in unison. A baby is coming to save the world. King Herod fears the child will be a king, come to threaten his power. On his orders, his men ride through the villages, slaughtering all the young boys.

Meanwhile, across the Atlantic Ocean, far from First Presbyterian Church, modern-day Herod's henchmen storm neighborhoods of their own, forcing Jewish families out of their homes and loading them like cattle onto trucks. The crowded transports are packed with adults and children, some bewildered, others paralyzed with fear; they do not know where they are going. The sign over the gate at Auschwitz cruelly promises ARBEIT MACHT FREI, "Work sets you free," but most will never be free from Hitler's evil plan; they will be starved or gassed to death. These innocents stand between Hitler and his vision for the future, an Aryan nation cleansed of Jews.

Not far away from the sermon, Jay Rebstock is just happy to have the whole day off. On Sundays at the Gulf Coast Military Academy, in Gulfport, Mississippi, if you aren't in trouble and doing penalty drills, you're free to head into town.

From nearby Bay Saint Louis, Rebstock played football for Saint Stanislaus. His team last season was 12–0, thanks mostly to its fullback, Felix "Doc" Blanchard. He was unstoppable, pounding his hulking shoulders through every defense. Everybody wanted Doc: Army, Fordham, Notre Dame. But when Jay went to the military academy, Doc headed to the University of North Carolina and eventually to West Point.[1]

Jay's dad felt that his son would benefit from a bit of military structure, and perhaps he was right. Most Sundays, truth be told, Jay was doing discipline drills, but on this particular Sunday, Jay settles into his seat at the Paramount Theatre on 26th Avenue. There was a long line for tickets and Jay and his buddies rushed through the lobby and scrambled for a row of seats together to watch Gary Cooper as Sergeant York, the most decorated soldier in all of the Great War.

The newsreel projector sends flickering images across the screen. Marching music fills the theater, and the booming voice-over tells the hushed crowd of Germany's onslaught on Moscow in its winter offensive on the snow-covered battlefields of Russia. In Washington, DC, Japanese ministers shuffle through the halls of the State Department, meeting with Secretary of State Cordell Hull. They carry a letter from the emperor with a proposal to avoid confrontation with the United States.

About forty minutes into *Sergeant York*, as York is grappling with his newfound Christianity and the realities of war, the projector rattles, sputters, and then fails. This is not uncommon, and Jay and pals join in the usual chorus of boos and hisses. The house lights come on, and the harried-looking theater manager scampers up the stage steps and faces the audience.

They assume he's about to say they can get their money back at the box office, but instead he is agitated: "You should all head home; the theater is closing for the day. The Japanese have just bombed Pearl Harbor!" The manager pushes his glasses back up onto his nose and stands there a moment, not sure what else to say to the stunned crowd. There is nothing more to say. He hurriedly steps down and hustles back to the office.

His words hang in the air over the theater. Waves of panic and concern float across the voices. "Pearl Harbor?" "Pearl Harbor." "Where is Pearl Harbor?" Rebstock asks. Suddenly he feels a tap on his arm. An older cadet standing behind him leans over and says, "I know where that is; it's in Hawaii. My brother is there on a battleship named *Oklahoma*."[2]

　　　　　　　　　　　　　　Ж

"God, please get us out of here." The silent, desperate prayer comes from Seaman First Class Stephen Young. Gasping, he struggles and bounces to stay afloat in an upside-down watery world.

Some twenty trapped sailors cling to beams, braces, machinery, a half-submerged ladder—grabbing whatever is within reach.

Seven blasts heard from their bunks signaled danger. Moments later, Japanese torpedoes ripped open *Oklahoma*'s port side. Now, eleven minutes later, water is gushing through the open watertight doors. *Oklahoma* rolls with the weight of it, and now he can feel it in his bones. She is going down.

Three of the Pacific Fleet aircraft carriers are safely at sea. But *Arizona* and the capsized *Oklahoma* bear the brunt of the losses; two-thirds of the dead are in their hulls on the ocean floor.

A sailor hoists a lantern above his head, bobbing in the rising water. It is just now sinking in, as they orient themselves, that they are in an air pocket in the hull. The sailor with the lantern turns it off to save the batteries. In pitch blackness, as the water creeps slowly higher, each man grapples with what has happened and what it might mean.

Trapped upside down and submerged, Young remembers how only a moment ago, he was upright, combing his hair, patting his wallet in his pocket, about to hop up that same ladder, to catch the liberty boat ashore for a beach date with a lovely Hawaiian girl he'd met only the night before. "My girl and I were going to Nanakuli, where the surf was much better than Waikiki and the beach not nearly so crowded. For once I had plenty of money—a ten and a one-dollar bill."[3]

Then came the blare of the bugle, the *bong, bong, bong* of the ship's alarm. "What's this bullshit on a Sunday?" The question flew off the lips of hundreds of running men in dress uniforms, work uniforms, skivvy shirts, and shorts.

The voice on the PA system froze them in their tracks: "All hands, man your battle stations! On the double! This is no drill! Get going— they're real bombs!"[4]

Young had made it to his battle station—the powder hoist handling room of gun turret 4, the lowest deck on the ship—when an enormous explosion made the deck beneath his feet rock.

Now he is trapped in an air pocket, the *slam, slam, slam* of the torpedoes still ringing in his ears. His home away from home, the *Oklahoma*, is mortally wounded, listing badly.

The ship is almost on her side. Then suddenly it begins lurching. The deck slips out from under him; his hands snatch at empty air. As the ship rolls over, he is pitched into a dark mass of dead and dying, and with them he is buffeted and tossed about. Then the dark waters close over him as the ship stops, resting upside down on the bottom of the harbor.[5]

He swims frantically, not knowing in which direction. Then he has broken into a bubble of air. It is all coming back to him. How long has he been here? He does not know.

❊

The harbor is about forty-five feet deep. *Oklahoma*, resting on the bottom, is just visible above the water line.

"No talking," orders a voice out of the dark. "We've got to save the air."

"For what?" someone asks, and there is no answer.[6]

"How about a cold beer? I'm thirsty," Young blurts out, feeling around for his shipmate next to him. "I'll bet you a dollar we'll suffocate before we drown."

"Okay, you're on," agrees the shipmate. "I say we drown first." Each somehow manages to fish a soggy dollar bill from deep in his pocket.[7]

Time creeps by. Hours, maybe. No one knows how many. Is anyone searching for them? Does anyone know they are still alive? Have the Japanese captured Pearl Harbor? Someone is banging on the outside of the hull! But they hear the voices and realize that it is just other trapped sailors, also helplessly floating in a bubble on the other side.

Outside the *Oklahoma*, the Japanese have not captured Pearl Harbor, but they have dealt it a devastating blow. Still, the bombs that tore through hulls and snapped masts of the ships at Pearl Harbor are just the beginning. In the coming hours and days, the Japanese will strike General Douglas MacArthur's forces in the Philippines and British forces in Singapore and Hong Kong. They will conquer Guam, Wake Island, Borneo, Java, Malaya, the Solomons, the Marianas, Burma, and the Dutch West Indies in an appalling torrent of aggression.

But back on *Oklahoma*, hours pass, and Young and the others shiver and wait. It was morning when their world turned upside down. Is it now night? Some talk to keep one another going. Others drift into and out of sleep, dreaming for a few moments, then rocking back to their dire reality. Young's mind is like a kaleidoscope, with morphing school years, his mother and dad, faces of girls, laughing and full of life. Then he feels desperately sad and alone. He shouts to all and no one, "Damn it, I'm not even twenty and I'll never know or love a girl again!"[8]

Time ticks by. Anger begins to rumble within him. "Why couldn't we have died in the sun where we could have met death head on? That was the way to die, on your feet, like a man. But instead, it was to be a slow, useless death, imprisoned in our dark iron cell."[9]

In time, anger passes. Then comes submission, which is oddly calming as it settles over their watery tomb. There is only God left to come.

"Oh, God, relieve us of our torment," Young whispers in his head. "If it is Your will that we die here, please watch over our families and comfort them. We are delivered unto You and ask to be forgiven for our sins."[10]

But time does not bring death. The teeth of the soaking and shivering sailors chatter as they go into and out of shaking fits, into and out of sleep, descending deeper into the darkest parts, the lowest place a man can be.

Then comes a hammering, far away. It stops. The black bubble becomes deathly silent as the men strain to hear it again, but it is gone. They hear it again. Perhaps they are just imagining it. Then it is faint, but there is definitely someone there, hammering in the distance.

They take a dog wrench and hammer away at the steel bulkhead. Three dots—three dashes—three dots—SOS!

"They're trying to get us," someone says. They pound "SOS" again and again. They tap out their story: "We've been here a day—a whole twenty-four hours in this awful place. We were thirty, but now we're ten. The others are gone."

Suddenly there is a piercing, grinding noise; a drill bit flashes through the steel from the next compartment. The release of air forces a surge of water into their side.

The cutting tool begins its slow, sawing tear through the wall on the other side, now filled with light. They can see that the next compartment is empty; those men are saved. But the water is rushing in faster, shoulder high.

"Please hurry, for God's sake! We can't stop this flooding!" Young scans the morbid scenario in his head. We will be the ones to drown like rats at the last minute, just when rescue is within reach! They watch as the cutting saw makes a square; they begin pushing it open. Bending down three sides, one by one they squeeze their soaked bodies through the jagged metal edges. Each time a man forces himself through, the metal bends open a bit wider. There it is! Blue sky fills their eyes.

"I emerged from out of the cold darkness into the warm sunshine of a new day. It was 9 a.m., 8 December. Standing on the upturned hull, I gazed about me. It was the same world I had left twenty-five hours before, but as I looked at the smoke and wreckage of battle, the sunken ships Tennessee, West Virginia, and Arizona astern of us, I felt that life would never be the same, not for me—not for any of us."[11]

✗

Young men across the United States knew their lives had been changed by that "day of infamy." There was no turning back. As Mark Antony knew, once the point of no return was met, the monarch's voice would "cry havoc and let slip the dogs of war!" The hounds had been released, and they would not return home until there was a victor.

And so they lined up and wrapped around blocks across the United States, young men straining to be unleashed against the enemy they called "the Japs." They wanted to fight; they wanted revenge. They poured into recruiting stations "in numbers unprecedented in the history of the nation."[12]

Their outrage was not fueled by a desire to save France and Great Britain. In fact, it had nothing to do with Europe at all. They wanted to come face-to-face with the bombers who had snuffed out the life of young men sleeping in their bunks or shuffling to breakfast. They wanted to end the Asian menace whose representatives talked diplomacy at the State Department while giving the order to annihilate our fleet at Pearl Harbor. Germany would declare war on the United States four days later, but to those men and boys on the long lines, the enemy that stirred their warrior blood was Japan.

At the University of Buffalo, the captain and star of the Bulls football team, Dominick Grossi, was one of them. Grossi's parents, Lena and Pasquale, called "Patsy," owned an Italian restaurant in their hometown of Lockport, New York. Dom was their adored son and big brother to Rose, Betty, Patrina, Marie, and his little brother, Junior. Dom left Buffalo early, packed his bag, and headed off to join the Marines and train at the University of Rochester. The Bulls' loss was U of R's gain as Grossi continued to take to the gridiron, but Grossi was turning his attention to the bigger battles across the ocean. He hoped to become an officer and head to the Pacific.

On December 10, the pride of the British Far Eastern Fleet, the battleship *Prince of Wales* and the battle cruiser *Repulse*, were hunted down and sunk by Japanese bomber and torpedo aircraft. Japanese forces took the Dutch oil fields in Borneo in mid-December and in the coming weeks managed to take over US- and British-built airstrips in Southeast Asia and the Philippines for their own use.[13]

In those early months of 1942, the existence of the United States was threatened in a way not felt since the dark days of the summer of 1814. Then it had been the rampaging British Army that swept Americans from their positions defending Washington, DC, and stormed the capital to destroy it. They breached the White House doors and helped themselves to the still warm food left behind in President James Madison and his family's hasty evacuation.[14]

The United States was now vulnerable again. The Japanese fleet had penetrated the ocean barrier and was moving undaunted across the Pacific. As with the British in their approach to the defenseless city of Washington, Americans were faced with the horror of the Japanese Navy sitting off our shores in a battle line between Hawaii and California.

With British and US naval forces destroyed or badly crippled, the Rising Sun flag was flying unchallenged in the Pacific.

※

Back in Tokyo, the forty-year-old Emperor Hirohito was a bit overwhelmed by his own success. His conquests had suddenly added 150 million new subjects in China and Southeast Asia to his kingdom. He told his lord keeper of the privy seal, "The fruits of war are tumbling into our mouth almost too quickly." The emperor had been told that he would likely lose a quarter of his ships in the early moves against the United States and Great Britain, but his only significant loss had been one destroyer. The Japanese war machine had surpassed all expectations. His imperial forces had vastly outmaneuvered the Allies with a larger and superior navy and air force and a masterful infantry that was better trained and more efficient. The days of just forty years prior, when the Japanese had been "awestruck at American ingenuity" and amazed by the technology of US ships, were long gone. Now they could see and taste dominance.[15]

This had been the plan for decades, and the work had gained momentum after the death of the Regent Hirohito's mentally ill father, Emperor Taisho, in December 1926. Despite the economic recession, the Imperial Diet had approved a yearlong enthronement extravaganza costing roughly the equivalent of $7 million, designed to deepen the bond of the people to their new leader in the tough economic times and dispel any tendencies toward communism that were simmering in the populace. The emperor's role as a god had to be reinforced, while any conspiratorial or radical movements against imperial rule had to be repressed. He was to be seen as father of the "divine land," a distant, all-powerful, benevolent leader. The distant part was a plus for Hirohito, who was awkward with people and plagued throughout his life by a "distinctly uncharismatic personality."[16]

The imperial court hierarchy sought to emulate the regal demeanor and pageantry they admired in the court of King George V, and with the dawn of mass media, albeit an obedient one, they sought to give Hirohito the royal treatment. It worked. A rapt nation witnessed his enthronement in Kyoto, which culminated with his oath "to maintain eternal world peace, and advance goodwill among nations through diplomacy." The final act of the ceremony involved donning ritual garments and traveling between three wooden structures in which he was purified; then he curled into the fetal position and was wrapped in a quilt to consummate his "marriage" to the sun goddess and his descent from the "plain of high heaven." This entire ritual was witnessed and assisted by members of the court.[17]

Twelve years later, the "maintenance of eternal world peace" was losing out to the ambitions of the Rising Sun. Now Emperor Hirohito and his minister of war, Hideki Tojo, were ready to seize opportunity.

On December 23, the US garrison at Wake Island surrenders to a Japanese invading force. On Christmas Day, the British at Hong

Kong also surrender, as US and Filipino forces hold out against overwhelming odds at Bataan, a province on the Philippine island of Luzon. In a horrific introduction to their ways of war, the Japanese force 70,000 prisoners, already weary from holding out, to march sixty-five miles north in the Bataan Death March. Thousands die along the way at the hands of the barbaric Japanese guards. Those who survive no doubt have many days when the alternative seems preferable, as they suffer at the hands of the inhumane prison guards, who take pleasure in beating and torturing them.[18]

The heaviest bombardment of the island known as "the Rock" comes on Hirohito's birthday, April 29. It is an all-day affair. Ten thousand shells blast the beach defenses. A powder magazine explodes, stripping the troops in the foxholes of their clothes and burning some men alive. The island is engulfed in flames and exploding ammunition that one ensign says made Dante's Inferno look like a backyard bonfire.[19]

One agonizing month after the fall of Bataan, the final US defensive stronghold in the western Pacific, Corregidor, falls. Thousands more Americans become prisoners of Japan.

They held the island for five long months after Pearl Harbor and, at the end of the battle on May 7, could hold it no longer. Defeated, the entire 4th Marines ceased to exist.

To all the Marines who watched events unfold in those early months of war, it is a gut punch. Though the Marines are seemingly always outnumbered, their fighting spirit captures the American imagination. The 147-man barracks at Guam fight tenaciously to the very end.

Major James Devereux's 449-man 1st Marine Defense Battalion on Wake Island seems to do the impossible. Devereux develops an Alamo-like defense that frustrates the Japanese, dashing their hope of a quick victory. Expertly deploying his guns and anticipating every Japanese maneuver, he blasts the Japanese out of the water, sinking two destroyers and an escort vessel. He damages two additional cruisers and two destroyers and destroys seventy-two Japanese aircraft.

Each morning, Americans at home grab their newspapers to follow the exploits of the daring Major Devereux. However, his men, who are the hope of bruised American morale, are up against the wall. They pin their hopes on a rescue naval force said to be racing to the scene. Americans read daily with bated breath, cheering on Devereux and his men. But the rescue never comes. Wake Island's brave defenders are finally overwhelmed two days before Christmas. The gallant Devereux and his surviving men become Japanese prisoners of war.

There is never any good news. The Japanese are never far away. There are muted reports that Japanese submarines are lurking along the California coast, shelling targets of opportunity. Then they are back at Pearl Harbor. Their mop-up operation frazzles Honolulu's already frayed nerves as the Japanese pummel the base with eight five-hundred-pound bombs, attempting to take out the dry docks and oil storage facilities they had missed on December 7.[20]

For all the young men standing in Marine recruiting lines, there are no illusions. The road back will be very long. They know next to nothing about what lies ahead. How many of them will it take? Will their little brothers be following them? These fresh-faced boys are eager to serve a cause bigger than themselves. If youthful enthusiasm could guarantee victory, then America was sure to win.

But the young warriors of the empire of Japan are also determined, and they are steeped in the "*bushido* spirit," based on the samurai code of honor. They embraced it for eight years in the bloody war in China, and they know in their bones that the code demands death before dishonor. Japan's minister of war, Tojo, made sure that each soldier has in his pocket his new booklet that explains the moral code of the fighting men: Running to your death, gun or sword raised high in a banzai charge, would be the only way to escape dishonor if your mission failed. Surrender would bring shame to everyone: the soldier, his family, his army, and the living-god emperor himself. The code demands, "Fear not to die for the cause of everlasting justice."[21]

They had little idea how fiercely that code would soon be tested.

4

The Changing Tide

The Rising Sun flew above the Dutch East Indies, it surmounted
the French tricolor in Indo-China, it blotted out the Union Jack in
Singapore. . . . Burma, Malaya, and Thailand were also Japanese.
India's hundreds of millions were imperiled, great China was all
but isolated from the world, Australia looked fearfully north to the
Japanese bases on New Guinea.[1]

—Robert Leckie, historian and World War II veteran

On December 22, as the United States reels from the attack on Pearl
Harbor, British prime minister Winston Churchill arrives in Washington, DC, to spend Christmas at the White House. He has invited
himself. President Roosevelt tried to dissuade him, warning of the
dangers of crossing the Atlantic Ocean, dodging U-boats and mines;
still Churchill is undaunted. The prime minister knows the attack at
Pearl Harbor has lit the fuse of the American people, but he is on a
mission to bend Roosevelt's will to take the fight to Hitler in Europe
first. He believes spending the Yuletide with the Roosevelts will help
his cause.

It is nearly Christmas, but war precautions dictate that holiday
lights are to be kept to a minimum. Cities are darkened at night, hoods
are placed over fireboxes, and neon signs in cities are left unplugged.
But that night, the Roosevelts and Churchill head out onto the South
Portico in front of a large crowd to light the White House Christmas
tree. In their respective homes in Arlington, Massachusetts, Gulfport,

Mississippi, and Lockport, New York, the Grays and Rebstocks and Grossis—and families all across the United States—sit in front of their radios to listen to their president and the prime minister. Churchill tells them that although he is far from his family and his homeland, he is glad to be among them in the country where his mother was born. He says that on this "strange Christmas eve," Americans should endeavor to "make the children happy in a world of storm," adding, "Now, by our sacrifice and daring, these same children shall not be robbed of their inheritance, or denied the right to live in a free and decent world."[2]

In the days that follow, Churchill and Roosevelt talk late into the night over cigars and scotch. The prime minister argues that the offensive against Hitler must push his forces back in North Africa first, while Roosevelt urges a France-first strategy. Churchill's stay stretches on for three weeks. He sleeps in the Blue Room and at times paces the room after his bath in just a towel and in at least one instance no towel at all, much to the surprise of President Roosevelt, who stops by to chat. The hours of talk forge a deep friendship and unshakable bond that Christmas of 1941 that will see them through the darkness to come. For each, the other is the one person who understands the enormous burden he bears.[3]

By January, Roosevelt is champing at the bit. He needs to punch back and soon. The American people must get the message that though they are down, they are not out. He wants to send Hirohito and Tojo a strong message close to home. He calls a secret meeting of his top brass at the White House. Huddled with the president are General Henry H. "Hap" Arnold, the chief of the Army Air Forces; General George C. Marshall, the chief of staff of the Army; Admiral Ernest J. King, the chief of staff of the Navy; Henry L. Stimson, the secretary of war; and William F. Knox, the secretary of the Navy.[4]

Roosevelt implores them to give him a plan that will bloody the nose of Japan and lift the sinking spirits of the American people. He pushes them again in a similar meeting on January 28. The obstacle is that the broadened ring of Japanese-controlled territory in the Pacific will require launching fighters from a great distance. But from where? The vast ocean offers no jumping-off point that is close enough to the Japanese mainland.[5]

The desperation of the president leads the military brain trust to propose a daring, if not impossible, plan. General Arnold lays it out to Roosevelt: The prime targets of the Japanese on December 7 were the United States' premier-class aircraft carriers. But by luck or the grace of God, they were not in the harbor that morning. Now those same vessels will be moved into position and act as floating airstrips, replacing the US strips on the nearby islands, which are now in Japanese hands.

The naval aircraft that typically launch off the carriers will not be used. They would never make it to the target. The plan calls for launching sixteen B-25 medium-range Army bombers (named for William "Billy" Mitchell) piloted by men from the US Army Air Corps from the deck of an aircraft carrier. There will be no chance of recovering the bombers since they were not built for a carrier landing; they are too big and have a nose wheel. They cannot be stored on the lower hangar deck, because they do not fit into the elevators. Instead, they will have to be lashed down on the flight deck, vastly shrinking the space left over for takeoff. The first plane will have just 467 feet to become airborne or plunge into the ocean.

To the crews who have trained on the carriers, the numbers do not add up. No aircraft with the standard 27,000-pound load has managed to become airborne in less than 600 feet. What they don't know is that the specially configured, stripped-down, combat-loaded planes, rigged with auxiliary fuel tanks, will tip the scales at a whopping 31,000 pounds. The aircraft, with their sixty-eight-foot wingspan, will somehow have to take off in less than 500 feet.

If they do make it into the air, they will need to fly 750 miles to drop their four five-hundred-pound bombs on targets in and around Tokyo, then hightail it for the Chinese coast, where, it is hoped, their pilots can locate the primitive landing areas marked out by the Chinese.[6] There are no guarantees; the pilots know that this is likely to be a one-way mission.

Ж

The secret plan to bomb Japan has been in the works for more than three months. But after the designated carrier, *Hornet*, is spotted on its way toward Japan by the patrol boat *Nitto Maru*, the timetable has to be accelerated.

At 7:25 a.m. on April 18, 1942, the elite bomber crews, led by the esteemed aviator Lieutenant Colonel James Doolittle, get the call to man their aircraft. Just hours before, Doolittle bolstered his men with a wry smile as he attached ribbon-tied messages for the Japanese to their bombs. Now his fellow pilots snap into their seats, flash smiles and thumbs-up, their voices drowned out by the buzz of the massive spinning propellers and the roar of thirty-two engines. Sixteen B-25 bombers stand stacked like elephants, trunk to tail, practically touching, on the deck of the *Hornet*, as it lurches up and down on the sea.[7]

The bombers rumble for takeoff, with one wingtip nearly scraping the carrier superstructure, the other slightly sticking out over the water. Two painted white stripes run down the length of *Hornet*'s deck. The pilots are to keep their left wheel on the left-hand stripe and their nose wheel on the right-hand stripe. Any deviation would be deadly.

A sailor up ahead, his signal flag blowing in the fierce winds, is just forward and to the left of the first plane. He is the focal point of sixteen pilots as they stare down the axis of the deck. For those at the end of the line, this figure, his deck uniform plastered to his body by the howling thirty-knot wind, is "first silhouetted against the skyline, and then against the horizon, and finally against the boiling ocean as *Hornet* rose and fell from one wave to the next."[8]

He is known as "Fly One," and one by one he signals the moment for takeoff. Timing is everything. He eyes the bow of the ship and the ocean dashing against it. Like a child picking the exact moment to dive into dueling jump ropes, he watches as *Hornet*'s bow completes its lift toward the sky and then is well into its descent into the trough of the next wave; then he turns to Doolittle and whips his flag like a matador's cape. Colonel Doolittle releases his brakes. The big bomber strains at the leash; now the fully revved engines propel it forward. The B-25 begins its roll forward, downhill, on the flight deck that is now dipping toward the boiling ocean.

Breathing seems to stop, every eye now pinned to the moving aircraft. It gathers speed, lumbering toward the end of the piteously short runway. Then, at just fifty miles per hour into a thirty-knot headwind, with just a few feet of runway left, Doolittle pulls back on the yoke. The nose wheel lifts just as *Hornet* surges upward to crest the next wave. As her deck rises toward the sky, the B-25 is catapulted into the air to the cheer of the sailors. With one bomber aloft, yet only twenty-five feet above the water to avoid Japanese radar, confidence shoots through one pilot after another. In short order they take to the sky as well and set their course for Japan.

Within hours and now some seven hundred miles away, high above enemy territory, one after the other they hit the release and drop their bombs. Tokyo and five other cities in Japan are rocked by explosions as "Doolittle's Raiders" release five-hundred-pounders onto their targets.

In the end the physical damage is limited, but the psychological blow to Japan is significant. The Japanese wake up to a world where bombs have fallen in their own backyard. Fifty people are dead, including some civilians, and four hundred are injured. Japan is no longer a proudly isolated, invulnerable island. The long arm of Uncle Sam has jabbed and bloodied Hirohito's bespectacled nose.

Back in the United States, the president says nothing. He knows it is no time to take a victory lap. Though the mission succeeded, the pilots never found the makeshift airstrips in China, and the planes crash-landed in China and Russia. Three pilots are dead, and eight are now Japanese prisoners.

It will be from foreign sources that the US press picks up the news of the raid. Roosevelt lets the headlines speak for themselves. The *Santa Ana Register* blares:

YANKS BOMB TOKYO.

In smaller print in the middle of page 1, subheadlines follow: "Naval and Industrial Bases of Three Other Cities Also Attacked; Raid on Tokyo Brings Elation to Washington."[9]

The *Los Angeles Times* hits the streets with a "9 AM EXTRA":

TOKYO, KOBE, YOKOHAMA
BOMBED!

On April 21, three days after the raid and with the press frantic for answers, Roosevelt finally meets with reporters. They jockey for position to hear what he has to say. The president remains stoic and coy.

"Would you care to go so far as to confirm the truth of the Japanese reports that Tokyo was bombed?" fires off the first reporter.

"No, I couldn't even do that," Roosevelt replies. "I am depending on Japanese reports very largely."[10]

It's an odd choice of words, "very largely." Indeed, the Japanese media reported the raid just hours after the bombs fell. The *New York Times* picked up the story, setting off a scramble to fill it in.

Roosevelt remains mum and feigns ignorance, insisting that the reporters know as much about the incident as he does. But members of Congress are not as content to remain silent and eagerly entertain reporters with their own speculations. The most common of which is that the attack had to have been launched from China.

Colorado senator Edwin C. Johnson immediately jumps on the bandwagon: "That is about the only place from which an air attack could have been carried out successfully."

Pennsylvania representative John Buell Snyder chimes in, telling reporters, "This will prove TNT in boosting morale, not only at home, but especially in China and Russia."

And Senator D. Worth Clark of Idaho echoes the exhilaration felt by most Americans: at last, we have been able to strike back. "This is the only way we are going to win the war—start right in bombing them at home."[11]

But astute reporters continue to press on the most curious strategic detail: "From where did the attack originate?"

Finally, Roosevelt calls the press together to reveal the answer. Pencils poised above notepads, the reporters are ready to race off to the phones to call in the story, but the president takes his time as they close in for the scoop. Again, they ask, "Mr. President, where did the raid take off from?" "Shangri-La," he replies.

)(

It is after midnight at 55 Welcher Avenue in Peekskill, New York, and Frank Bowes is at his workbench. He had taken a map out of the newspaper back when Hitler invaded Poland and put it on the wall there. He had marked it up and put pins into it to follow the expansion of Nazi territory. He had always wanted to go to Europe, and now he wondered if there would be a Europe when the war was over. He looked at the red pin he had pushed into Pearl Harbor.[12]

Now he holds a clipped newspaper headline and tacks it near Tokyo, where the Doolittle Raiders had hit. He steps back and takes a long draw on his pipe, the scent of which eventually wafts its way upstairs, letting Helen and Betts, already in their beds, know that he is still down there, deep in thought. The newly added pin seems defiantly alone, its gold color shining like a beacon on the western edge of his battle map. His young nephew, Harry Gray, now fifteen, is already itching to get in the fight. Uncle Frank has assured him that it will all be over by the time he is old enough to go. Frank wants Harry to stay right where he is on Linwood Street, in Arlington, not far from where he spent his own teenage years. He hopes maybe Harry will head off to Holy Cross for college and follow in his footsteps. Yes, he wants Harry to stay safely at home.

By May 6, 1942, any optimism Harry's uncle Frank had had about the Tokyo raid has vanished. In the Philippines, General Jonathan

Wainwright surrendered the US and Filipino forces that had bravely withstood the Japanese onslaught for five long, horrendous months. Though the details were scarce, stories of the Japanese forcing US soldiers to march hundreds of miles, many of them to their death, were starting to hit the home front. Americans could hardly bear the tales of their boys being mutilated, tortured, and starved to death, many left by the roadside unburied. It was simply unfathomable.

)(

After the Doolittle Raid, Japan lashes out against the Chinese, who they discover had laid out crude landing areas intended for the American pilots.

Japan's next priority is to shore up its southern defensive perimeter. That line is to run to the north of Australia and New Guinea. Japan has never lost a military confrontation at sea, and Hirohito, the 124th emperor, is determined to continue the unbroken chain of military success.

On the morning of May 4, 1942, the United States detects Japanese ship and troop movements toward Port Moresby, New Guinea. Admiral Chester Nimitz, the commander of the US Pacific Fleet, dispatches a naval task force. Severely depleted by the attack at Pearl Harbor, it is made up of some of the surviving cruisers and destroyers, which form around two of the last four carriers, *Lexington* and *Yorktown*. They make their way into the Coral Sea south of the Solomon Islands, searching for the enemy with orders "to destroy enemy ships, shipping, and aircraft at favorable opportunities in order to assist in checking advances by the enemy in the New Guinea–Solomon area."[13]

On May 7, 1942, a "favorable opportunity" arrives. The fleets spot each other on radar and signal for air attacks. Neither fleet sees the ships of the other side. But each land deadly blows, sinking ships in a storm of torpedo and dive-bomber attacks. In the end, the combatants back off to lick their wounds and count their casualties. The Japanese light carrier *Shoho* has sunk to the bottom of the ocean under the pounding of thirteen bombs and seven torpedoes. It was under attack only a short fifteen minutes.[14] The second carrier, *Shokaku*, lumbers along, wounded by the direct hits of six dive-bombers. The Japanese turn tail and abandon their mission to invade New Guinea and occupy Port Moresby.

But the US carriers are also hit hard. Gasoline fires roar across the deck of *Lexington*. Sailors scramble to put them out. Then the tank explodes in a fireball. The stinging smell of fuel burns in the sailors' nostrils and eyes, like Pearl Harbor all over again.[15] A gigantic column of dense black smoke rises skyward, and in the early hours of May 8, the order comes to abandon the "Lady Lex." US destroyers come in to finish her off, sinking her to the depths of the Pacific.

Yorktown, down but not out, sets course for Pearl Harbor for repairs. The Navy is now down to only two carriers, *Hornet* and *Enterprise*. Both sides have lost about seventy aircraft, and 1,500 sailors and aviators are dead.[16]

What neither side knows is that in this battle, in these days in May 1942 in the Coral Sea, the Japanese vision of southern territorial expansion by sea has been stopped cold in its tracks. But the battle-grounds to come lie dotted along stretches arching west and east on the path to the Japanese mainland.

※

For the second time in three weeks, American newspapers hit the stands with screaming bold headlines. This time it is the battle news from the Coral Sea. *The Sun* of New York trumpets in big black letters:

15 JAP SHIPS SUNK,
LEXINGTON IS LOST,
IN CORAL SEA FIGHT[17]

That evening, Frank Bowes turns back the pages of the newspaper to the detailed maps, to read the reports of what unfolded on the Coral Sea. Helen sits in her maroon velvet chair and leafs through the papers as well. She is still in her dress and pumps after a long day at work. Betts scampers down the front staircase in her pajamas, her wet brown curls combed, ready for bed. She and her aunt Jane went to Woolworth's that afternoon after school, and Betts picked out a small box of American flags on pins. Helen looks over the top of her newspaper with a slight smile, watching as Betts holds them out in her small hands. She looks up at her father with her proud bright hazel eyes. "Daddy, these are for your map."

He smiles at her and pats her wet head. "Thank you, Betts. Tomorrow we will find Port Moresby, but now it is off to bed for you!" He holds her hand as they walk upstairs with Helen.

※

One month later on June 7, days of press speculation continue as sketchy details emerge of yet another naval battle going on near the island of Midway. There are reports that the Americans are inflicting some real damage on the Japanese.

The *Sunday Telegram* of Elmira, New York, blares across page 1:

13 TO 15 JAP SHIPS SUNK OR DAMAGED
GREAT VICTORY IN MAKING, SAYS NIMITZ

There's more. The subhead reads:

2 OR 3 CARRIERS WITH PLANES AMONG ENEMY MIDWAY
LOSSES; BATTLE RAGES INTO THIRD DAY.[18]

A third day! Day three spells doom for a fourth Japanese carrier, which follows their carriers *Kaga*, *Akagi*, and *Soryu* to the ocean floor in a crushing blow for the Rising Sun.

It had begun, in the days prior, as the massive Japanese naval force moved toward Midway Island to push their eastern defensive line closer to Hawaii, and draw the United States' remaining aircraft carriers into battle.

Admiral of the Fleet Isoroku Yamamoto had sailed the Japanese Combined Fleet to the east in two battle formations. The first group of the huge armada had four carriers, two battleships, three cruisers, eleven destroyers, and five supply ships. On board the carriers, lined up head to toe, were 275 attack aircraft and the crews to man them. Several hundred miles to the rear were seven more battleships, one light carrier, three cruisers, and twenty destroyers. It was a daunting naval caravan as far as the eye could see.

On *Hornet*, *Enterprise*, and *Yorktown*, sweating work crews were still fixing and hammering and patching, as they sensed the enemy far out there in the distant rolling waves. But the Japanese commanders misjudged the location of the US carriers, believing them to be somewhere between the Coral Sea and Pearl Harbor.

They were wrong.

In fact, the Americans were less than an hour's flight from the Japanese carrier force.[19] The Japanese dive-bombers may have swept in on unsuspecting sailors on December 7, 1941, but six months later, at Midway, it was the Japanese who never saw the attack coming.

The American attack began midmorning on June 4, and within moments, three Japanese carriers and a heavy cruiser were ablaze. The fourth carrier, *Hiryu*, was the only one to initially escape major damage. It launched an attack against the *Yorktown* and severely damaged the American carrier. But by 5:00 p.m., dive-bombers delivered disabling attacks on *Hiryu*, and it, too, was scuttled by the next morning.

After Midway, the Japanese could no longer claim naval or air superiority in the Pacific. The four enemy carriers they lost were all attackers at Pearl Harbor. Unfortunately, the patched-up *Yorktown*, named for the pivotal battle of the American Revolution, also saw her last day at sea in the Battle of Midway. Torpedoed by the Japanese submarine I-168, the crew tried desperately to save her, but she was lost.

The morning after, Admiral Nimitz sent a message to his task force commanders: "You who have participated in the Battle of Midway today have written a glorious page in our history. I am proud to be associated with you."[20]

X

Weeks earlier, Frank Bowes had wondered how a sea of red and black ink could cover so much of the world map—and whether it was only a matter of time before it would cross the ocean to California and the US mainland—but tonight he and many in America have hope. The Battle of the Coral Sea has stopped the Japanese Empire's southern expansion, and the Battle of Midway has hemmed it in on the east. The bleeding has stopped, and it appears that the pushback is slowly getting under way.

X

Frank welcomes Harry for a visit just before his sixteenth birthday. It isn't often that the Bowes family have a boy in the house or that Anne can buy her son a train ticket, but everyone is glad to have Harry around. The house is too quiet much of the time with just one child, but Harry punches a hole through the silence with his laugh and hilarious stories about him and his friends sneaking into the movie theater in Arlington and taking their dates to the roller rink. Betts sits at the dinner table staring at him and hoping no one will shush him when he talks about teenage things with her parents. She loves the banter and how different her dad seems around him, since they are both "boys." Harry loves the change of scenery. Plus, he got to take the train and feels very grown up.

Talk turns to the war, as it does at every dinner table in 1942. When Harry talks about it, he gets that glimmer in his eye. He wants to be old enough to go fight the "Japs," as he calls them, and the Nazis. He doesn't want the war to pass him by. He wants the United States to win, yes, but not before he can get there. "I'm going to do it, Uncle Frank. I'm going to sign up as soon as I can," he says, gulping down his dinner. "I'm going to be a Marine."

Frank cuts his steak and nods. He knows just how Harry feels. But

Uncle Frank has told him not to enlist. "Wait to be drafted, Harry. You are the man of the house. Your mother needs you. Just be patient." But "patience" is a word wasted on sixteen-year-old boys. Frank knows that Harry looks up to him; he also knows when he looks in those bright green eyes and Harry smiles that warm, sweet smile back at him, as if nothing can touch him, that he isn't listening and there isn't much that Frank or anyone else can do about it.

So Frank does the only thing he can: every Sunday at the Church of the Assumption, when he is on his knees, he prays to God that it will all be over before next June 13, when Harry turns seventeen.[21]

5

What Hirohito Knew

I had presumed the news of the terrible losses sustained by the naval forces would have caused him untold anxiety, yet he was as calm as usual. He ordered [the Navy chief of staff] to ensure that future operations continue bold and aggressive.[1]

—From the diary of Koichi Kido, aide to Emperor Hirohito

The shock was all-encompassing. The Japanese navy once achieved great victories over its formidable foes China and Russia but now was suffering blows that cracked open the door to defeat by America and its allies. To the emperor, the first six months of 1942 seemed inexplicable. Until April 18, there had not been a shred of good news to bolster the flagging spirits of Americans and their allies. After April 18, good news was elusive for Japan.

Who deserved the blame for the catastrophe at Midway? The British and Americans had been on their knees. Had his leadership failed? Had his generals failed him? The Japanese had expected to push back the Americans in the central Pacific, but now the opposite was happening: they were losing dominance in the South and Southwest Pacific as well. The differences in culture and tactics appeared to be hurting the Japanese efforts rather than giving them an edge. They were now part of the wider world, and the forces against them were daunting.

After Commodore Perry pierced the veil of Japanese secrecy in 1853, Japan's rise as a military power was built on its own "rules of war." Those rules were formed in part by the fifth-century B.C. military strategist Sun Tzu, but largely, they were the creation of the Emperor Meiji, who came to the throne at age fifteen in 1867. Meiji brought Japan out of its dark age and into the light as a thriving industrial society with the military might to defeat China.

Meiji dictated "Japan will attack without warning."[2] And why not? Sucker-punching a nation with which you are at peace was anathema to the West, but Meiji's dictum was to conquer. Western rites of "proper" engagement were of no concern to him. An ancient samurai motto seemed to sanction it: "Win first, fight later." It was in sync as well with the great Sun Tzu's maxim: "In war the victorious strategist only seeks battle after the victory has been won."[3]

But the maxims of the samurai and Sun Tzu assume that hostilities have begun and two nations are at war; they propose that he who is victorious without fighting does so by presenting such a powerful posture that victory is certain. Meiji may have contorted his attack-without-warning strategy to resemble the win-first dictum of Sun Tzu. If so, he missed, or ignored, the second line of that dictum: "He who is destined to defeat first fights and afterwards looks for victory."[4]

※

On December 25, 1926, at the age of twenty-five, Prince Regent Hirohito, a grandson of the late warrior Emperor Meiji, ascended the throne as the 124th emperor of Japan, after the death of his father. The Shinto religious ceremony celebrated him as the descendant of Amaterasu, the sun goddess, who had created the Japanese archipelago from the drops of water that fell from her spear.[5] In conformance with the custom of naming the upcoming era, Hirohito took the name "Showa," meaning "Enlightenment and Peace."[6]

Meiji possessed absolute divine rule. Hirohito was destined to struggle with a covey of powerful and often conniving advisers, but in all matters, he had the final word. He aspired to emulate the British model of constitutional monarchy, but two years into his reign, financial catastrophe thwarted his plans for the evolution of his government. First came the 1927 financial panic and the ensuing depression, then the calamity of a worldwide depression in 1929.

Japan's fragile economy could not risk any form of democracy in this fragile moment. Instead, Hirohito looked across the sea to China with a clenched fist. What China had, Japan must take; rich farmland, plentiful mines and coal. The Chinese were an easy target, and Manchuria was the obvious point of entry.

The United States had firmly signaled that Manchuria belonged to China, but Hirohito's prime minister, General Giichi Tanaka, had other ideas. He brazenly told his cabinet that a takeover of Manchuria was necessary.[7] So began the Japanese era of conquest, usually cloaked in multiple layers of deception, fraud, and feigned indignation. The drive for natural resources was the initial goal, but the taste for a growing empire was seductive. That hunger pulsed through the upper echelons of Japanese military and imperial advisers, but Hirohito, as sovereign, head of state, and supreme military commander, clearly wanted to make his mark on the world and prove the superiority of his dynasty and his people.

His father, Emperor Taisho, had been a weak leader, plagued by mental illness. As one story goes, on a rare occasion when he actually addressed the Imperial Diet of Japan, he stood before them all, rolled up his speech, and looked at them all through it, as if it were a spyglass.[8]

Hirohito took over as regent for his ailing father in 1921, becoming the effective ruler as Taisho retired to the country and died in December 1926.

Any suggestion that Hirohito was a bystander who watched as history unfolded is challenged by his every action. In 1928, many Japanese companies operated in Manchuria and defense was an integral part of the growing military-industrial complex. Rebellious soldiers plotted an "incident" to provoke China. Anticipating that it would work, the Imperial General Staff drew up secret operational orders to mobilize the army in Manchuria on May 22, 1928. But US intelligence uncovered the Japanese movements in Manchuria, and, suspecting that something was afoot, the US government demanded to know what Japan's intentions were, making clear that in the eyes of the West, Manchuria was Chinese territory.[9] The United States emphasized that any deviation from that understanding would constitute "a most serious matter."[10]

Tokyo got cold feet and backed down. But the rebels were furious and devised a plot to keep moving the ball forward. On June 4, 1928, at 5:20 a.m., a bomb they planted exploded under the railcar of a Manchurian warlord and killed him. Japanese soldiers approached the scene to investigate. They spotted three suspicious Chinese whom they approached to question. When one suddenly hurled a bomb, they were compelled to stab and kill two of them; the third escaped.

The three were in on the ruse and had been hired by the Japanese as backup assassins who were to rush in and finish off the warlord in case the bomb did not do its job. They did not know that the plan included killing them and, with them, their knowledge of the plot. But the third man escaped, made his way to the son of the slain Chinese warlord, and revealed the whole sordid plot.[11]

To stoke instability, the rebel soldiers went about bombing the homes and offices of Japanese residents as if it were the Chinese doing it, then offered the services of the Japanese Army to restore order. The plan fell flat on its face. In the end, the rebels' failures revealed their own duplicity.

Word quickly reached the Imperial Palace in Tokyo, and anxious advisers argued that the emperor be informed and the agitators punished. Others said no, fearing that escalating the situation would reflect badly on Japan and ignite rumors that the treachery had been sanctioned from the top.

Finally, the prime minister, Tanaka, went to Hirohito with the truth. The emperor demanded that the conspirators be punished. When it was not done quickly, he repeated his command. But there was no punishment; the Army secretly would not allow it, and the emperor let it lie. Some of the guilty officers resigned. Officially, the Army declared the incident closed, having found no evidence. In July 1929,

Tanaka stepped down in disgrace. In the end, Hirohito let those who had been responsible live, but their careers were over when the cabinet essentially collapsed.

It was not the last time Hirohito would butt heads with his military leaders. In 1930, despite enormous Japanese military and civilian opposition to the proposed London Naval Treaty, which sought limits on submarines and shipbuilding, Hirohito overcame the opposition and backed the treaty. Without him it was doomed to failure. The treaty was approved and ratified.[12]

A year later, the restless forces in the Japanese Army took another surreptitious run at amassing control over parts of Manchuria. Again Hirohito feigned disapproval, but his silence suggested otherwise. By the end of 1931, Manchuria was firmly under Japanese control. Like the parent of a rebellious child, Hirohito chose to look the other way while his officers moved in on Manchuria, stopping short of disciplining them as they achieved the desired goal. Japan signed an "agreement" with the last emperor of China, Puyi, in 1932, to demonstrate legitimacy in the eyes of the world, and established Manchuria as a puppet state.[13]

After a resolution by the League of Nations condemning the actions in Manchuria, Japan withdrew from the world body.

Japan was doubling down on its warrior culture, dynastic rule, and religious sovereignty of the emperor and moving farther away from any dream of constitutional monarchy. Hirohito embraced it. His father had been a weak ruler. His own personality was uncharismatic and awkward. He moved to bolster his stature as a deified leader. The Army instituted the Imperial Way with its patriotic pledge: "The Emperor, the people, the land and morality are one and indivisible."[14]

The youths of the nation were "reeducated" in the religion of emperor worship: "The entire nation regard[s] our emperor as a Living God." They were taught to die willingly for the emperor; they must always attack—never retreat.[15] Their training was brutal. Had he chosen to, Hirohito could have reined in that resurrection of the *bushido* code. But he did not. In the years to come, young men from the United

States would be astonished as Japanese soldiers ran into oncoming fire and exploded grenades into their own torsos, rather than humiliate their families and emperor by surrendering.

While the nation was being programmed in emperor worship, the Army officers continued their headstrong ways. On February 26, 1936, Army assassins mobilized to eliminate seven key figures in a coup of the Tokyo government leadership. They cloaked their actions as an effort to shore up the Divine Showa Restoration—done, of course, for the emperor's benefit.

Hirohito called in his minister of war and ordered that the rebellion be put down. Those who had surrounded the targets of assassination were now themselves surrounded by soldiers obeying the emperor's orders.[16] Despite the surreptitious moves and plots of his military to chart its own destiny, somehow Hirohito always had an inside track to their deviousness. He was leading from the shadows of the palace, always.

As Japan moved steadily toward its goal of Asian dominance, 1937 brought yet another opportunistic "incident" on the Chinese mainland. On July 7, a single Japanese infantry company decided to maneuver into a most unlikely area of the Twenty-ninth Chinese Army. In the confrontation, shots were exchanged on the disputed area of the Marco Polo Bridge. A cease-fire document was hastily drafted, but the Japanese left it unsigned for two days. At home the Japanese newspapers reported government-sanctioned accounts of the skirmish. It was a tale of anti-Japanese racism and exaggerated stories of Chinese atrocities.

The incident at the Marco Polo Bridge served the Japanese military's purpose of pushing the area of engagement beyond Manchuria into north China. The military leadership then went on to claim that the area of hostilities now went beyond north China and in fact that all of China was now in the Japanese sphere of influence. It was an argument made purely to justify the protection of Japanese interests wherever and whenever the Imperial Army saw fit. The military leaders pressed the emperor further and argued that, given the new circumstances, military reinforcements were necessary. They said it would take less than a month to subdue Chiang Kai-shek's armies and create peace in China.[17]

The emperor listened, fully aware that such a move would pull his country deeper into an aggressive path in Asia. He was told that five divisions from Japan, in addition to the existing army already in China, should do the trick; his advisers counseled that it wasn't really an act of war, more a show of force against the Chinese to *prevent* war. Hirohito gave the royal nod and his approval for the extended operation.

With that, he gave not only his blessing to the military leaders' lust for war but his confirmation of their distorted reasoning for the mission creep in China. He then unlocked the imperial war chest, without which his ambitious military advisers would be impotent.

Hirohito did not choose to weigh down progress with an over-attention to reason or thought when the possibility of a widening Japanese Empire was dangled before him.

Within a month, Hirohito was getting anxious. The promised quick victory was now nowhere in sight. The unsophisticated but fanatical Chinese Army was willing to sustain enormous losses against the modern Japanese Army. Hirohito called for an end to the fighting. A diplomatic solution would include land concessions, and that would be a win for now.

But it was too late. One "incident" or skirmish led to a response and then another, and now there was a full-scale mobilization of the Chinese armies and the emperor was left with no choice but to fight fire with fire.

Future apologists for Emperor Hirohito would proclaim that he had been personally opposed to war but had been powerless to stop it. The invasion that followed the incident at the Marco Polo Bridge refutes that notion, but a further examination of the events of the Second Sino-Japanese War proves that the emperor was very much in charge. Any doubt about his convictions was swept away that December in the Rape of Nanking.

By the end of 1937, the Japanese had the Chinese capital completely surrounded. Day and night, they pummeled the city with artillery and air strikes. Once the city was brought to its knees, the
Japanese soldiers began a six-week massacre that would go down as
one of the most brutal in the history of the world. It was a scene of
unbounded degradation, torture, mutilation, and murder. Unborn
children were sliced from their mothers' wombs. Sexual mutilation by
the insertion of bayonets and sharpened bamboo poles into women's
vaginas and breast amputations were giddily carried out and photographed by the rampaging Japanese soldiers.

The historian Edwin Hoyt attempted to explain the origins of the
Japanese bloodlust:

> It was a result of the policy of brutalization of the troops from
> the day of enlistment. In the name of discipline, the most violent
> and inhumane actions had been taken against these soldiers . . .
> and had destroyed most of the admirable tender elements of the
> Japanese character. The new bushido had made them brutes, and
> they acted like brutes.[18]

That December, Reverend James M. McCallum, an American
working at a hospital in a demilitarized enclave, made safe under German auspices and flying the Nazi flag, wrote in his diary:

> Never have I heard or read such brutality. Rape! Rape! Rape! We
> estimate at least 1,000 cases a night and many by day. In case
> of resistance or anything that seems like disapproval, there is a
> bayonet stab or a bullet. . . . People are hysterical. . . . Women
> are being carried off every morning, afternoon and evening. The
> whole Japanese army seems to be free to go and come as it pleases,
> and to do whatever it pleases.[19]

On December 23, 1937, George Fitch, an American Protestant
missionary in Nanking, wrote that Nanking "is a city laid waste, rav-

aged, completely looted. . . . It is hell on earth. Hundreds of innocent civilians are shot before your eyes or used as bayonet practice. . . . A thousand women kneel before you crying hysterically, begging you to save them from the beasts who are preying on them. This is a hell I had never before envisaged."[20]

The butchery went on unmitigated for weeks. The officers saw a purpose in it. One of the regimental commanders confided to Hirohito's uncle General Yasuhiko Asaka that "the best bayonet training in the world was to let the troops work on people."[21]

Throughout the atrocities, Hirohito remained silent in his palace in Tokyo.

In Japan, newspapers glorified the butchery. One headline read:

Contest to Cut Down a Hundred!
Two Second Lieutenants Already Up to Eighty[22]

That was the headline on a story by Asami Kazuo and Suzuki Jiro on the murderous exploits of two Japanese officers, Mukai Toshiaki and Noda Tsuyoshi.[23] The two lieutenants bragged about their hand-to-hand combat with enemy soldiers, all of whom they claimed to have vanquished and dispatched with their swords alone. It was like a national sporting event to kill one hundred enemy soldiers first, and the Japanese public followed along. Every few days in December, the papers flashed updates and tallies of the kills until the final score was announced, 106–105. Both Japanese warriors outlasted more than two hundred Chinese rivals, somehow without sustaining even a scratch.[24]

But underneath the swashbuckling samurai spirit and *bushido* was a far less sportive, far more grim reality.

The truth leaked out rather ignominiously when one of the two lieutenants went home and detailed his exploits as if unaware of the lore. It turned out that the killings had been nothing more than extermination of prisoners. Neither of the Japanese warrior soldiers had suffered a scratch for the simple reason that none of the Chinese had been armed. They hadn't even been fighting back. After they surrendered, he admitted, "we'd line them up and cut them down, from one end of the line to the other."[25]

The soldiers in the Japanese Army were behaving just as they had been taught to. They had been conditioned to believe that they were part of a superior race. They pledged obedience to their officers and worshiped their emperor as a god. They were taught that anything or anyone non-Japanese was beneath them and therefore disposable.

It was all to the same ends to tell tales of valiant fighting that actually amounted to no more than systematic extinction. Lieutenant General Nakajima Kesago described his plan to murder the thousands of Chinese prisoners now under his control: "Divide them into groups of two hundred . . . and deal with them."[26]

In January 1938, Koki Hirota, the Japanese foreign minister, wrote, "I investigated reported atrocities committed by the Japanese army in Nanking and elsewhere. . . . Convincing proof. Japanese army continuing [to] behave in fashion reminiscent [of] Attila and his huns. . . . 300,000 Chinese civilians slaughtered [in] cold blood."[27]

That damning note found its way into the hands of a Nanking resident, Harold John Timperley, a reporter for England's *Manchester Guardian*. He immediately sent it on to the *Guardian* in enciphered English, which was intercepted and decoded by US intelligence and sent on to Washington.[28]

If Hirohito's foreign minister knew about the Nanking holocaust, how could the emperor not know? Hirota was not some low-level military officer on the faraway Chinese battlefield; he was part of the imperial cabinet and in the emperor's inner circle.

The rest of the world slowly became aware of the horror happening on the other side of the ocean, as diaries and photographs of Japanese soldiers murdering and raping helpless victims began to appear with all the ghastly details, including people being doused with gasoline and set afire. Their testimonies removed all doubt that anyone, anywhere could pretend not to know what was happening under the rule of Emperor Hirohito, who had taken for the name of his reign Showa, "Enlightenment and Peace."

In fact, it was a family affair. General Asaka, a prince of the royal family, had been personally appointed by the emperor, and the Nanking massacre had been carried out under his direct command. Hirohito himself had removed the constraints of international law for the protection of Chinese prisoners. For Hirohito, there was no such thing as a Chinese POW.[29] Neither Hirohito nor his uncle Asaka had stepped in to command an end to the slaughter that dragged on and on in Nanking. The historian Yoshida Yutaka wrote of the triumphant return of Asaka, who came bearing as gifts objects pilfered from the devastated city. He presented Hirohito with several Chinese art objects, saying, "We always bring back such things as booty."[30]

※

After the Doolittle Raid, the Japanese captured eight elite US Army Air Corps pilots. They were taken prisoner after they dropped their bombs on and near the Japanese capital and then crash-landed their planes. All of the pilots had known it was a mission from which they were unlikely to return.

General Tojo opposed putting them to death, fearing retaliation against Japanese citizens in the United States. The army generals urged the execution of all eight, to send a message. Hirohito commuted the sentences of five of the pilots and sanctioned the execution of three. Since all the prisoner-of-war records were later destroyed, no one knows why he let the five live.[31]

In 1942, after the Battle of Midway, US forces began to mobilize for what lay ahead. Midway had stopped the eastward expansion, but to the west lay the empire's hundreds of heavily fortified fortress-island outposts. The US Marine Corps's mission was to attack across the vast central Pacific, defeat the island-chain defenders, convert the captured islands into stepping-stones, and attack the heart of Japan. The young Marines who were unaware of the gruesome reports from Nanking enjoyed an innocence not shared by those who had paid attention. For them the images of how the Japanese had treated their vanquished were seared into their minds as they set sail.

6

The First Step: Say a Prayer for Your Pal on Guadalcanal

I've got spurs that jingle, jangle, jingle / As I go riding merrily along / And they sing, oh, ain't you glad you're single?

—Kay Kyser Orchestra, "Jingle Jangle Jingle" (1942)

Harry Gray hums along, "And that song ain't so very far from wrong." He likes what he sees in the mirror. He has grown at least another inch in the past year and is shaving pretty much every day now. Looking at his reflection, he can't help but smile a little, rubbing some Brylcreem into his hair and making a clean part to the right. The wide teeth of his comb carve his blondish-brown hair into a wave like ripples on the sea. He buttons up his shirt as he hears the *click-clack* out the window of Nancy, riding his creaky silver bike up the driveway. It is five o'clock, so she is just back from her route slinging *Saturday Evening Post*s on front stoops up and down the neighborhood streets.

"Oh, Naaaan-cy!" he hollers singsongy from upstairs as her saddle shoes slap up the front steps.

"Junior, I don't have any money!" she yells and runs like lightning into her room, slamming the door.

It's always the same: she adores her big brother, but she can't for the life of her figure out where his money goes. Every week she stuffs the $1.35 she makes for the magazine deliveries into the very back of her night table drawer. She is saving up for a bike of her own. But there he is again now, rapping lightly on her door. "Nance?" He cracks the door open just a bit, and she looks up at his sixteen-year-old eyes bearing down on her. "If you just lend me one dollar, I will pay you right back as soon as I get paid, and I will let you play touch football with me and Tom tomorrow after Mass." She looks up at him, trying to hold back a smile. She already has the dollar in her hand. It's a bargain he knows she will strike.

Tom is the handsome boy next door. He has a fox terrier named Riot. Nancy loves to play with them and race across the yard, squeezing the football tight in her arms. Sometimes her friends stroll by on the other side of the street, watching her running and laughing with the big boys. Other times, Harry puts Riot into the basket of his bike, and Nancy squeezes onto the front of the seat with him behind her, his arms on either side holding the handlebars, swerving from side to side and laughing as she screams, "Stop!" They come within a hairsbreadth of a tree or a fence or a parked car, but somehow at the last second Harry steers them onto the grass in front of the Linwood Street house, bumping up over the curb. Anne stands in the doorway watching it all, pretending to be just a little bit mad.

So of course Nancy gives him the dollar. He kisses her head and takes off like the wind. She swings around the doorway, watching him run down the stairs, hands hitting the walls instead of the banister as he goes and singing "Jingle, jangle, jingle . . ." The scent of his aftershave hangs in the air.

Tom and his sister, Kitty, pick up Harry, and they drive through town, the car windows down in the warm, still summer night. At a stoplight, Harry looks over at the old Winchester Savings Bank; a poster hangs in the window: "Even a little can help a lot—NOW." On the poster a little blond girl and her big sister crouch over a war stamps book, licking stamps and sticking them onto the page. Next to them on the floor lies a soldier's cap.

Harry feels a twinge of guilt about borrowing money to go bowling, but damn it, he wants to do more than lick stamps, he wants to lick "Japs." He is so ready! He kicks the floor of the car in frustration.

He does not want to wait another year. He can't imagine waiting another year. Three miles down the road, they pull up to Bowl Haven. Candlepin bowling on a Saturday night in New England; walk in the door, and you can forget all about the war. Taking a look around, Harry pushes his hands down into his pockets. The place is packed. The floor rumbles as balls roll down the alleys, pins crashing, steel bars slamming down to sweep them noisily into the pit. Underneath the sound of the balls shooting back up the ramp like earthquake tremors, teenagers jostle on the benches, one on each bench sitting at the lit score pad, pencil in his teeth, asking, "What'd you get? Are you sure?" They are whistling and slapping each other on the back. Harry takes it all in. There's that song again. It's on all the time: "Aren't you glad you're single?" He sips his Coke and settles onto a bench as Tom strolls up to roll his first ball. He takes another look over his shoulder; his eyes land on a slim blonde in the last lane. She is laughing and putting her hands over her face. Behind her, a ball meanders like a drunken sailor ever so slowly down the alley before plopping into the gutter. She slides onto the curved seat next to a boy about his own age. She has cherry-red lipstick and long legs crossed over each other under a straight skirt that skims the top of her smooth knees. Anybody going off to the war would want a picture of a girl like that in his pocket, thinks Harry. Staring over his shoulder, he watches her a bit longer. It suddenly seems as if there isn't anything else going on around them. If she were his girl, he would write to her every day from wherever he was, whoever she is.

"Harry, wake up, pal! What are ya looking at? Come on! It's your turn!"

--- ⋊⋉ ---

Charlie Gubish married his girlfriend, Ethel, on May 11, 1939, and their two boys, Charles and Richard, followed quickly thereafter. They live on a farm in Wassergass outside Hellertown, Pennsylvania. Their place isn't far from where Charlie grew up on his parents' 132-acre farm.

When Charlie gets home from a long day at work at the fire department at Bethlehem Steel, he plays with the boys, and sometimes when he looks at them, he sees the old days. In his family, as he was growing up, there were twelve brothers and sisters. Three of them died as babies, gone before they were five months old. Two were stepbrothers. Charlie left school at the age of twelve to help out on the farm, which was not unusual back then. His father needed the help. But it wasn't all work. Charlie and his sister, Helen, would run over the hills and into the woods when the work was done for the day. One spring day, they discovered what looked like a "tin man" propped up in the trees. Helen screamed, and then Charlie thought he saw the strange creature move, and they ran as fast as they could all the way home to tell their father about the strange man in the forest. Charlie's dad's face grew stern, and he looked them both square in the eyes. He scolded them for going that far and told them not to tell anyone what they had seen. In time, Charlie figured out that the "tin man" was busy making whiskey out there in the woods, during Prohibition. No doubt the men snuck a bit of it, when the whole family gathered at the Gubishes' farm on the weekends. The men would play cards and the women would cook for everyone.[1]

Charlie smiled thinking about it.

He bounces little Charles on his knee, and his thoughts turn to the present. Working at the mill makes him and the other men exempt from the draft since they are supporting the war effort. But when Charlie watches the young men shipping out in their smart uniforms, there are times when he longs to get onto a ship and sail away, see the world and maybe even a bit of action against the Japanese.

)(

In the summer of 1942, the US victories in the Coral Sea and on Midway begin to dim a bit in their ability to keep Americans' spirits high. On the ground, the reality is that "our boys" are in a helluva fight against the soldiers of the Third Reich and those of the Rising Sun.

Field Marshal Erwin Rommel and his vaunted Afrika Korps appear to be unstoppable in North Africa as they capture Tobruk. On the eastern front, the Red Army reels under the devastating German onslaught; gruesome death is everywhere and casualties climb into the millions.[2] Americans do not know how bad it really is. By the end of the year, 35,000 of our brave young men will be dead: shot down in the air or blown up on the sea or the land.

Back home, American factories kick into high gear, working overtime to build the machines to fight the war. The auto factories that built 3 million cars in 1941 turn out only 139 new cars during the war years. Women flood into the workforce, as they did during World War I in England. Each morning, they pour through factory doors, lunch boxes and tools in hand, to build fuselages at Chrysler and engines at General Motors. At Ford, massively converted assembly lines build B-24 Liberator bombers, turning out one every sixty-three minutes.[3]

But the men to fly the new planes and fire from their gun turrets are nowhere near ready yet. As Americans sit in their cinema seats gazing up at newsreels of goose-stepping German soldiers and hearing reports of the treatment of our young men at the hands of their Japanese captors, they harbor secret doubts.

The United States' fighting strike force in the Pacific numbers only 15,000. What is that in the face of enemy armies in the millions? They are the men of the 1st Marine Division, a curious lot of holdovers from the 1930s who developed the new doctrine of amphibious warfare. They are the Marines who endured the privations of constant training, desolate posts and training grounds, and long separations from just about everyone and everything. The Corps is their home.

During World War I, Captain John Thomason wrote from France that the strange collection of fighting men were:

> a number of diverse people who ran curiously to type, with drilled shoulders and bone-deep sunburn, and a tolerant scorn for nearly everything on earth. They were the Leathernecks, the old breed

of American regular, regarding the service as home and war an occupation.[4]

Their home base was one only a "leatherneck" could love, New River Base, North Carolina: a recent Marine Corps acquisition described as "111,710 acres of water, coastal swamp and plain, theretofore inhabited largely by sandflies, ticks, chiggers, and snakes."[5]

To those being forged in that crucible, the grueling training and deprivations were to be not simply endured but relished and embraced as the path to a new level of esprit, camaraderie, teamwork, and disdain for all those who could never measure up. It was the chance for the new men to attempt to attain the never-to-be-attained title of "Old Breed."

Though that high-minded goal was not necessarily foremost in the minds of the Marines striving to achieve it, the idea of the ordeal itself was not lost on them. "This is the way they want things," growled one salty veteran. "You don't make a good fightin' man if you're in love with everybody. You got to be mad, so sore at everything you'd slug your best buddy at the drop of a pisscutter [slang for garrison cap]."

Recreation, when it came, was the occasional movie night, boxing match, or homegrown Marine talent show. Even the USO shows avoided the swamp in North Carolina. The men were largely shut off from the world, except for their rare, shared copies of the *Onslow County News*. Its editor seemed as salty and pissed off at the world as the Marines, hawking his weekly product as "the only paper in the world that gives a damn about Onslow County."[6]

That band of brothers, bound by their isolation and seemingly abandoned by all, wore their moniker, "the Raggedy Ass Marines," as a badge of honor. There was indeed a 2nd Marine Brigade stationed on the West Coast, but the Raggedy Asses delighted in distancing themselves from those "candy asses," and since the 2nd Brigade occasionally furnished Marines to the film industry, they labeled them "the Hollywood Marines," with all the disdain that the title conveyed.[7]

A Marine private's pay was $40 a month,[8] and the mess hall or field rations kept him fed. The Corps provided a roof over his head every night—even if it was a starry or stormy sky—and soon a refrain spread among them: "In the Corps, every day's a holiday and every meal's a banquet!" To many, they seemed a strange lot, but to one another, they were Marines.

In February 1941, the collection of "Old Breeders" that had been the nucleus of the 1st Marine Brigade since 1934 became the 1st Marine Division. During the seven previous years, the brigade had been the very essence of amphibious doctrine. It had conducted six fleet landing exercises training all services, and it had honed its unusual skill in warfare to the highest level. Now, on the day of its formation as a division, the men had no time for celebration; they embarked for Culebra for yet a seventh exercise.

A personnel officer noted of the new men, "The average age of the enlisted personnel is very low, probably not 20 years—about 90 percent of them enlisted since Pearl Harbor. They are full of patriotism and have the up-and-at-'em spirit."[9]

The naval brain trust, led by Admiral Ernest J. King, the chief of naval operations, was well aware that Japan's forces continued to fortify its outer-island defense system. Few people even knew where those far-flung places were, but during their whirlwind 1942 military expansion, Japanese forces had seized Rabaul in the previously British-held Northern Solomon chain. The rest of the chain, which ran from northwest to southeast, was also to be seized and fortified as an impregnable line blocking all communications and supply lines with Australia and New Zealand.

The historian John L. Zimmerman wrote of the Japanese, "In Rabaul they secured a prize of great strategic worth . . . as a point of departure for further offensives to the south . . . toward the all-important, slender U.S. line of supply and communications from the Hawaiian Islands to Australia and New Zealand."[10]

Despite the heady successes in the Coral Sea in the waters to the south of the Solomon chain and at Midway Island in the central Pacific, what was now at stake was complete control of the southern

Pacific Ocean and the installation of a phalanx of interlocked, fortified Japanese defensive lines. The foothold the Japanese had on those two spots enabled progress on two potential fronts. The northern route, from Pearl Harbor, could move from Tarawa to Saipan to Guam to Japan's own Iwo Jima. The southern route, up from New Zealand, would start with Guadalcanal, Leyte Gulf, Hong Kong, and on to Japan's own Okinawa. Both routes would involve amphibious assaults on heavily fortified Japanese bases. Most would require deadly close-quarters combat in order to drive out every last Japanese soldier. Battles at sea can sometimes provide easy victories, but there would be no easy land victories in the South Pacific. Every inch of wet jungle and barren rock would be paid for in blood.

Admiral King was determined to move the small band of leatherneck fighters along with his depleted navy to a position closer to possible combat. He ordered two-thirds of the 1st Marine Division, under the command of General Alexander Vandegrift, to Wellington, New Zealand. Vandegrift balked, complaining that the final combat training had not been completed. King assured him that combat was not expected to occur before January 1943, and there would be plenty of time, at least six months in Wellington, to complete training.

So on May 19, 1942, the 5th Marines sets sail from Norfolk. It passes through the Panama Canal, then continues toward the South Pacific. The 7th Marines was detached in April and assigned to the defense of Samoa, and it provides a ready force to be deployed to the Canal Zone if necessary. The 1st Marines, also bound for Wellington, will take a different route and has been entrained to the West Coast to sail from San Francisco.

The Marines who sail for the Pacific in May 1942 are the boys who first flocked to the recruiting stations in the aftermath of Pearl Harbor. Some enlisted fraudulently (they were too young); others, not yet eighteen, came armed with their parents' permissions; others came without their parents' permission but with forged parents' signatures; and the eighteen-year-olds stepped across the line on their own.

Thousands of other younger ones stand and watch their older

brothers and cousins board trains to bases for recruit training. Mothers, sisters, and girlfriends wave and weep. Each young boy who watches his hero brother wave good-bye is counting the days until he is old enough to join him.

X

Jay Rebstock is one of these boys. Back on December 7, when the theater manager announced the attack at Pearl Harbor in the middle of the afternoon at the movies and Jay heard the boy near him say, "I know where that is; it's in Hawaii. My brother is there on a battleship named *Oklahoma*," he scrambled out of his seat and ran to the nearest pay phone. The line at the phone booth wrapped around the block that afternoon as theatergoers frantically called family members to make sure they were okay and to talk about the shock and the "What next?" and try to understand what lay ahead. After Jay stood in line for three hours, change for the phone sweating inside the hand clenched in his pocket, Jay's father picked up the phone back home.

Suddenly, focused as never before, Jay said, "Daddy, I'm quitting school to join the Army to fight the Japs." His father at first was silent and then delivered his curt answer: if Jay walked away from school, the elder Rebstock would give him more fight than any Jap could ever give him. End of subject.[11]

X

Nineteen-year-old James Russell worked as a spot welder at a steel company in New Orleans, in a dark world of burning embers and blinding lights. As a barrel banged off the roller, Jim grabbed it, squared it, and hit a button on the robotic spot welder, which set into motion an impressive explosion of fiery bolts as the welder tacked the seams before the barrel moved along the belt to the next stop.

Russell was constantly snuffing out burning bits of metal that rained down on him. Goggles protected his eyes, but about every fifteen minutes he was handed a new pair of gloves, because that was how long it took for them to get riddled with small burn holes. For his work he earned sixteen cents an hour.

One day after work, one of the guys egged Jim on to join the service with him. It had to pay better than this, and it would get them out of the smoky inferno for a while. Jim thought it was a capital idea and told his grandmother that night that he was shaking off the dust of that factory and moving on. Like most families, she was stoic about his news, but her heart sank at the thought of him, just a kid really, facing the frightening menaces of the war. She tried to dissuade him, reminding him that in battle, some people get killed. But like most boys, he was fairly sure it wouldn't be him.

"Granny," he said. "Well somebody has to get killed, but it's better than that stupid spot welding!"[12]

※

Pulling into King's Wharf in Wellington, New Zealand, the Raggedy Ass Marines, now known as the 1st Marine Division, hear a band playing. It is playing for them: "From the halls of Montezuma to the shores of Tripoli . . ."

It is June 1942, and these Marines are moving into the Pacific theater to train closer to the action. Wellington is the other side of the world in every way: a city in a mountainous and green foreign land. The Raggedy Ass Marines have kissed good-bye the sweaty boxing matches and bad talent shows under the hot, dingy tents in New River. The slithering snakes, chiggers, and sand fleas of that hellhole are now distant memories as they press together against the rail, craning their necks for a look at this first foreign port. Locals of all ages are waving and smiling up at them, and the band keeps playing welcome songs. The crowd's jubilance is an expression of their relief that the Americans are here to help defend them against the Japanese. They have watched the fall of Hong Kong and the surrender of Singapore; they have seen the British warships *Prince of Wales* and *Repulse* sunk; and they fear that their green island home will be next.

As the Marines come down the ramp, there begins a boisterous trade of coins for oranges and cigarettes; there are robust hand shaking and eye searching and crowd scanning as Marines lock eyes here and there with Kiwi girls and hearts on both sides race at the possibilities. Combat is still at least six months away. They will train for what lies ahead on the islands between here and Tokyo. But that day on the wharf, they drink ice-cold bottles of fresh farm milk offered to them from rattling carts, and for the moment, they forget all that lies ahead. The milk tastes so good, and this place looks more like home than anything they have seen in a long time.[13]

For the first time in a year and a half, these young men are "going ashore."[14]

But six days later, everything shifts. After his arrival in Auckland, General Vandegrift and his staff report to headquarters on June 26. They are there to meet with Vice Admiral Robert Ghormley, the commander of the South Pacific Area. Expecting that the first order of business will be the plans for training the division and coordinating activities with the New Zealand authorities, Vandegrift is handed a piece of paper. The Marine general quickly reads the thirty-seven words of an official military dispatch from the Joint Chiefs of Staff of the United States:

Occupy and defend Tulagi and adjacent positions (Guadalcanal and Florida Islands and the Santa Cruz Islands) in order to deny these areas to the enemy and to provide United States bases in preparation for further offensive action.[15]

Vandegrift asks who will be responsible for the occupying and defending. He is more than mildly shocked when the admiral blithely informs him that he and his 1st Marine Division are to execute the order—not in six months but in five weeks. The operation is provisionally set to begin on August 1, 1942.[16]

Unbeknownst to General Vandegrift, the change in plans has been set into motion by new movement of Japanese troops in the Solomon

Islands, especially at Tulagi. A Coastwatcher, British Colonial Service district officer Major Martin Clemens, from his hideout on a hill overlooking the Lunga River on Guadalcanal, has spotted a large Japanese force crossing the thirty miles from Tulagi to the northern shore of Guadalcanal. Two thousand Japanese troops and construction workers are now there building an airfield.[17]

Guadalcanal and Tulagi are small islands sitting at the southeastern end of the Solomon Islands chain. Guadalcanal is ninety miles long and twenty-five miles wide. It is separated from tiny Tulagi by Sealark Channel. The recent, frantic Japanese construction efforts are a red flag to Admiral King.

Admiral King seems to be almost alone in his urgent exhortation that the United States has to attack, seize the initiative, and do it now. This is no time for vacillation. It is time for the type of daring, offensive thinking that led to the stunning victory at Midway. The Japanese are on the march in the Solomons and in short order will complete the seizure of the entire formerly British island chain. There is no one to stop them. Their success in fortifying the Solomons would sever any and all lines between the United States and Australia.

Step by step the admiral manages to overcome all interservice rivalry, foot-dragging, and bickering, and Operation Watchtower comes to life.[18] The historian John Zimmerman describes Admiral Ghormley's understrength naval and Marine Corps force that is now to sail to confront the powerful Japanese forces surging ahead in the Solomon Islands:

> Taken all in all, Ghormley could rely on a small, highly trained striking force . . . of less than one Marine division . . . surface forces of fluctuating and never overwhelming power (which nevertheless represented the maximum which Admiral Nimitz could spare), and an extremely scanty array of land-based aircraft. He had no assurances of reserve ground troops for the coming operation.[19]

It wasn't much, to be sure, but the commanders know that waiting is perilous and it is better to fight now with what they have than miss the moment to strike. Having lost *Lexington* and *Yorktown* at Coral Sea and Midway, they are down to three aircraft carriers. *Enterprise*, *Saratoga*, and the carrier *Wasp*, which had recently been transferred from the Atlantic, form the front line, along with the newly commissioned battleship *North Carolina* and a number of cruisers and destroyers.

In mid-July, from his lookout post, Clemens reports that the new Japanese airfield is nearly complete, and Admiral Nimitz orders the 1st Division to seize and hold it before they can get it done. The new invasion day will be August 7.[20]

The timeline advance is not enough, though. On August 5, one of Martin Clemens's native scouts reports to the Coastwatcher that the airfield on Guadalcanal has been completed (actually, only 2,600 feet of 3,800 feet has been finished) and will soon start receiving aircraft. Clemens is distraught. Japanese bombers will now be able to strike all surface ships bound for Australia, and Australia's isolation will be complete.[21]

But on August 7, the US naval force manages to arrive at Guadalcanal and Tulagi undetected, thanks to the cover of overcast skies and rain squalls. The weather has grounded all Japanese air activity at Rabaul.[22] The stealth and silence of this remarkable approach are broken at just after 6:00 a.m., when the bombardment fleet opens fire on the invasion beaches with its big guns.

The convoy carrying the 1st Marine Division anchors its transports, and under the lingering cloud cover the Marines begin disembarking. Almost 1,000 Marine officers and 18,000 Marine enlisted men begin the first US offensive against Japan. Tulagi and Guadalcanal are now under simultaneous attack.

Wellington is just a sweet, distant mirage as they shoulder eighty-four-plus pounds of gear (making them the most heavily weighted foot soldiers in the history of warfare) and pull all that weight over the side of the ship, clambering down the cargo nets, in their first death-defying feat of the attack.

There is no initial opposition upon landing. As Marines make it to the airfield, they discover full rice pots, still hot. The Japanese had run for the hills when they realized the Marines were there. Looking at the island, the first jungle most of these Marines have ever seen, they see the sweltering, hellish place that will be the arena of their first combat, the torrid jungle that will inspire their fellow troops to "say a prayer for your pal on Guadalcanal."

During the first two days of the landings, the Japanese soldiers work to disrupt further landings of troops and supplies. But a greater Japanese force is on the way. Late on August 8, a powerful cruiser force is dispatched from Kavieng and Rabaul with orders to "attack and destroy enemy transports in the Tulagi-Guadalcanal area."[23]

The vulnerable US troop transports are guarded by three cruisers and two destroyers of the Northern Group off Tulagi and two cruisers and two destroyers of the Southern Group off Guadalcanal. Separating the two groups positioned on opposite sides of Sealark Channel is the circular-shaped Savo Island.

At 1:30 a.m., August 8, the seven Japanese cruisers and one destroyer steam at twenty-six knots on a course to pass to the south of Savo Island. The Japanese attack force enters the channel waters undetected and closes on the unsuspecting ships of the Southern Group. As they come to bear on the US ships in their attack column, each ship in the column fires torpedoes. Explosions rock both heavy cruisers, inflicting damage—one later sinks.

Not missing a beat, the flying Japanese column now swings around Savo Island as if it were a revolving door, splits into two columns, and opens fire on the Northern Group.

Illuminating the US ships with searchlights, they open fire with their main deck guns at nearly point-blank range. The devastating fire rips through the US ships and sinks all three cruisers, and the Japanese sail away into the night. They have inflicted one of the worst losses ever on the US Navy.[24]

The rest of the transport ships and their escorts quickly leave the area. As dawn breaks, the Marines on shore look out on the now-vacant waters of Sealark Channel to discover that they are all alone with no sea or air support. In their isolation they nickname the Battle of Savo Island "the Battle of the Five Sitting Ducks."

)(

On a steaming summer Wednesday, August 12, Frank Bowes settles into a sticky seat on the train on his way home to Peekskill and opens up his folded *Boston Post*.

"Gains on Solomons" blares the headline, and beneath, "U.S. Fighters Outpunching Japs in Invasion of Southwest Pacific Islands." Another item near the bottom catches his eye: "Clark Gable in Army as Private: Actor Joins to Be Airplane Gunner."[25]

The *Los Angeles Times* reports on the screen idol and Oscar nominee:

Just as many another American male of proper physical, mental and moral qualifications is doing these days, Clark Gable, he-man of the motion-picture screen, yesterday held up his right hand and repeated the oath of enlistment in the Army of the United States.[26]

Gable, forty-one years old and devastated by the tragic death of his third wife, Carole Lombard, in a plane crash, decided to do his part. He enlisted in secret to avoid the crush of fans that swarmed his buddy Jimmy Stewart when he enlisted.

Gable says about being a man and a soldier, "He must be ready to choose death before dishonor without making too much song and dance about it. That's all there is to it."[27]

Although the Guadalcanal headlines are vastly encouraging to Americans at home, the death Gable speaks of is cutting down scores of boys no one ever saw on the silver screen in ways no one at home could even imagine.

※

For the next six months, the Marines on Guadalcanal desperately cling to their island stronghold while the Japanese battle ceaselessly to evict them. The opposing forces on shore also have front-row seats at the nightly sea battles that rage in the waters offshore. While the US Navy mostly controls these waters during the daylight, at night the battle line of Japanese ships, nicknamed "the Tokyo Express," plows through "the Slot," the channel between the outer islands of the chain, to engage in the desperate struggle for control.

Each struggle brings more sunken ships, shelling of the Marine defenses, and bombardment of the crucial airfield. These attacks routinely crater the runway before it is frantically patched the next day. Some hits damage it to the point of full or partial shutdown.

There is never a day that Henderson Field is not under bombardment. "Almost daily, Japanese bombers from Rabaul attacked Henderson Field at noon during August, September, and October . . . warships and submarines sailed into Sealark Channel nearly every night to shell the airfield."[28]

The Henderson Field defenders call the noontime onslaught "Tojo Time." "There would be 18 to 24 of them, high in the sun and in their perfect V-of-V's formation. They would be accompanied by 20 or more Zeroes cavorting in batches of 3, nearby. Their bombing was accurate, and they would stay in formation and make their bombing run. . . .

"And the men would pull the chin straps of their helmets tighter and tense their muscles and press harder against the earth in their foxholes. And pray."[29]

Then: WHAM! (the first one hit) WHAM! (closer) WHAM! (walking right up to your foxhole) . . . WHAAA MM! (Oh Christ!) WHAM! (Thank God, they missed us!) WHAM! (the bombs were walking away) WHAM! (they still shook the earth, and dirt trickled in). WHAM![30]

As bad as the daily bombing is, the men prefer it to the naval shelling. That is much worse. "A bombing is bad," said one defender. ". . . But a bombing is over in a minute. A shelling, however, is unmitigated, indescribable hell. It can go on for a few minutes or four hours. When the shells scream overhead you cringe expecting a hit and when there is a let-up you tremble knowing that they are getting their range and the next one will be a hit."[31]

Then there is the other kind of trembling, the one that racks the body with dengue fever or malaria. On Guadalcanal, the men are as likely to die from the depletion of their bodies by these ravaging diseases as from bombing or shelling. And then there is the hunger that sets in after the supply ships leave. Men pick the maggots out of their white rice gruel or they just get used to eating them. The sun burns the men's skin daily, and when the rains come, it is never-ending deluge. Every day is like the next ring in Dante's Inferno.

The first two months in Guadalcanal hell is just a prelude to the next onslaught by the Japanese. The historian John Miller writes:

Shortly before midnight of 13 October, a Japanese naval force including the battleships *Haruna* and *Kongo* sails unchallenged into Sealark Channel. While a cruiser plane illuminates the target area by dropping flares, the task force bombards the airfield for eighty minutes, the heaviest shelling of the campaign. The battleships fire 918 rounds . . . of which 625 are armor-piercing and 293 high explosive. They cover the field systematically. Explosions and burning gasoline light the night brightly.[32]

The bombardment has closed the field to US heavy bombers, and the perpetual shortage of aviation fuel is now dire.

In the weeks leading up to the October attack, the Japanese are unrelenting in their drive to fight hand to hand on the beaches and in the jungle to recapture the island. Though US air forces constantly interdict and destroy supply and troopships and bomb suspected Japanese assembly areas, some 27,000 Japanese soldiers try, on at least three separate occasions, to advance to the Marine lines and hurl themselves against the dug-in leathernecks. They are on a mission to break through the Marines' defenses and recapture the vital airfield, which now has a rudimentary secondary fighter plane strip that the Americans have simply demarcated on the bare ground. (This airstrip housed the famous Cactus Air Force, "cactus" being the code name for Guadalcanal.)

The desperate ground attacks surge against the line, and night after night the Marines hurl the banzai attackers back, ejecting them with frightful losses. Morning light reveals piles of broken bodies on and in front of the battle line.

In mid-September, on the orders of Lieutenant General Kiyotake Kawaguchi, 6,000 Japanese, laden with equipment in the hot swamp, cut a road through the thick mosquito-infested jungle. They attempt to fall on the Marine positions just south of the airfield, but are confronted and destroyed by Marines of the 1st Marine Raider Battalion and the 1st Marine Parachute Battalion. When it is over, 600 broken Japanese dead lie close to the Marine line on the ridge itself, smashed beyond recognition from point-blank artillery fire delivered into the charging mass.

To the extent that the military allows, reporters and their newspapers try to convey to readers back home the horrors of the first battle of the Pacific, but the message is often delayed, at times weeks or months later. But in time, Americans learn that the United States has lost yet another aircraft carrier, *Hornet*. The precious carrier force, after all the building and repairs the services have been working at breakneck pace to carry out, is now shockingly back to post–Pearl Harbor levels.

On October 30, the *Boston Daily Globe* tries to capture the vicious terror of the Japanese banzai attacks, but the paper reports that the Marines are equally ferocious in their response:

MARINES REPULSE JAPS 3 TIMES
GUADALCANAL TROOPS PLUG HOLE CUT IN LINE[33]

By mid-November, there are signs that the Japanese are being beaten. Their fleet pulls out of the battle area. Those still stuck on Guadalcanal continue to fight. Action will drag into February, but there are no more attempts to retake the island by ground attack. The Marines there have finally completed their mission; they have captured and completed Henderson Field, and they did it using the equipment left behind by the Japanese.

In the end, 24,000 Japanese soldiers are dead. The Americans have lost 1,600 and have 2,400 wounded. Several thousand more die from the diseases that infest the island. The six naval battles that raged in the waters around Guadalcanal have cost each side twenty-four ships and thousands of additional craft.[34] The waters off Guadalcanal, littered with sunken ships, become known as "Iron Bottom Sound."

Unbeknownst to the US Army command, now in control of the actions on Guadalcanal, Japanese plans are in motion to rescue more than 10,000 soldiers from the death that awaits them if they are left on the island.

On Christmas Day 1942, senior military officers of the Japanese Army and Navy meet at the Imperial Palace in Tokyo. The Army and Navy blame each other for the defeat at Guadalcanal. For days the two sides rage at each other. They must rescue their men from an island now held by US forces. The evacuation, which they plan for January, will require Hirohito's approval.

His Majesty is not at all happy to hear that his army and navy have been unable to drive the detested Americans from Guadalcanal in spite of more than four months of exhausting effort.[35] Hirohito is especially irked about the lost airfield. Why did it take Japanese construction crews more than a month to build an airfield when the Americans did it in days? Henderson Field was the key to the success or failure of the Japanese expansion and fortification in the Solomon Islands. It was the airfield that had triggered the US attack. He presses and grills his military leaders, putting them on the spot for another two hours before doing what he must: approving the troop withdrawal.[36]

With that, the emperor seals and sanctions the humiliating loss.

In a series of three-night evacuation operations the first week of February, Japanese destroyers rescue 10,828 soldiers. It is called Operation KE, and the US command assumes that the steady, increased naval activity is an attempt to reinforce the island for yet another attack, when exactly the opposite is the case: the Japanese are in retreat.

The rescued soldiers struggling off of the western shore of Guadalcanal are in terrible physical shape, hardly fit for a return to battle in the near future, or ever. The rescuing crews on the destroyers look aghast at the sight of the walking skeletons.

A Japanese officer on one of the destroyers writes that the pitiful men "wore only the remains of clothes . . . their physical deterioration was extreme. Probably they were happy but showed no expression. All had dengue or malaria . . . diarrhea sent them to the heads. Their digestive organs were so completely destroyed [we] couldn't give them good food, only porridge."[37]

The Marine Corps has struck the first successful blow in what will be a long trek across the vast expanse of the Pacific Ocean. The thinning, illusive ranks of the legendary "Old Breed" who were the minutemen of 1942 are now refilled.

ﾒ

In February 1943, Frank Bowes places American flags on the tiny black specks of Savo, Tulagi, Santa Cruz, Guadalcanal, and Tassafaronga. How can these places, so small that some are barely on the map, matter so much in the effort to save the world? In the depths of his imagining, he cannot come close to understanding what is playing out on those godforsaken specks so many miles away. Americans in places such as Peekskill, and all across the land, have no idea what "their boys" are enduring overseas. Newspapers and newsreels do not report the horrors that will linger forever in the minds of the survivors, even into old age. These men will forever be haunted by tripping through darkness over charred limbs on beaches and in the jungles; the night sky lit with flares that shed light on the face of a buddy, his eyes wide open, a gaping wound deep, wet, and red across his midsection where his uniform was moments ago. Last night he was snickering with you about the absurdity of it all; now he is still. You can only move on; there is no time to stop and weep for him.

A Marine named Sid Philips remembers being sent with other troops to recover the bodies of US troops on Guadalcanal. When they found them, "they had been beheaded, their genitals stuck in their mouths." After that, says Philips, shaking his head, "we never took another prisoner."[38]

The *New York Times*, on February 10, 1943, spoke for Frank Bowes and so many others: "Every American heart must have thrilled yesterday at the news that the battle of Guadalcanal was over and the victory was ours."[39]

Although Frank knew there was so much sacrifice on the part of so many, he prays the silent prayer of parents and sweethearts across the country: "Just let it end before they need our boy."

※

Harry Gray is determined to cross paths with the pretty blonde from the bowling alley. He sneaks the keys to the car while his mom is working late and drives by the house where she lives. He and his friends follow her and her friends as they head to the roller rink one night. Harry strolls in just a beat after she crosses the threshold, acting as if it is just the strangest coincidence to see her again. She is not with the boy this time, and Harry is not about to waste this golden opportunity. He sits next to her on the bench as she is putting on her roller skates and catches her eye. She locks onto his gaze and says yes, she does remember seeing him the other night. Her voice is harder than he imagined when he had watched her bowl and sway and sidle up to the older boy in the booth. Harry wants to know, so he asks. "Was that your boyfriend you were with at the bowling alley?" "No," she says, "well, not anymore." And then it is clear, she is not going to say any more about that. Harry doesn't care to hear any more on the subject, either, beyond that confirmation of what is relevant to him, and says, "Would you like to skate together?" Dorothy smiles and nods, and with that simple exchange, he and Dorothy skate off into the night. After that, they see each other pretty much all the time. He sometimes picks her up in his mom's car and takes her for ice cream on a weeknight. On Fridays, they go roller-skating. But on Saturdays, he takes her to the movies. He wants to sit close to her and put his arm around her shoulder. He slides his knee over to rest against hers and then moves to put his hand on her knee, which sends a quiet shiver through them both.

When the *tick-tick* of the newsreel begins, a different shiver courses through his veins. The movie rattles from the projector, and the audience tips up their heads in unison to get a good look at Hitler's army triumphantly goose-stepping past the Führer. Hitler, after suffering devastating blows the previous year, is imploring his people not to lose heart and to stand behind him.

Then the scene changes to the Pacific. The Marines are packing up and leaving Guadalcanal. Harry watches as they march thin Japanese prisoners in shirts and long white undershorts off the island. The grinning Marines have hollow cheeks, and their ribs jut out beneath their bare chests.

Harry knows the great landmarks of Europe. He has painstakingly drawn them in his sketchbooks. He wants to see the world and knows that if Hitler is not stopped, he never will. It is clear to him, though, that if the war lasts long enough, he will likely be sent to the Pacific. He wants to be a Marine. His friend Jim, who lives at the bottom of his street, has joined. He and Harry spent endless hours sitting on his front steps talking about how it isn't worth going if you aren't going in as a Marine. When Anne hears Harry coming up the front steps, she asks, "Where've you been?" If the answer is "At Jim's!"

she nods, her heart sinking a bit. She knows that Jim is filling his head with stories of the valiant Marines. If Harry has to go, she wants him to join the Navy. She tells him, "Harry, if you join the Navy, you'll sleep in a bed; if you join the Marines, you'll sleep in a ditch."[40]

Once the movie begins, Dorothy lets her head fall to the side against Harry's temple. He couldn't care less what is on the screen once the newsreels are over. He has it all planned out. He will enlist as soon as he turns seventeen. He will likely be part of the attack on Tokyo, and then he will come home a hero. He and Dorothy will get married and have a nice party at his mother's house, and then he will spend the rest of his days smelling Dorothy's skin and feeling her curls brush his cheek. She makes him happy, and he is 100 percent sure that he makes her happy, too. It's nice when life looks clear ahead; he can see it all perfectly.

On their way out of the theater, it starts to snow. Dorothy slips her arm into Harry's as they walk. Out of the corner of his eye as they pass the barber, Harry sees Tojo's toothy grin staring at him from a war bond poster saying mockingly, "Don't buy defense bonds, make me so happy—Thank you!"[41] Harry doesn't have any money to help the war effort, but before long, he will be doing his part against Tojo.

7

1943

A million men cannot take Tarawa in a hundred years.

—Admiral Keiji Shibazaki

Joseph Stalin could not make it to the Anfa Hotel in Casablanca, French Morocco, to discuss the next phase of the war with Churchill and Roosevelt in January 1943. His Red Army, which would ultimately lose 11 million men, was in the midst of the raging Battle of Stalingrad. Two-thirds of Hitler's forces were there fighting on the eastern front. On January 9, the Red Army would encircle Stalingrad, forcing Hitler's army to surrender there in a matter of weeks. To the north, it was on the verge of recovering Leningrad, and in the south, they were weakening the Germans' hold on the Caucasus.

Churchill and Roosevelt met in North Africa, and determined they could accept nothing short of unconditional surrender by the Axis powers. The first priority was to drive Hitler's Third Reich to its knees, followed by the complete capitulation of Imperial Japan.[1]

Churchill urged Roosevelt not to cross the English Channel to take on the Germans in France. The memories of trench warfare in France in World War I were still too fresh in the minds of the British people, and Churchill was determined to begin the pushback of Hitler's acquired territories in North Africa, then on to Italy.

By February, the Allies were on the offensive in Tunisia, where Hitler had given Field Marshal Erwin Rommel and General Hans-Jürgen von Arnim orders to "fight to the last." Rommel was a most dangerous opponent, and inexperienced US commanders and troops would learn the harshest of lessons in the hot sand before eventually starting to beat back "the Desert Fox."

While all eyes were on Europe, the Americans ran into a bit of luck combined with shrewd intelligence in the East. In April 1943, sixteen P-38 fighters took to the skies from Henderson Field and headed to Bougainville Island, based on intelligence that the revered Admiral Isoroku Yamamoto would be going there to inspect his troops. The poker-playing, Harvard-educated naval genius and architect of the Pearl Harbor attack called himself the sword of Emperor Hirohito and claimed that he would ride down Pennsylvania Avenue on a white horse and dictate the surrender of the United States in the White House.[2] As the plane carrying the commander in chief of the Japanese Combined Fleet was approaching the island, it was shot down by two of the P-38 fighters in a dramatic ambush and crashed into the jungle. His loss was devastating to Hirohito, who never discovered that US code breakers had deciphered intercepted messages detailing Yamamoto's location and itinerary for the day.

In May, Churchill and Roosevelt met at the Third Washington Conference in Washington, DC, code-named Trident, to plot the bombing in the Pacific theater, as well as the push to Sicily and then up the boot of Italy. Plans for an invasion of France across the Channel by combined US-British forces were also now well under way.[3]

On July 22, General Patton took Palermo, forcing the surrender of the Fascist dictator, Benito Mussolini, who had aligned himself with Hitler. Mussolini had been a miserable military failure, earning the ire of his own people. (Mussolini would hunker down in Milan until 1945. Under increasing pressure, he and his mistress, Claretta Petacci, tried to make a run for the Swiss border, but they were caught and their car was surrounded by Italian Communist partisans in a village near Lake Como. They were shot and hanged in the town square just two days before Hitler committed suicide.)

Hitler's soldiers would spend eighteen months in vicious combat to hold Italy, under strict orders from the Führer not to fail. The Allies lost 60,000 to 70,000 men before finally succeeding in the treacherous terrain of places such as Anzio and Monte Cassino. Meanwhile, in California, Washington, and Oregon, the fears of Hirohito's prime minister, Tojo, had come to pass. Tojo had argued that the US pilots who had been captured after the Doolittle Raid should all be allowed to live, fearing that if they were killed, there would be retribution against Japanese Americans. In 1943, President Roosevelt issued Executive Order 9066, forcing some 117,000 Americans of Japanese descent from their homes. They were put onto trains with only a suitcase and the clothes on their backs and forced to live in drafty one-room shedlike houses behind barbed-wire fences in internment camps in the West until the end of the war.

Ж

Across the Pacific, with Guadalcanal now secure, the southern Solomon Islands were firmly in US hands. The way forward would come only after an internal showdown between the powerful men leading the US Army and Navy.

Admiral Ernest J. King was the driving force behind the investment of men and resources in the Guadalcanal battles. But General George C. Marshall, the Army chief of staff and closest confidant of President Roosevelt, had done everything he could to sidetrack the venture. He wanted General Douglas MacArthur's army to lead the way. MacArthur was convinced that the way to the heart of Tokyo and victory was the western route through New Guinea and the Philippines. As far as King was concerned, Admiral Chester Nimitz's South Pacific route was the way to go. He felt the main thrust must be led by the Navy, under the command of Nimitz. After all, MacArthur and his troops were a thousand miles away from the battle area. King stood his ground, concluding his note to Marshall emphatically, "I think it is important that this [seizure of the initiative] be done even if no support of Army Forces in the South West Pacific is made available."[4]

Whatever the course, the Japanese military bulwark of Rabaul on the island of East New Britain in Papua New Guinea had to be taken. After the island's capture by the Japanese in 1942, it became a remote headquarters of the imperial forces in the South Pacific. General George Marshall wanted the Rabaul attack to be under the command of MacArthur, but the Navy balked. Admiral King was reluctant to turn command over to the Army, since the operations would not be possible without massive Navy ship participation.

King called for a unified strategic command under Admiral Nimitz. However, while the Third Washington Conference was under way to discuss the way forward, it was MacArthur's plan for the advance on Rabaul that was presented. The Navy would seize airfields in the Central Solomons, while MacArthur's forces would take airfields in the New Guinea area. Then, in subsequent stages, the Navy and Army would seize more airfields and other objectives in the tandem march to converge on Rabaul.

The plan they laid out would require five additional divisions and forty-five more air groups, a total of another 1,800 airplanes. The Washington brain trust balked. They saw the plan as impossible. Even if they were to commit a fraction of the aircraft and personnel to it, they wouldn't be able to transport them to the battle area.[5] MacArthur's people laid out their demands to the stunned gathering not as a suggestion but as a necessity. The conference adjourned in shock.[6]

Roosevelt had committed to Churchill's Hitler-first-and-then-Japan plan. He couldn't divert the Army's planes now; they were conducting a massive bombing campaign against the heart of Germany. The joint directive to the British and US air commanders had been unambiguous: "Your primary object will be the progressive destruction and dislocation of the German military, industrial, and economic system, and the undermining of the morale of the German people to a point where their capacity for armed resistance is fatally weakened."[7]

However, politically, Roosevelt could not let up on the Pacific push. The memories of the burning ships at Pearl Harbor and the loss of young sailors trapped in the *Arizona* at the bottom of the harbor had stoked the fire of revenge in the hearts of Americans. It was Japanese pilots who had dropped the bombs, and Japan must pay the price. "I'm going to kill Japs!" That was the cry of the boys on the recruiting lines and the fervent goal of the president who had declared that the day of the Pearl Harbor attack was a day of infamy and that victory over Japan was the only option.

Admiral King shared that desire. After the botched presentation of the MacArthur plan, King argued that if they didn't have the assets to take Rabaul, they would use what they had to neutralize the base. It would still require a large commitment of ships and naval assets in the advance to the northwest, up the long axis of the Solomon Islands. The advancing ships would be operating in confined waters and exposed to attack by land-based Japanese aircraft. To Admiral King, this was all unacceptable. The valuable carrier task forces should not be exposed to that danger.

At the Casablanca Conference, the British had given less-than-enthusiastic approval for a US drive against the Gilbert, Marshall, and Caroline Islands in the central Pacific once Rabaul was neutralized. To Admirals King and Nimitz and all of the other naval officers who had spent their entire careers embracing the dogma of War Plan Orange, that path must have looked very familiar.

In Washington, that new approach to a central Pacific offensive was met with favorable nods. It was a three-thousand-mile path across tiny islands clustered in groups like stepping-stones leading to the Philippines and to Japan itself. Even a novice tactician could see that there were no confining waters to hinder carrier operations or large landmasses that could provide bases for enemy air forces.

To the Navy, the central Pacific was the perfect operating area. Since the beginning of the war, it had been the opinion of the US Chiefs of Staff that Japan "could best be defeated by a series of amphibious attacks across the far reaches of the Pacific."[8] But there had been no chance to initiate such an offensive. The Marines' response to Japan's maneuvering in the Solomon Islands had been one of necessity, not of choice, to prevent the building of the airstrip at Guadalcanal.

A central Pacific drive was exactly what the old War Plan Orange had envisioned. If the enemy's navy chose to come out and challenge for control of the sea, so much the better, as it had been at Midway. If the enemy chose to defend an island, he could be isolated with little chance of reinforcement or resupply; and any attempts to reinforce or resupply would face interdicting attacks by US ships and aircraft.

On the other hand, there were disadvantages: Any attacking US force would be restricted in its tactics. It was not possible to land an overwhelmingly superior force against a smaller force of dug-in defenders. It would become a point-blank slugfest, ensuring many casualties on both sides, perhaps even to the point of mutual annihilation. How many men was an attacker willing to lose hurling itself against a rock-ribbed defensive position manned by defenders sworn to die at their posts? Would victory be so costly and the numbers of killed so ghastly that those on the home front would recoil in shock and demand a change of direction?

Plus, the defender would get to choose the battlefields. He controlled the islands the attackers would have to assault. The attacking Americans could never choose to bypass an island and let its defenders "die on the vine" if that island had an airfield. An advance to the next island could never proceed with an active enemy airfield left in the rear.

The Strategic Committee now decided that the central Pacific would be the primary approach with the Southwest Pacific thrust continuing as the secondary front.[9] The Japanese would have to deal with both drives. The committee's directive ordered the US forces to "maintain and extend unremitting pressure against Japan with the purpose of continually reducing her military power and attaining positions from which her ultimate surrender can be forced."[10]

On July 20, 1943, over vociferous objections from General MacArthur, the Joint Chiefs instructed Admiral Nimitz to capture bases in the Gilbert Islands and prepare detailed plans for the leap into the Marshalls.

Ж

Tarawa is an atoll of sixteen islands in the Gilberts, so small they can't be seen on most maps. The triangle they create lies across the equator, some 2,400 miles southwest of Pearl Harbor. Here Marines will battle first coral reefs and then malevolent tides that seem to be allied with the enemy; if and when they make it past that gauntlet, they will face a tightly constructed Japanese defense network designed to draw them to the island and its airfield and then make as many of them as possible sitting ducks.

These otherwise idyllic islands have on their western tip a tiny islet called Betio, the home of the Japanese airfield. Between two tips of the triangle is a submerged coral reef that opens in only one narrow place, the only unobstructed passageway to the beautiful, calm lagoon. Pilots say that Betio is shaped like a parrot, a long pier its feet. The whole thing is just two miles from head to tail, and at its widest point, it is not even seven hundred yards across.

Admiral Tomonari Saichiro does not want to see a repeat of Guadalcanal. When the Marines landed there, he began his work on Betio. He made the island that is home to the Tarawa airfield an impregnable fortress. Betio will be defended by massive firepower from sea and air, its beaches made into an obstacle course, creating a killing field for the unsuspecting Marines. The Japanese word for such a plan is *yogaki*, meaning "waylaying attack." "*Yogaki*'s purpose, to teach the Americans the prohibitive cost of invading fortified islands."[11]

Long-range bombers from Rabaul and short-range aircraft from Truk will provide decisive air support to Tarawa. The waters around the atoll will be teeming with Japanese vessels, ready to attack US shipping on the surface and with submarines from below.[12] It will be a repeat of the Tokyo Express, as it was in the waters around Guadalcanal.

In August 1943, Admiral Keiji Shibazaki arrives on Betio to oversee its final fortification and prepare to command the defense against the anticipated US attack. The admiral walks the entire perimeter, admiring the best-fortified position the world has ever seen.

The southern shore, with the airfield at its center, is heavily defended, aided by natural obstacles; the convex shape of the shore means
that anyone trying to land there will be extremely vulnerable. It is also
constantly lashed by winds and rough water. Thus the only way to
approach Betio is through the coral reef and into the lagoon on the
northern shore.

So it was there that Admiral Saichiro constructed his killing field.
Twenty yards off the beach, he had his men build an ingenious coconut-
log barrier wall. Pairs of logs were driven vertically into the earth less
than two feet apart to form end supports for long logs stacked in rows
on top of each other, creating four-foot-high walls. The whole wall
construction was anchored and strapped at every point, and any gaps
were filled with sand and coral.

The Allied attackers coming off the beaches will be forced to
climb the wall in a hail of deadly grazing small-arms and automatic-
weapons fire. If they choose to stay huddled behind the wall, they
will be framed in a shooting gallery for preset mortar and high-angle-
weapon fire. But even before they hit the unforgiving beach, they will
need to make it across the eight-hundred-yard-long coral reef alive.

The approach will be possible for the "amtracs," tanklike vehicles,
designed to claw their way up and onto the reef and grind across the
coral, but most of the boats will never make it across, forcing the Marines up and out of them. As they wade into shore for hours, most will
be shot and killed or wounded and drowned before they ever reach
the sand.

Those who make it will then have to dodge fire coming from the
pillboxes, blockhouses, and massive concrete-reinforced bunkers, some
two stories high, that house every type and caliber of Japanese weapon.
These fortresses are dug in, hardened against any aerial attack designed
to soften the islet's defenses. In them are more than a hundred machine
guns that can sweep every square foot of the battlefield. Twenty-three
37 mm antitank guns are dug in and concealed to back up thirty-four
pieces of heavy artillery. Topping the list are four 5.5-inch and four
huge 8-inch coastal guns, brought all the way from Singapore to do the

job. They are capable of blasting holes in anything, including offshore ships. Almost 5,000 Japanese defenders man the bastion, each armed as well with an array of individual weapons for close confrontations.[13]

A 1942 Japanese order defined the mission:

Wait until the enemy is within effective range (when assembling for landing) and direct your fire on the enemy transport group and destroy it. If the enemy starts a landing, knock out the landing boats with mountain gunfire, tank guns and infantry guns, then concentrate all fires on the enemy's landing point and destroy him at the water's edge.[14]

Admiral Shibazaki surveys it all from atop his two-story bomb-proof command post. He proudly announces to his assembled staff, "A million men cannot take Tarawa in a hundred years."[15]

※

Ever since Private James Russell had given up his sixteen-cents-an-hour spot-welding job and joined the Marine Corps in February 1943, boredom was no longer his problem. After surviving twelve grueling weeks at boot camp and three more weeks on the rifle range, he was off to several weeks of advanced infantry training at Camp Pendleton, California. He received orders that sent him to Tulagi while the Guadalcanal campaign was wrapping up, not to one of the regiments of the 1st Division but to the 2nd Division. After further training at Tulagi and New Hebrides, Russell sailed to Wellington, New Zealand, to become part of the cutting edge of the Marine force in the Pacific.[16]

Camp Wellington was a training ground the likes of which Marines had never seen. It wasn't just tactics and fire and maneuver that filled the training day, it was hours and hours of training for attacking a fortified beachhead. Previous training had stressed finding the least defended part of an enemy line and massing against it, overwhelming it with superior force. The training at Wellington stressed charging ashore from landing craft and immediately engaging the well-entrenched enemy. There was no room to maneuver; everything was a frontal assault.

If the men could bypass a position, they should bypass it, but they must keep moving, stopping for nothing, especially not to assist a fallen comrade. That would just slow down the impetus of the assault. "Move, move, move!" the sergeants screamed in their ears. They were to let follow-up forces finish off bypassed positions.[17]

Russell got his first glimpse of a landing vehicle, tracked (LVT) "Alligator" during that training. That latest addition to landing craft inventory was indeed revolutionary. It looked similar to a standard tank, but the Alligator could travel at seven miles per hour in the water and twelve on land. It didn't have to stop at the water's edge to discharge its troops; instead, it carried them up onto and over the beach. Men didn't exit the LVT, as they did a Higgins boat, by charging out the bow once the coxswain dropped the ramp. Instead, the outside ranks of the four columns of embarked troops did a low-profile roll-out over the sides, followed by the inside columns.

The Kiwis shared an easy camaraderie with the Marines from the United States. When the Japanese had been on their doorstep, looking south from already conquered lands with an eye on the green of New Zealand, the Marines had swept in to bolster the country's defenses. They had stood like pit bulls on the shore, looking north and forcing the Japanese to consider what they needed to defend, rather than prosecuting what had seemed to be a very appealing push into Oceania. Now the New Zealanders were returning the favor. They "adopted" the Marines of the 2nd Division, filling their bellies with home-cooked meals, listening to their stories, and giving them a bit of "home." For some it went beyond cooking; in the end, five hundred US Marines either stayed forever with Kiwi brides or took "down under" girls home to the United States as their wives.[18]

In mid-October, Russell watches as three battalions of his 2nd Marines quietly pack up, one battalion at a time. He is told, as he embarks on the USS *Biddle*, that they are heading for a final training exercise and then they'll all be back for a farewell party. The hotels in Wellington fill to the gills as dates and wives in party dresses anxiously await their return for one last shindig. The hours tick by as the women go from eager anticipation to frustration and then dismay as they realize their dates are not coming back. They slip off their white gloves and heels and put them away, wiping back tears with perfectly pressed handkerchiefs. They, like so many others back home, are sacrificing their happiness for the war; they will wait and pray for their young Americans to return safely.

The 2nd Marine Division sails as part of a naval task force for parts unknown. On the troop transports rumors spread like wildfire. "We were always going to Truk," says Russell. "Most Marines didn't know one place from another, but everybody seemed to know Truk. It was a nasty place with lots of Japs, and it would be a bitch to attack. It didn't matter where you were going, the speculation was always Truk."[19]

On November 14, the Marines on USS *Biddle* finish their morning exercise on deck and are called to a briefing. A lieutenant, brandishing a handful of maps and charts, points to the many islands of Tarawa Atoll and says the operation is code-named Galvanic; the target is the tiny island of Betio, the one shaped like a parrot.

Russell and the men of Company K, 2nd Marines, will land in LVTs on Red Beach 1 in the vicinity of the bird's neck and attack the large guns near the bird's beak. Rear Admiral Howard Kingman sends an unequivocal message to the landing force: "Gentlemen, we will not neutralize Betio. We will not destroy it. We will obliterate it."[20]

Three battleships, four cruisers, and more than twenty destroyers pummel Betio with three thousand tons of ordnance for two solid deafening hours. The bombardment ships are four miles off the western tip. On the decks of the transports, Marines wait for the order to roll over the sides and down the rope net into the landing craft, as they had practiced so many times. Suddenly, to the south, the bombardment fleet opens fire with salvo after salvo, like the finale at fireworks without the colors. The enormous cloud of smoke that hangs around afterward hovers and the whole two-mile island virtually disappears under the plumes. Cheers and hollers and whistles rise from the transports as for a moment it appears the job may already be done. Who could survive that?

But as the island shudders under the blows, Admiral Shibazaki, in his fortified two-story blockhouse, knows the attack is just beginning. He has built a fortress, but he is not without concern. The air and naval support he was promised has been siphoned off in recent weeks.

The US dual offensive has sent Japanese forces spreading out to cover their bases. To keep up their air strength in the Northern Solomons, they have borrowed from the airpower earmarked to support Tarawa. Naval vessels that had been held at Truk for the defense of the Pacific perimeter were sent to check the US forces' advance toward Rabaul. Adding insult to injury, the ships diverted to Rabaul were ambushed as they were about to refuel. US planes dived in, attacking with bombs and torpedoes. Of nine cruisers, seven were so crippled that they had to be sent back to Japan. As is often the case in a war of limited assets, the backup Shibazaki relied on is never coming to Tarawa.

The Americans, too, will see that on Tarawa, despite the briefings, nature and the enemy can combine to scoff at your plans. On the morning of November 20, 1943, the first three waves of LVTs cross the line of departure and head for Betio's Red beaches. Churning the water as they run, the Marines turn their eyes to the skies; they watch the final runs of fighters and bombers as they blast away, poking the bull of Tarawa like picadors stabbing to weaken it for the matador. But they soon notice that when the aircraft have banked off after dropping their last bombs, the tractors are still a good twenty minutes' distance from the beach. The crescendo of protective fire has ended, but the denouement is not yet ready to unwind. A heavy silence sets in.

Russell looks over both sides of his craft; the invasion line is well formed, and the tractors are advancing in unison. But in the momentary quiet, with no covering fire to pin them down, Japanese gunners begin to get the range on the advancing assault line. The lull is pierced by overhead whistles from the island and then the splash of geysers of water as exploding shells hit between and around the advancing Alligators.

Russell's tractor approaches the reef, its shallower green waters taking the place of the deep blue that had surrounded it, and then it hits the coral with a dull thud, throwing them forward a bit. The coxswain guns the engine, and the Alligator's tracks churn and jerk and lurch until it is on the reef. The beach is still well off in the distance, and what looks like a brown wall stretches across the sand.[21]

First on the beach are the assault forces of the 3rd Battalion, 2nd Marines, and two LVTs carrying part of Russell's Company K. The two Alligators have barely crawled ashore on the west end of Red Beach 1, when they are hit with raking fire coming from a position up to the left.

The blistering fire torches the Company K vehicles, stopping them in their tracks.[22] An LVT of Company I lands there as well; now it, too, is under the fire pounding at it from a hidden pillbox. Within moments, all the vehicles are knocked out; the steel hulks heave their last and sputter as they line up like dead whales on the beach.

Russell's LVT is taking a steady drumbeat of bullets on its port side when suddenly, to the left, a blistering hot orange flame shoots up as the next tank over explodes in a ball of fire. "Japanese fire whistles over our heads, and in the next instant, a large-caliber shell slams into the side of our LVT, killing both the coxswain and his assistant!"[23]

"Get out!" is the frantic order, and Russell rolls out, not over the side as he had practiced but anywhere—which turns out to be over the stern. He falls heavily on the sand, half in, half out of the water. "The rest of the men were out, running in a low crouch, crawling toward the wall. In their scramble out of the stricken vehicle, ammunition and other ordnance was dropped or left in the vessel."[24]

In the chaos of two hours, Companies I and K lose half their men and more than a third of their LVTs.[25] As the survivors run, they glance back across the beach at an eerie sea of bobbing bodies. Those who fought their way up the beach, only to be cut down, lie twisted as they fell, crumpled on the narrow strip of sand or pinned against Shibazaki's coconut-log trap.

Ironically, the destroyed LVTs have made it to precisely where they were supposed to land: at the neck of the bird. But in a gruesome plot twist, that has put them right into the path of Shibazaki's entrenched guns.

Now the surviving men from the two boats of Company K crouch on the sand and press against the wall as the world explodes all around them. The enemy fire is relentless and deafening. A sergeant named Gresham takes charge, yelling, "Move! Move!," exhorting the men to crawl west, toward the bird's beak. They scrape their way across the scrub and beach, dragging five of their wounded with them.

There is no other choice. Going left would take them away from their objective and into the teeth of the Japanese gun that blasted them from Red Beach 2. Going over the top of the wall would definitely be suicidal. Above their heads, certain death whistles over them; machine-gun bullets send a constant cascade of sand and log splinters down onto their heads and blurring their vision. The noise is so loud that they can only read their sergeant's lips and follow his hand signals.

Inch by inch they crawl along, dodging death, until Gresham's head turns toward the sound and he points at the sea. It is happening again: the tractors of the second wave are bearing down on the beach in a hail of gunfire and exploding shells. The Marines watch from their position as geysers erupt, shrouding the vehicles in walls of water and smoke. Some LVTs are knocked sideways like toys tossed in a stream; others erupt in flames as desperate Marines scramble to the water to escape the inferno.

Using the wall as continued cover, Jim Russell and his small band of Marines slowly muscle their way through the chaos, managing to skirt past one pillbox and then another until they hit a barbed-wire entanglement. One Marine deftly clips his way through with wire cutters. Their westward advance pushes them up against a third bunker, and now they are taking incoming. Japanese snipers are pinning them down. But now they have a position, and for the first time, they are firing back. Russell is unleashing a barrage of staccato fire from his Browning automatic rifle.

Popping up from behind the wall, firing, and ducking down again, for thirty minutes they chip away at the concrete surrounding the bunker's aperture. Some of their rounds are bull's-eyes inside the hole, and the shooters inside go silent. Gresham's group inches away under cover, crawling toward the bird's beak.

Russell's heart is pounding in his chest; he is a long way from the barrel line and right where his grandmother feared he would be. In a place where everyone seems to be dying, he finds his way to the beach and crouches down over the bodies of his fellow Marines as they float into and out of the water. He turns them, looking at their faces and wet uniforms caked in sand. He rifles through their pockets, looking for more ammo, just as he was taught to do. He finds some, but no grenades, the weapon he needs the most right now.[26]

Finally, as the unit moves along, there is water on both sides. The men have made it to the islet's tip—the bird's beak. They see that one large 8-inch gun has been knocked out by naval gunfire; but there is another, just inland, and it hammers away at the incoming Marines. As each round explodes, they watch helplessly as it cuts down their men.

The handful of still operational LVTs goes back for the rest of the invasion force, who are stuck waiting in Higgins boats at the edge of the reef they cannot cross. They were told that the tide would be with them, that the water would cover the reef and they would be able to float over. But the reading on the tides was wrong—dead wrong. One after the other, Higgins boats hit the reef. The Marines abandon their boats, climb out into the water, and wade across the jagged reef, through four hundred to five hundred yards of fire and water.[27] The men stretch across the lagoon, dotting the horizon, wading in, guns overhead, as they are picked off by Japanese fire, falling and sinking into the water over and over, going down in brutal, heartbreaking repetition, alone or in twos or threes as they stay in their lines. In a cruel twist of fate, the wounded Marines who cannot wade in lie on the reef waiting to be rescued, only to drown as the tide rises over them.

It is semi-ordered chaos. Communications have broken down, so small units resort to waving and shouting to one another. "There is no way to communicate with other units. The radios were inoperative, either from immersion in the salt water, or because they were riddled with machine-gun bullets."[28]

Russell and the rest of the Company K survivors dig in to defend their position on the bird's beak. They know nothing of the fate of the rest of their company, or what is going on beyond their sight lines. Their commander, Major John Schoettel, is hung up on the edge of the reef, trying to make it to the beach. He has some communication with parts of his three companies and seems to know the difficulties facing Companies I and K on the extreme right. He sends a message to Colonel David Shoup, commander of the 2nd Marines and the senior commander ashore, who has been blown out of his LVT and has taken shelter in the center of the landing area under the long pier. "Receiving heavy fire all along beach. Unable to land all. Issue in doubt."

Eight minutes later, with his remaining troops in the water and beginning the long wade-in with their rifles held over their heads, he signals, "Boats held up on reef of right flank RED 1. Troops receiving heavy fire in water."

Shoup signals back that he should try to land more to his left, toward Red Beach 2, and then try to work his way to the west. But during the short time between messages, the fate of Schoettel's wading Marines has become dire, and he transmits, "We have nothing left to land."[29]

There were 700 men in that battalion. How could there be none left?

He and his staff frantically wave to the Marines wading through the lagoon. Gaining their attention, they direct them to change direction and head for the pier. The pier will provide some shelter, at least, under which they can make their way to the beach.

For the Marines, who are chest high in water and laden with combat gear, currents swirling around them, shifting direction is nearly impossible. For some it is their last move. Japanese gunners in the trees follow them with their sights and pick them off; Marines tragically drop beneath the water one after the other. Those who make it to Shoup's position grab on to the wooden pilings of the pier like shipwreck survivors. (Shoup, who was born in a place called Battle Ground, Indiana, rose quickly through the ranks. He will win the Medal of Honor for his bravery at Tarawa and later become a general who is outspoken against the Vietnam War.)

Then, at the bird's beak, the small Marine force looks seaward and detects what looks like little "bobbing corks. In small groups and clusters, these bobbing objects move across the reef toward the shore. . . . Russell is held spellbound as the fourth assault wave wades in."[30]

As the Marines approach the shore, Japanese bullets pinging all around them, they make themselves into the smallest possible targets. They rest their rifles on their helmets and wade in with only their helmets above the water. On the extreme western flank of the reef, well removed from the main line of Marines struggling toward Red Beach 1, is a spread-out group of several hundred men. They are wading away from the line of approach to Red Beach 1 and directly toward the bird's beak.

They make better progress, and the Japanese fire is not as heavily concentrated against them, perhaps because the 8-inch gun has been destroyed and Russell's group has taken out some of the enemy on that shore.

This group is led by Major Michael Ryan with men from H&S Company and his own Company L. While waiting at the edge of the reef, his attention is diverted from the Red Beach 1 landing area to the extreme edge of Betio by the beak. His eye has caught sight of a solitary Marine from Company K jumping over the wall.

"It looked like a hopeless situation on Red Beach 1," Ryan will later say, "the boats hung up on the reef and the amtracs disabled.

Marines were forced to walk or crawl ashore directly into heavy fire, and it looked as if only a handful were surviving. I veered off to my right to avoid the guns on the left."[31]

It takes an hour for Ryan's group to wade in on this alternate line, and Japanese gunners are able to take down a third of the men. Finally, Ryan's men stagger into the Company K perimeter. The total force now on the northwestern tip of Betio is close to two hundred strong, and Major Ryan takes command of them all.

Out to sea, another strange procession seems headed for the bird's beak. A group of landing craft, mechanized (LCMs) carrying six medium Sherman tanks has discharged the Shermans at the edge of the reef, and the tanks have begun their crunching run in. Walking in front of the amphibious tanks and subjected to hostile fire are reconnaissance men carrying small flags to mark obstacles and potholes in the coral. When one flagman is shot, another heroically takes his place.

Only two of the tanks survive the harrowing trip to shore. Ryan takes command of them to spearhead an attack to the south, attempting to gain the upper hand on Tarawa for the first time. They will parallel the west coast along Green Beach and blast the enemy positions. Ryan's infantry will follow closely and clean out pockets of defensive positions.

At 2:00 p.m., the attack begins. The tanks blast the Japanese bunkers, but in the first minutes of the attack, the Sherman tank called *Cecilia*'s main gun is damaged when an enemy light tank gets off a round from its 37 mm gun and strikes the turret.[32] The other tank, *China Gal*, blasts the Japanese tank, and *Cecilia* continues on with her machine gun.

Russell and the other Marines follow in a furious charge, rolling up the Japanese positions, and in short order, they emerge on the other side of Betio, facing the blue water of the Pacific Ocean. The Marines have crossed the three hundred yards separating the contested Red landing beaches from the southern shore and have, unbelievably, outflanked the entire Japanese defensive force.[33]

The Marines dig in. They scrape out shallow holes to form a hasty defense facing the broken and shattered trees to the east. With their backs to the water, there are no Japanese defenders to confront them. Still, Major Ryan is uneasy in this advanced position. He has no way to signal anyone that he has outflanked the defenses of Betio and is on the southern shore. No one knows that Green Beach is secure for possible use. If the enemy counterattacks, he and his men will be alone.

He has two choices: to stay in his advanced position with the risk of being cut off or withdraw to his original position and try to establish communications.

Ryan is a veteran of the Guadalcanal campaign, and he understands Japanese cave and bunker fighting. The first grenade he threw into a bunker came flying right back out. He said, "I also learned that positions reduced only with grenades could come alive again a little later."

He has walked part of the battlefield at Tanambogo and observed that despite "a prolonged bombardment before the invasion . . . [there were] little mounded fortifications out of which scores of Japanese erupted in a kamikaze wave to push the Marines off the beach they had secured."[34]

All around him he sees many such innocent-looking mounds and bunkers that have undergone a massive shore bombardment but have never been cleaned out.

"When we managed to overrun most of the turrets and pill-boxes on the beak of Betio, I was convinced that without flamethrowers or explosives to clean them out we had to pull back the first night to a perimeter that could be defended against counter-attack by Japanese troops still hidden in the bunkers."[35]

He orders his force to withdraw. When Jim Russell hears the order to go back across the island to their original position, he cannot believe his ears. This is their only success of the day, and now they are going back? The tanks rumble alongside as they retrace their steps.

The sun is slowly setting on the wretched day. Exhausted, Russell stares out into the lagoon. Bodies float everywhere, swaying where the currents go. He is alive. Equipment and vehicles jam the beach, emasculated. Now their only service is as cover for the survivors who huddle behind them, shaken by their first combat day and first close-up views of death. They are so utterly exhausted that even these haunting images cannot keep them from sleep, fitful and short as it is when it comes.

To Russell's left and front, the Japanese still hold most of the island; at no time does their deadly fire seem to slacken. He and his fellow Marines dig in on the beak for a second time. They have no way of knowing that their landing and foray across the island have been the one enumerable success of the day.

X

The Marines welcome first light on D + 1. The shattered state of Japanese communications has made a night attack impossible.

But during the night, Japanese soldiers reoccupied some of their old positions, including the hull of a sunken ship in the lagoon that provides a commanding view. Their bunkers along the beach are mostly intact. Few Marines have attempted to climb over the deadly coconut-log wall. The Japanese fields of fire are still as deadly as they were on D-Day.

The first new Marine attackers across the reef cross the line of departure in boats, expecting that the tide will lift them over. But the water is still shallow, and an agonizing repeat of D-Day is under way. Once again, boats catch on the reef and grind to a halt.

Japanese gunners in their blockhouses zero in on the stationary targets and blast away. *Time* correspondent Robert Sherrod lands on the first day and from his position on the beach watches the wholesale slaughter. "One boat blows up, then another. The survivors start swimming ashore, but machine gun bullets dot the water all around them. This is worse, far worse than yesterday."[36]

On the bird's beak, Major Ryan's force faces to the south for a renewed attack to clear the area behind Green Beach. During the night, a few stragglers joined him. Among them is Second Lieutenant

Thomas N. Greene, a naval gunfire spotter, who has a working radio.[37] Headquarters now knows their location and that they were able to make it across yesterday.

At 11:10 a.m., on this blistering hot Betio day, Ryan is ready to attack. The tanks are revving as the Marines watch the land in front of them explode in a thunderous display of naval gunfire. Lieutenant Greene, handset to his ear, rattles off adjustments to the ships offshore, the exploding salvos smashing into the Japanese defenses.

"Ryan's Orphans," as they will come to be known, wait for the bombardment to lift so they can step off into the attack. They have barely enough weapons, only what they managed to carry out of the initial attack. Jim Russell carries a single bazooka he found in the flotsam and jetsam on the beach, but there are only two rockets for it, and one of them has a damaged fin. The bazooka is a new weapon, and no one in the group has ever trained with it or fired it. As they have no hand grenades, explosives, or flamethrowers, this is the only weapon that can engage a bunker. No flamethrowers made it across the reef; the seventy-two-pound weapons had either been jettisoned or had dragged their gunners to the bottom.[38]

Overnight, Japanese soldiers found their way back to a large bunker that is so well hidden, it looks like a sand dune. Attacking it with naval gunfire is out of the question, and if *China Gal* were to try to maneuver into position for a shot, she could easily be blasted by the bunker's cannon. That would be the end of the armor on that end of the island.

Jim Russell is pinned down by enemy fire behind a large coconut log. Marines are returning fire at the bunker, to little effect. Russell knows they can't move on until the bunker and the men in it are cleared.

Russell and fellow Marine Private First Class Joseph Herberski discover that the large eighteen-inch log just in front of them rolls rather easily and they can move around behind it, changing their position without exposing themselves to the machine gun.

Major Ryan peeks out from his covered position to plan his next move and sees a large log suddenly roll forward with the two Marines pushing it from behind. Russell is dragging the bazooka and his single rocket along with him.

The Japanese gunners also see the rolling log and fire a burst in its direction.

At a turtle's pace, the log-rolling Marines get to the base of the bunker's slope. They are gasping for air and soaked in sweat, their muscles cramping and aching.

They move to lie on their backs with legs crouched against the log. They dig in the edges of their boots and push as hard as they can. The log rolls about a foot up the slope. Russell jams some rocks behind it so it can't roll back on them. Then they get behind it and crouch and push again, and again and again in this rhythm. Crouch, push, chock . . . crouch, push, chock!

They use their heads, arms, and shoulders as chocks to stop the log. The other Marines are firing at the bunker to keep the Japanese from firing at the log, but bullets are flying in both directions over the heads of Russell and Herberski and at the log. In one of their synchronized moves, Herberski gets too far above the log in his thrust and is hit, shot in the throat. Russell rushes to bandage him, but Herberski is undaunted, insisting it's just a nick. Sweating, straining, and under fire, they are now within fifteen feet of the bunker's shooting aperture. Herberski struggles with the bazooka and loads it, but he has lost too much blood and has no strength left to fire, so he passes it to Russell.

The other Marines are laying down tremendous fire that drives the Japanese gunners from the aperture; Russell braces himself for what he knows is his one and only shot. As the Marines pour fire into the bunker, he bolts upright to a kneeling position, takes a quick aim, and squeezes the trigger of the bazooka.[39]

The back blast of the weapon creates a dust cloud as the rocket sails straight into the bunker and detonates. The explosion knocks the log loose, and it rolls back down the hill, flattening Russell and Herberski.

The next bunker is eliminated with the help of the Marines' one Bangalore torpedo, and the Marines suddenly find themselves again looking at the blue waters of the Pacific off the southern shore.

Lieutenant Greene continues his calls for thunderous salvos of naval gunfire, and by 12:30 p.m., the western end of Betio has been swept clear of enemy resistance. Ryan's Orphans advance several hundred yards to the east and dig in.

Ryan signals back his success, and shortly afterward, the 1st Battalion, 6th Marines, lands without opposition, not in landing craft but in rubber boats, on Green Beach. The next day, they sweep the island in a flanking attack and roll up holdout Japanese positions. Knowing that the fight is over, most of the remaining Japanese soldiers run at the Marines in a suicidal banzai charge.

Russell and Herberski will receive the Navy Cross for their heroic actions at the bunker. But Joseph Herberski dies of his wound later that day. He is one of the 3,407 casualties in the 2nd Marines in just seventy-six hours of fighting. Among them more than a thousand lost their lives on Tarawa.

Some of the assault companies of the division lost more than 50 percent of their numbers. More than a hundred critically wounded Marines died of their wounds on board ships returning to Hawaii and are buried at sea.[40]

Of the 5,000 Japanese fighting on Tarawa, only 17 survived after the banzai charge. They were taken prisoner.

※

For the first time, back on the home front, Americans begin to really see the war. They see US Marines, not shiny faced and heading off to war, but lifeless and fallen in the unnatural crumpled posture of death by gunfire and shelling. They see young boys who will never come home floating facedown, tossed back and forth at the water's edge, thrown like shells crushed by waves, scattered on the shore. The Canadian illustrator Kerr Eby wrote, "Tarawa was a time of utmost savagery—I still don't know how they took the place."[41]

President Roosevelt was persuaded to sign off on the release of Norman Hatch's movie *With the Marines at Tarawa*, filmed during the battle. Hatch would later remember the stench of death and thick black smoke everywhere. His camera had captured the dead "just as they lay. This was the first time this type of death was shown; floating in the water . . . and this was just before Thanksgiving Day, which made it even worse."[42]

※

As Christmas 1943 approaches, Dominick Grossi writes home from boot camp at Parris Island. After a big send-off that made the newspapers in Buffalo, Grossi and his fellow University of Rochester football players turned enlisted men are now just head-shaven "numbers," like everyone else, getting taken down a few pegs and then built up stronger through the rigors of Marine training.

Grossi sends a postcard home to his younger siblings:

Hiya Kids,
    Just returned from a movie. I called my rifle a gun and the sergeant had me write 100 times on toilet paper, "One hundred thousand Marines have a rifle, I'm lucky I've got a gun." You see we aren't supposed to call our rifles, guns.

Love to all, Dom.[43]

In Arlington, Massachusetts, Christmas and the end of 1943 turn Harry Gray's thoughts to his coming springtime graduation from high school. He will be eighteen then, and as he promised his mother, he will stay until graduation and then head to Parris Island to become a United States Marine. He will spend the next Thanksgiving and Christmas in the central Pacific.

8

Cracking the Inner Ring

Anne Gray, like her brother, Frank, now has a good job at Liberty Mutual Insurance Company. She is an executive secretary, a trusted employee, and her boss relies on her greatly. Anne is marching forward, and if she feels overwhelmed raising her children and holding down a full-time job, she keeps it to herself. Although life is very different for Nancy and Harry without their dad, they soldier on, without self-pity or complaint. They do not have much, but they have what they need and each other, as well as their grandmother, who still lives with them to keep an eye on things while Anne is at the office. The war, though, hangs over everything. "After the war, we will get a new car" or "After the war, when the boys come home" is a common refrain in every conversation. Life is suspended.

Harry is speeding through his senior-year spring homework and spending what seems like hours on the phone with Dorothy. The Grays share a party line with the neighbors, so Anne tells him all the time to keep it short. But as long as no one chimes in and barks at you to get off, you can get away with it, which they do. Anne is a bit concerned about all the time they spend together. She doesn't know all that much about Dorothy, just that she lives in a small house in a nearby town and has a job at the glove shop. They are still very young. She can't help but wonder what Harry Sr. would say. He'd probably tell her to leave them alone and let 'em have fun. If he were here, he would talk to Harry about it all.

On the home front, Americans are doing all they can for the war effort. They flatten their metal cans to be turned in to make weapons and save their bacon fat to be used to fuel explosives. It is a national way of life, and the Gray family does their part. They line up for butter only when it is Thanksgiving or someone's birthday. Nancy waits in line with her mother and smiles all the way home, thinking about spreading it on her bread when she gets home.

But Americans happily wait in line to go to the movies, which are the great wartime escape, even when they focus on the war. They are fascinated by the bombers and submarines being built across the country, and they thrill to watch them in action, with their boys—winning, of course—in films such as *Guadalcanal Diary* and *Cry Havoc*. Eighteen-year-old George Colburn and his buddies of Medford, Massachusetts, are among those at the Capitol Theater in Arlington, who settle in on a Saturday afternoon to watch *Guadalcanal Diary*. The picture lures them in with beautiful, sunny beaches and palm trees, and right then and there, George and his pal Bob decide they'll join the Marines and head to the Pacific. After all, their friends who had already enlisted were in Europe, where it was freezing cold and snowy.[1]

But the stories bring home the dark side of the war as well, revealing the barbarism of the enemy. In *Behind the Rising Sun*, a young Japanese man who has studied in the United States returns home, only to be sent to fight against the Chinese. He is horrified by the brutality of Japan's officers against the Chinese and he speaks out but is reprimanded by his commanding officer. He ends up hardening his heart for war but is then shot down in his plane. The movie's brutality gets it a rating of "not suitable for general exhibition."

The blockbuster musical *This Is the Army* shows the lighter side of military life and features Irving Berlin's showstopping "God Bless America." It seems as though everybody has a son in the war or one about to go or a husband or a future husband or an uncle or a brother.

All across the United States, people wait in long lines to be transported to their world or forget about it all. Each in its own way slightly eases the weight of the war at home.

In Japan, images of Midway, Guadalcanal, and Tarawa bring home a different reality. These losses have jolted the emperor and his top brass. As Japan's Navy and island defensive forces scramble to reposition themselves for the next US onslaught, Admiral Nimitz's Fast Carrier Task Force is retooled to iron out some of the deadly glitches of their equipment, such as the Alligator vehicles' difficulties on the reef at Tarawa. Now they are ready to strike again.

None of this feels good at the Imperial Palace, and Japanese leadership turns to the potent weapons of fantasy and denial to keep spirits up. Censorship is their weapon at home, to prevent the Japanese people from getting a "glimpse of the fate of their nation."[2]

The Battle of Midway was the first defeat in Japan's naval history. As its wounded fleet was limping home, Radio Tokyo was making up stories: two US carriers, a destroyer, and a cruiser had been sunk, it gleefully reported. If victory was an illusion, facts were pliable. In reality, only one US carrier and a destroyer had been lost. Radio Tokyo didn't stop at exaggerating the United States' losses; it also pretended that the devastation of the Japanese fleet was a mirage, wiped away easily. It gleefully lied to the people of Japan, telling them they had lost only one carrier and another sustained a bit of damage. Clearly a victory for the Imperial Navy!

But the truth was this: all four of Japan's carriers were gone, as was a cruiser, and a second cruiser had been damaged, as had two destroyers, an oiler, and a battleship. Suddenly all the burning metal and dead sailors vanished into thin air as far as the Japanese media were concerned. Also unmentioned was the staggering loss of 322 planes and the better part of their highly skilled crews. Many of the planes had been incinerated on the exploding carriers or shot down by US fire. Some of the Japanese pilots had been killed when they came in for landings on carriers that were no longer there. Having no other choice, they had plunged into the ocean.

The Japanese leaders decided to hide the losses for the time being. Like gamblers, they bet that a later big win would make up for a dismal hand now. So when the rest of the fleet arrived back in Japan, the survivors disembarked under the cover of darkness and were essentially sent into hiding.[3] "All the enlisted men of the sunken carriers were sent to naval bases, confined to the bases, and shipped out . . . to the far reaches of the empire, such as Truk. So were many of the junior officers, and the others were sworn to secrecy."[4]

No one asked about the four missing carriers of Pearl Harbor fame or about the men who had served on them and had not returned home.

Fantastic reports of Japanese naval and air prowess, as well as incredible victories, were fed to the people in a steady stream. For the most part, they accepted it. They believed a report issued after Guadalcanal that thousands of US planes and 245 warships had been sunk during the previous four months—more than the United States could have ever produced—but no one dared to ask the obvious questions: If there had been such destruction of the enemy's forces, how was it possible for that enemy to be sitting on the doorstep of Japan's bastion at Rabaul; or, How did Guadalcanal and Tarawa fall?

On October 21, 1943, one month before the invasion of Betio, a senior literature student from Tokyo Imperial University, Shinshiro Ebashi, delivered an impassioned speech on the occasion of his call-up for military service. He was one of thousands of university students now called to fill Japan's burgeoning need for replacement manpower, especially in aviation. Those thousands were to march in a patriotic parade witnessed by 65,000 of their proud relatives and friends, wives and girlfriends.

Prime Minister Hideki Tojo was also there, proudly standing in the front in full military regalia. The parade was to be witnessed by thousands more and end at the Imperial Palace, where the students would shout a rousing triple cheer of "Banzai! Banzai! Banzai!" to honor the emperor. Such spectacles had been stoking the fervor of Japanese pride for years, but on this day, there was something decidedly different. A heretofore unspoken fatalism was expressed in Ebashi's speech: "We, of course, do not expect to return alive as we take up guns and bayonets as we embark on our glorious mission of crushing the stubborn enemy."[5]

Why would that be? Had not earlier Japanese warriors returned alive after their years of expansion, annexation, conquest, and "crushing the stubborn enemy"?

He then addressed those in the audience not yet called to service. He predicted that they "would follow in our footsteps, in the not distant future, and march over our dead bodies to win victory in the Greater East Asia War."[6] This was the *bushido* spirit that would characterize the coming months: the belief that the nation led by the emperor would win, even in losing. Ebashi's speech sent a prescient message: "Fight to the death, die proudly." In other words, the student told the people of Japan, we need your sacrifice, but wake up, things are not going well.

And what of the emperor? He would forever maintain that he, too, had been given rosy, deceptive reports. But did he really not know that his ships had never made it home? Could the descendent of the sun goddess be so much in the dark? As Prime Minister Tojo received the triple "Banzai!" cheer from the university students at the end of their march, did he feel a pang of guilt about sending off new recruits who could have no expectation to return alive?

In March and April 1946, shortly before the Tokyo war crimes trials were to begin, Hirohito would give eight hours of secret interviews about the war. In them he would reveal some of what he had thought during the war years, working to spin how he should be perceived in it all. He and his advisers had furiously worked to destroy any paper trail in the two weeks between surrender and occupation, and now he was filling in the blanks before the coming trial of his military leaders.

He stressed his "noninvolvement." He was a constitutional monarch, he said, not a supreme military commander.

The record and transcripts of the interviews disappeared shortly after their completion. They were never given to General MacArthur, and they remained missing for more than forty years, until they turned up in 1988 in a Wyoming home in the hands of the daughter of one of the interviewers.[7]

One interview segment was labeled "Table Talks on the Pacific War." In it, Hirohito revealed that he had been very much in command. He had been well aware of Japan's aggressive expansionism. He had been especially determined to hold on to his land acquisitions in the south and central Pacific. As the US offensive began late in 1942, he would say, "We can't give up our [newly-won] resources in the south half-way through exploiting them."[8]

Though the Japanese survived on the truism that to the victor go the spoils, the Americans upended it. The Japanese, living on an island nation with few resources of their own, considered a growing empire built on war to be the only path to long-term survival. The Americans, blessed with nearly unlimited resources, fought wars only to end them.

Hirohito further stated, "We thought we could achieve a draw with the US, or at best win by a six to four margin; but total victory was nearly impossible. . . . When the war actually began, however, we gained a miraculous victory at Pearl Harbor and our invasions of Malaya and Burma succeeded far quicker than expected."[9]

Hirohito declared that he would have sought for peace then, while he still had the upper hand, but he had been stymied from doing so. He blamed the Germans for having ruined his plans for seeking peace. He said he had been handicapped by the terms of a corollary agreement to the Tripartite Pact that he had signed with Germany. That corollary agreement forbade seeking a separate accord with the United States.

The emperor continued, "I knew we had lost any hope for victory when we failed to hold the Stanley Mountain Range on New Guinea."

This is nonsensical, since that battle in New Guinea went on late into 1942, while Japan was still actively expanding its empire to the south, into the Solomon Islands, and threatening Australia. The battle for Guadalcanal was still being fought, and it, too, was in doubt.

Hirohito himself indicated that he was hardly willing to fold before he had fully exploited his new landholdings.

He then again laid all blame for his continuing the war on the Germans: "I hoped to give the enemy one good bashing somewhere, and then seize a chance for peace. Yet I didn't want to ask for peace before Germany did because then we would lose trust in the international community for having violated that corollary agreement."[10]

So according to the emperor, Japan had continued the war while waiting for Germany's permission to surrender!

As Nimitz's Fast Carrier Task Force prepared to assault the inner ring of the Japanese defense line in the Marshall Islands, the emperor would have another opportunity to administer a good "bashing" to the Americans.

⋈

Legend has it that Admiral Isoroku Yamamoto, the commander of the Japanese Combined Fleet and architect of the Pearl Harbor attack, once said, "I fear all we have done is to awaken a sleeping giant and fill him with a terrible resolve."

At the end of January 1944, a massive US fleet plows its way through the Pacific. It moves westward toward the Marshall Islands, 620 miles northwest of Tarawa, along the War Plan Orange trail. Commanded by Vice Admiral Marc Mitscher, it is an armada the Japanese could only dream of building. Known as Task Force 58, it is actually a massive collection of four separate Navy task forces. Twelve aircraft carriers carry seven hundred planes, and these carriers are surrounded by eight new battleships and a ring of prowling cruisers and destroyers.[11]

For Japan, after the loss of Tarawa and the Gilbert Islands, the massive expanse of the Marshall Islands becomes the new forward rampart of her defense. But that rampart is not prepared for the aerial blitz that Mitscher unleashes with his 700 aircraft against 130 defending Zeros on January 29, 1944. The Americans swoop down like falcons from above and make short work of the Japanese planes; after two days, there are no more of them.

For the young Marines of the 4th Division, who attack into the Marshall Islands, this is their first action and the first fight of the division. There is no division history, as there was for the 1st and 2nd, which assaulted Guadalcanal and Tarawa. There is no Belleau Wood, Château-Thierry, Tripoli, or Chapultepec in their past. They are not part of the Old Corps or the Old Breed. They are the new Marines, a new breed that has expanded the Corps from 50,000 to a force now approaching half a million.

Their transports depart San Diego on January 13, 1944, and except for a twenty-four-hour layover in Hawaii, they are continuously at sea, zigzagging on a five-thousand-mile, eighteen-day trek to the battle. Several miles out of Hawaii, commanders show the eager Marines the operational maps and details of Kwajalein Atoll, in the heart of the Marshall Islands: a massive cluster of 32 atolls, more than 1,000 islands, and 867 reefs.

Yet in that vast expanse of ocean, reefs, and islands, the 4th Marine Division is focused on the tiny pinprick of a double island nestled within the huge Kwajalein Atoll called Roi-Namur. One look at the details of these twin islands evokes comparisons of the ordeal at Betio. On Roi there is an airfield, much like the one on tiny Tarawa Island; on Namur there are fifty-two pillboxes, coastal defense guns, heavy and medium antiaircraft guns, and numerous trenches, blockhouses, and tangles of barbed wire. Neither Roi nor Namur amounts to a square mile of land.

On the plus side, there are enough tractors for the attacking force and there will be no long wade-in across an exposed reef in the face of murderous enemy fire. And the massive force moving to attack Roi-Namur is far larger than that committed to Tarawa. It is comforting for the young Marines to stand at the rails of their transports and feel dwarfed within the body of the great naval task force that surrounds and escorts them.

One Marine, Private First Class Robert F. Graf, is eager to finally get his turn. Too young to join just after Pearl Harbor, Graf is among the legions of boys who envied the older ones who had gone off to fight the enemy and strained at the leash to join them. He will later say, "As I thought of the landing that I would be making on the morrow, I was both excited and anxious. Yes, I thought of death, but I wasn't afraid. Somehow I couldn't see myself as dead. . . . I was headed for great adventure, where I had wanted to be. This was just an adventure. It was 'grown up' Cowboys and Indians, it was 'grown up' Cops and Robbers. . . . Now it was my turn to 'carry the flag' into battle. It was my turn to be a part of history."[12]

Two days before the invasion, the US warships and aircraft carriers begin to bomb and shell every square yard of Roi-Namur. The battleships move into a bombardment position as close as 1,900 yards from the beach and fire into the island defenses. Waves of carrier planes sweep in for bombing and strafing, and the combined bombardment lays six thousand tons of steel on the twin islands.

The amphibious assault begins on February 1. The first wave of the 23rd Marines hits the beaches at noon, and as the Marines move inland, they are virtually unopposed. Immediately they see why: the devastating bombardments have left the airfield strewn with destroyed aircraft and caved-in defensive positions. The dead are everywhere; a few hundred dazed defenders are quickly mopped up. The rest of the force has fled to the more formidable positions on neighboring Namur.[13]

In fifteen minutes, Roi is neutralized, and at 12:15, a jubilant communications officer signals to the commanding general, "This is a pip. Give us the word and we'll take the island."[14]

After additional naval gunfire prep fires, the Marines continue the attack at 4:00 p.m. with tanks rolling ahead of the assault line. At 6:00 p.m. the island is secured in the quickest battle to ever be won in the Pacific. Hundreds of Japanese soldiers lay sprawled over the Roi battlefield. The bombardment caught them in various stages of fleeing for their lives and mutilated their bodies horribly.

Across the small causeway connecting the two islands, Namur is not a "pip." Not only are there multiple hardened defensive positions, but there is thick vegetation, concealing and camouflaging the enemy everywhere. The men of the 24th Marines hammer the Green beaches and are met with heavy gunfire as they are assaulted on the left. Scores are cut down within seconds of coming down out of their landing craft; all around them rifles and guns are firing at them at close range.

On the right, the Marines press ahead about two hundred yards and come upon a large enemy blockhouse. A lieutenant named Saul Stein leads his men to surround the building, and on his signal, a Marine carrying a shaped charge, used to penetrate concrete and steel, advances and places the explosive against the wall. After triggering the charge, he retreats to cover with the other Marines. The deafening blast rips a hole through the wall.[15]

The Japanese pour out from inside, firing wildly in all directions while making their escape. The surprised Marines fumble and scramble to engage them. Stein shouts for his men to throw in satchel charges in case any Japanese are still in there. The Marines hurl the charges with hissing fuses through the hole.

Within seconds, the world on the island of Namur explodes. An immense tower of black smoke and rubble jets into the sky, turning the heads of every man on shore and at sea toward the detonation. The cloud rises a thousand feet into the sky. From a ship offshore, an officer reports, "The whole of Namur Island disappeared from sight in a tremendous brown cloud of dust and sand."[16]

Major Charles Duchein, a Marine artillery spotter circling in an aircraft above the battlefield, suddenly feels his plane violently forced upward. "Great God Almighty!" he exclaims. "The whole damn island has blown up!"[17]

Men on Namur are knocked to their knees by the shock wave; they scramble for cover as tons of debris fall from the sky. One officer recalls, "Trunks of palm trees and chunks of concrete as large as packing crates were flying through the air like match sticks. . . . The hole left where the blockhouse stood was as large as a fair-sized swimming pool."[18]

The blockhouse was crammed with tons of torpedo warheads. Lieutenant Stein is among the twenty Marines who are killed by the massive detonation. Another hundred men are wounded. That evening, the attacking 24th Marines digs in for the night, fully expecting a Japanese night attack from the desperate surviving enemy, now pinned in a pocket against the northern shore.

It comes in the early-morning hours in the drizzling rain across the bombed-out landscape illuminated by star shells. Shrieking "Banzai!," several hundred Japanese begin the charge against the lines of the 3rd Battalion. The Marines pour fire into the onrushing enemy line. But the Japanese re-form their line and come on again. The firefight drags on for hours and at one point pushes the Marine lines back to a secondary defensive position. But the Marines charge back, regaining their ground, and in the end the attack fails.

In the early afternoon of the following day, Namur is declared secure. The operation is barely twenty-four hours old. As at Tarawa, the Japanese force is virtually annihilated, many of the soldiers committing suicide rather than surrender. Unlike the 3,400 casualties at Tarawa, the Marine casualties at Roi-Namur are 313 dead and 502 wounded, with 3,500 Japanese soldiers dead. Emperor Hirohito's wished-for "good bashing" has not materialized.

In a simultaneous attack, the Army secures the island of Kwajalein on the southern end of the atoll. In the Marshall Islands campaign, Japanese deaths reach a total of 8,122, twenty-seven times the number of Americans lost.

The swift wins in the Marshalls move up Admiral Nimitz's timetable by twenty weeks. US forces are now within 1,100 miles of the Mariana Islands, which will put them into a position to strike Japan with long-range bombers.

At home, in theaters across the United States, the dramatic voice of Hugh James of Movietone News narrates "Marshalls Invasion!" A preliminary image leads to the narration: "The victory is a major step in the Central Pacific offensive on the Road to Tokyo."

The short film, shot by Coast Guard, Navy, and Marine Corps combat cameramen, shows the great armada moving to battle and then the battle at Roi-Namur itself. The shore bombardment with its shattering sound vibrates the movie seats. The tractors running into the beaches as low-flying airplanes dropped their final bombs are high drama for Americans anxious to see victory.

James booms, "Enemy parties were wiped out in a war to the death." An orchestra plays "The Marines' Hymn" in the background, and there is a final tribute to those who did not make it out alive: "Americans who were defending their country's cause made the supreme sacrifice on a distant shore."[19]

9

Willing to Fight

As long as justice and injustice have not terminated their ever-renewing fight for ascendancy in the affairs of mankind, human beings must be willing . . . to do battle for the one against the other.[1]

In April 1862, the British philosopher John Stuart Mill penned those words about the American Civil War. As Mill saw it, the Union forces needed to prevail, and the citizenry of the Northern states needed to fight and defeat the new Southern Confederacy and end the perpetuation of the evil of slavery.

To Mill's way of thinking, the war was not to be won by military maneuver and a few defeats on the battlefield or even "by taking military possession of their country, or marching an army through it, but by wearing them out, exhausting their resources, depriving them of the comforts of life, encouraging their slaves to desert, and excluding them from communication with foreign countries."[2]

In a future time, Mill could have written those same words to describe the ongoing world war against Nazi Germany and Imperial Japan and the necessity to defeat their evil, totalitarian attempt to enslave the rest of the world.

The Casablanca Conference, in 1943, had called for the Allies to bring about the unconditional surrender of the Axis powers, not some negotiated peace that could leave their evil institutions intact.

Making peace would have meant "giving up the original cause of quarrel," Mill wrote.[3] Bringing about victory would require freedom-loving people to be willing to fight. Mill chastised those who were unwilling to fight and were willing to turn a blind eye to evil for the sake of peace in their time. In the 1930s, appeasement had enabled Hitler, Mussolini, and Hirohito to spread their subjugation and enslavement of innocent people under their vicious totalitarian rule. Now the wages of that unwillingness to fight would be paid by a new generation called upon to restore freedom to the world. Mill wrote:

> War, in a good cause, is not the greatest evil which a nation can suffer. War is an ugly thing, but not the ugliest of things: the decayed and degraded state of moral and patriotic feeling which thinks nothing worth a war, is worse. . . . A man who has nothing which he is willing to fight for, nothing which he cares more about than he does about his personal safety, is a miserable creature who has no chance of being free, unless made and kept so by the exertions of better men than himself.[4]

In Arlington, Massachusetts, "better men" had picked up the torch of freedom in 1775, when they had gathered to confront the British Army at Lexington and Concord. Dr. Joseph Warren, the president of the Massachusetts Provincial Congress, was willing to fight the tyranny of King George III. "To the persecution and tyranny of his cruel ministry we will not tamely submit; appealing to Heaven for the justice of our cause, we determine to die or be free."[5]

On a hot June graduation night in 1944, Harry Gray sits on the risers at Arlington High School, in cap and gown, sweat rising on his back. He is listening to the mayor talk about the history of Arlington and the battles at Lexington and Concord. As a little boy, he imagined himself in the spring of 1775, fighting for freedom and the future of a new kind of country. His mind drifts off to the place he dreamed up years ago. It puts him at the heart of the action.

He is a young minuteman, running, his worn boots covered in New England mud. Slung over his shoulder, a musket, and a hunting knife is deep in his pocket. He is racing back from the surprise attack at the North Bridge, his cheeks and jacket spattered with dirt and sweat. The cool Massachusetts air whips across his chest; his heart is pounding as he catches his first glimpse of the redcoats.

They are swarming the ridge in front of him in full retreat from the battle at Concord. Harry is crouching down behind the rock wall at Dr. Warren's farm. Watching them, breathing hard, he braces his musket against the rocks.

Before dawn this morning of April 19, 1775, the tensions between the local militias and the redcoats finally boiled over. At first light, the British marched out of Boston, and on Lexington Green the minutemen lined up to defy them, the tension between them rising in the air with every cool breath on that April morning. The redcoats, in their crisp uniforms, despise the scrappy bands of rebels and militiamen in mismatched farm garb. The rebels, though, have had more than enough of the stranglehold the king has on their money and their freedom. At some point, no one knows from whose rifle, a shot is fired, and within moments eight are dead on the ground, another ten are wounded,[6] and the stunned colonists fall back.

The poet Ralph Waldo Emerson wrote of the moment, "Here once the embattled farmers stood / And fired the shot heard round the world."

Down the road, the patriots at Concord have been tipped off. Paul Revere has warned the Massachusetts militias. Family by family, mile by mile on horseback, he bellowed the alert to the eleven towns between Lexington and Concord.

The militia scrambled to arm themselves, well aware that this day could be their last, as it was for their neighbors on Lexington Green. They are outmatched, outnumbered, undersupplied, and woefully trained. The only thing they have in spades is outrage.

At Concord there is a second skirmish, much like the one at Lexington, but this time the colonists have cobbled together more men than the redcoats, as they face off at the North Bridge. A first shot is fired that quickly deteriorates into a general melee, and the outgunned

British detachment falls back to rejoin the main column. Its officers, sensing that things have gotten out of hand, signal to the main column to begin retracing its steps back to Boston.

Now the colonists, amazed that the British are retreating, go in for more confrontation. They harass the red column on both flanks, ambushing them from all sides. The British, stunned by their mounting losses, hasten their retreat. This is where Harry sees them coming into Arlington over the ridge; he stays crouched down behind the stone wall.

The British column enters Arlington (known then as Menotomy), ripping through the town, looting along the way, reeling from the ferocity of the firepower from the mixed bag of farmers, armed with whatever they could find in the homes and barns.

But the spark has been lit, and the furious citizens simply won't stop shooting at them. Townsfolk gather, and the ambush is growing. Their weapons bristle and flame from every conceivable position: from just off the road, from behind the stone wall, from the taverns and the mills, even from the old cemetery.[7]

Lord Percy barks out orders for the British soldiers to clear every house and eliminate all snipers' nests. The soldiers bully their way in, ransacking and looting, then torching what is left. Flames soon engulf the buildings, and a black, choking cloud hangs over the streets.

Harry the minuteman hears the screams of his neighbors, bolts from the wall to Jason Russell's house, and takes cover with others in the cellar. Heart pounding and sweat streaking down the sides of his face, he braces his back against the cool stone cellar wall and holds his musket with his finger on the trigger.

Overhead, the redcoats stomp up the steps and into the house. Those in hiding hear Mr. Russell struggling with them and trying to push them back, then he cries out in agony and hits the ground above.

The redcoats are coming his way now. Harry's finger takes up the slack in the trigger as he hears the door creak open, and now black boots are on the step above his head. He holds his breath, as the boots take another step. Then he sees, through the open slats of the cellar stairs, the tips of the red coats. The others crouch back behind Harry, and he prays that they will stay still. As the redcoat comes down the steps, Harry waits a beat and then pulls the trigger. The flame leaps two feet from the barrel, and the recoil of the weapon drives Harry back. The slain redcoat's body drops heavily onto the stairs and then to the cellar floor. Harry hears the redcoats scatter from the house upstairs and rests his head on his musket as blood pools under the soldier on the floor. He has shot him squarely through his back; he is not breathing. Harry sneaks out the cellar door and sees the last of the redcoats making their way out of town.[8]

Harry's mind snaps back to the present, at his graduation, as the mayor goes on about the spirit of the patriots of the American Revolution and how that spirit is now at work in the world once again. He pays tribute to all the men in towns like theirs who are off fighting the war, now not in their backyards but in Europe, in the bombed-out villages and fields of France, and across the Pacific, facing the foe that killed so many at Pearl Harbor. Now Harry is getting antsy.

Finally they are calling names; his lifelong friends stand and walk across the stage, grinning as they receive their diplomas. "Harry . . . Eugene . . . Gray." Harry pops up with a big smile and strides across the stage. He shakes the principal's hand and shoots a side smile over at Dorothy, who is sitting with two of her friends. Then he finds his mom and Nancy, sitting in the bleachers. He can see how proud his mom is. She sits tall and holds the program against her chest, her hands folded over it. Her eyes are glistening a bit, and he smiles right back into them. The truth is that six years after his father's death, they are doing pretty well, and it is all because of his mom. She has held them together, kept a roof over their heads and shoes on their feet. For his part, Harry kept them all smiling. All in all, he thinks as he takes his seat, they are doing pretty okay.[9]

When Harry gets home, there is a small party under way. The table is full of pies and sandwiches. A couple of his buddies are there; they pat him on the back and mess up his hair. Everyone congratulates him. These are the pals he has played football and baseball with over on the sandlot ever since he was little. Two of Mom's friends from work are there and some of the neighbors. Looking around the room at them all, he sees them talking and laughing, but he feels somehow apart. So many boys have already left, and soon he will be on his way. Time has been standing still, but now he is about to leave Arlington and all of this behind. Uncle Frank sent him a graduation card and put some money into it for him. He said he knew Harry had worked hard and he was very proud of him. He signed it, "With lots of love, Uncle Frank and Aunt Helen and Betts." He is grateful for Uncle Frank's easy way and guidance over the years. Uncle Frank has never tried to tell him what to do; he always seemed to say just what Harry needed to hear when he needed to hear it. He knows that Uncle Frank did not want him to enlist. But he's glad he understands that Harry has to do what he has to do.

Suddenly his eyes are drawn to the doorway, and there is Dorothy. She looks perfect in her yellow fitted dress with a white collar and full skirt and her white gloves, her red lips and her short blond hair curling just below her ear. He excuses himself from Mrs. Newley, who has been talking his ear off, and slips through the crowd to her. Dorothy doesn't really know any of these people; Harry isn't sure *he* knows all of them. She is holding a cake on a plate. He smiles at her and takes it to free her hands. "Hi, Harry, congratulations," she says.

Harry smiles down at her. "C'mon, let's go put this in the kitchen." They work their way to the kitchen, and Harry puts the plate down on the table. "Did you make this?" he asks.

"Of course I did," she says. It has chocolate icing.

"What's inside?" he inquires with a sly smile.

"More chocolate," she answers, smiling back. Their words are just words; they are too busy staring into each other's eyes. Neither wants to talk about what the day means, which is that now there is nothing standing between Harry and leaving Arlington. Dorothy picks up the cake and goes through the swinging kitchen door, placing it prominently in the center of the desserts. He stands in the doorway and watches her. But then he catches his mother's eye. She is watching them as well. She looks at Dorothy. She worries that they've moved too fast, and the only thing she doesn't mind about Harry enlisting is that it will give him some time to figure it all out.[10]

)(

That June, Admiral Chester Nimitz's Fast Carrier Task Force is again on the move to the west. With the Gilbert Islands and the Marshall Islands secured, the next stop is the Mariana Islands, the inner ring of the Japanese defenses.

In Washington, the Joint Chiefs of Staff ponder the next Pacific objective and, after much discussion and argument, opt for a daring, far-reaching triple operation, to be called Operation Forager. The aim is to seize the islands of Saipan and Tinian and to recapture Guam, lost to the Japanese during the first days of the war. If the move is successful, the US forces will be just 1,250 miles from Japan[11] and within the range of a new long-range bomber coming off the assembly lines: the B-29.

The invasion force is already training in Hawaii. The 4th Marine Division, veterans of Roi-Namur, are on Maui; the 2nd Marine Division, veterans of Tarawa, are on the Big Island of Hawaii; and the Army's 27th Infantry Division is on Oahu.

Replacements have flooded into the 4th Division to fill the gaps left by the casualties suffered on Roi-Namur. They are green recruits and have completed only basic training, not nearly the training necessary to attack a fortified island. Lieutenant John C. Chapin will later report:

> Most of these replacements were boys fresh from boot camp, and they were ignorant of everything but the barest essentials. Week after week was filled with long marches, field combat problems, live firing, obstacle courses, street fighting, judo, calisthenics, night and day attacks and defenses, etc. There were also lectures on the errors we'd made at Namur. . . . We worked with demolition

charges of dynamite, TNT, and C-2 [plastic explosive], and with flame throwers till everyone knew them forward and backward.[12]

Late that spring, final maneuvers and practice landings are under way for the three divisions that will attack Saipan. The massive assault force that assembles at Pearl Harbor comprises eight hundred ships and more than 70,000 Marine and Army troops. This is a far cry from the dark days of 1942 and Guadalcanal, when a meager US naval force risked everything to face down the enemy in the Solomon Islands; or the even darker days during the Battles of the Coral Sea and Midway, when all that stood between survival and Japanese naval domination was three US aircraft carriers.

Now Task Force 58 is a juggernaut. Its main ships include sixteen fast carriers and seven new battleships, ringed by thirteen cruisers and fifty-eight destroyers.[13] The fleet weighs anchor from Pearl Harbor on May 25, 1944, to begin the 3,700-mile trek to the Mariana Islands.

Nine months earlier, in August 1943, the First Quebec Conference, code-named Quadrant, did not paint a rosy picture of the war in the Pacific. The conference had been convened to discuss strategy and a timetable for Europe, but at the end of it, the planners presented a timetable for the defeat of Japan. It was hardly encouraging for a quick end to the war.

The conference anticipated the defeat of Germany in 1944, but it envisioned a long-drawn-out conflict with Japan. "The plan called for capture of the Philippines, Formosa, Malaya, and the Ryukyus [Okinawa] in 1945 and 1946, with final operations against Japan itself to commence in 1947 and continue into 1948."[14]

※

Jay Rebstock graduated from Gulf Coast Military Academy in May 1943. He walked onstage on crutches to receive his diploma—he had torn cartilage in his knee playing football. He had intended to join the military service as school ended, but he had been declared 4F, unfit for military service. The surgery to remove torn cartilage had been successful, but the 4F classification had remained. His family was delighted.

From the day at the movies in 1941 when the manager had stopped the film to announce that Pearl Harbor had been bombed, he had been itching to get at it and join up. His father had shot down the idea in no uncertain terms.

Now that he was nineteen and free to do as he pleased, the doctors said no. None of his appeals to the recruiters were working. He dragged himself off to the Louisiana oil fields and became a roughneck doing backbreaking work on a drilling rig; he bitched every day that the strain on his knee as a roughneck was far worse than basic training.[15]

He tried to enlist in the Air Corps in Biloxi and was turned down; then he went to the merchant marine recruiter at Pass Christian, Mississippi, and was turned down. He could follow the war only as old men and shirkers followed it, through the newspapers and Movietone News. The billboard outside the recruiting office had said, "Uncle Sam wants you!," but he didn't seem to want Jay Rebstock. The headlines came and went: Midway, Guadalcanal, Bougainville. The war was passing him by. His friends were "over there," and he was over here. Like any young man who was still around at that point, he suffered taunts of "chicken" and "draft dodger," and he was tired of explaining his bum knee.

As the war progressed, the manpower shortage called for a mandatory draft; there would be few exceptions or deferrals. Rebstock decided to give it one more try. He hitchhiked from the oil fields to the town of Thibodaux and visited the draft board. He gave his name, and within two weeks, his summons came. He was ecstatic. At last he had found a way in.

His father was not pleased and told him it was a stupid move. Jay was adamant and told him that everybody was in this because of the sneak attack, and he felt left out and wanted to go. He argued that because his father was the head of the ration board, people were saying that he was pulling strings to keep his son out of the war.

Finally he reported to New Orleans for processing along with hundreds of other young men. He talked with some of his friends and said he wanted to go into the Marine Corps and especially mentioned the famous Raiders. He had read about their exploits in *Reader's Digest*. Echoing his bravado, his friends agreed and backslapped each other that they were going to be elite, too.

They were called to line up, and a series of recruiters spoke to them, outlining each service. The Army, Navy, and Coast Guard recruiters addressed them kindly: "Gentlemen" this and "Gentlemen" that and "Please fill this out" and "Please line up over there."[16]

The Marine Corps recruiter was altogether different. He was small and wiry, a sergeant who looked like a street fighter masked in his sharp, impeccable uniform: tailored shirt, military creases, and the distinctive red stripe down his trouser legs. He was a veteran of Guadalcanal, the newest of the Old Breed. His address to them was short, sneering, and caustic. The words that flew out of his mouth included "maggots," "scum," and "worthless."

Finally, standing with his arms folded in front of him, he called out to anyone "who thought they could make it in this man's Marine Corps" to take two steps forward and assume the position of attention. Young Jay did just that and even clicked his heels together after his two steps. The sergeant approached him and sent him right off for his physical exam.

It was then that Rebstock looked about and noticed that he had been the only one to step forward. His big-talking buddies were shaking their heads and avoiding his eyes. The sergeant told Rebstock to make sure that he revealed to the doctor any identifying scars; that "was so someone could identify your dead ass after your face was blown off."[17]

The exam was quick; he passed and sighed in relief. The young doctor asked him if he had any identifying scars, marks, or tattoos. Jay showed him every nick and cut, delighted that he was finally in. Then he showed him the large surgical scar on his knee, and he was suddenly out. The doctor shook his head and rejected him.

Rebstock's eyes welled up, he was so frustrated. He stammered out all the reasons he should not be rejected: he'd been working hard at manual labor; the knee never bothered him; he could bend his knee all the way—which he couldn't; and he could do anything anyone else could do. It wasn't fair.

The doctor was moved by the young man pleading with tears running down his face and gave his okay. Jay Rebstock finished boot camp at San Diego in December 1943 and joined the Raider Battalion for the toughest of training.

"You never went to bed without your weapon," said Rebstock. "You never took a shower without your weapon. There was no such thing as walking—everyplace you went you sort of jogged. When you got up in the morning, you brought a sock with you to the mess hall. They didn't care if you had been wearing it or if it was new, but you had to have a sock.

"When you got into that breakfast line, they gave you a handful of rice, a handful of raisins, two potatoes, and two slabs of Canadian bacon. You put that into your sock and tied it around your cartridge belt and that was your noon meal. It was long hours and lots of training. The Raiders were tough."[18]

Sometime in January, the paratroopers and the Raiders were broken up and he was assigned to the newly forming 5th Marine Division: Company E, 27th Marines. Rebstock promptly got himself a new "identifying mark," a tattoo of the Marine Corps emblem.[19]

※

That June night, after the small party at the house breaks up and the last guests have gone home, Harry takes Dorothy for a walk. They head down Center Street in the middle of town, past the movie theater and the soda shop. Harry takes her hand and walks her into the park near the *Menotomy Indian Hunter* statue, and they sit down on the bench.

"So, Dorothy, in a few days, I'll be off to Parris Island." She nods and looks at him. He is taking his time. He is nervous, she can tell.

"But I will always be thinking about you and telling everyone I meet about you, as much as they'll listen. They'll complain, because I will go on and on . . . about your sparkling blue eyes, your soft blond curls, your sweet red lips . . ." He touches her lips. She laughs and pulls away a bit, listening for what is coming next. "And when the guys pull out the pictures of their girls, I'll save mine until last. They will all go crazy when I show them your picture. But I'll say, 'Uh-uh-uh,' and I'll snag it back. 'She's mine, fellas, no more looking!'

"I'm keeping it right here in my pocket, always, wherever I go. I'm going to write you every day, every chance I get. And when I come back . . . I want us to get married, Dorothy.

"Will you marry me when I come home?"[20]

She puts her arms around his neck. "Yes, I will, of course I will, Harry!" She hugs him with all her strength. Then she pulls back. "But, Harry"—she takes a long pause—"why don't we get married now? You could take a job like your father at Olmsted-Flint, and we could get a little place right here in town. I don't care where we live. But we can start our lives together, we don't have to wait. Harry, maybe you don't have to go. Like your uncle Frank said, you're the man of the house, and the war will be over soon, anyway. Everyone says so."

"Listen to me, Dorothy. If I don't go now, I'll be drafted for sure. It won't be long, and I will be back, I promise."

He pulls her in to him, and she rests her head against his chest. He smells her hair against his downturned face and inhales it; he wants to be able to bring it all back when he is off at training. He closes his eyes and feels her heartbeat. He will lock all this away in his heart and take it everywhere he goes. One day they will look back at tonight and tell their kids about how they promised themselves to each other just a few days before Harry went off to the war. It is all going to turn out perfect. Harry is sure about that.

They talk some more and kiss good night, agreeing to see each other tomorrow and talk about it all some more.

Harry walks in the door after taking Dot home and sees the light on in the kitchen. His mom is sitting at the table, paying some bills. He tells her that he plans to marry Dorothy when he gets back.

Anne takes a deep breath. She is a bit taken aback. "Son, I know you feel grown up now that you've graduated, but trust me, Harry, you are still so young. You have your whole life ahead of you, and there will be other girls along the way." She puts her hands gently on his cheeks and looks into his eyes.

"You're just eighteen, and, my goodness, Dorothy's only sixteen. Give it a bit of time." Harry looks down at the floor and doesn't look as though he's going to say any more. So she changes the subject. She feels she's gotten through to him. He doesn't really want to get married now, she is fairly sure of that.

"Listen to me, Harry. Promise me you'll keep your head down and you won't volunteer for anything. If there's a safer job to be done, that's what you raise your hand for, do you hear me, son?"

He just looks at her. Her words falter, and she takes in a long breath. It is moments like these when she feels inadequate. It is too hard to be both mother and father, and sometimes she finds it easier not to say anything than to risk saying the wrong thing to her son.

She smiles. "I know you will be busy. But please write to me and your sister as often as you can. She is going to be so lonely here without you, Harry. She thinks you hang the moon, you know. Even though you battle sometimes, she's so proud of you, you know that's true, don't you? And write to Uncle Frank, he worries about you so. Send a note to Betts when you can. She is such a darling, and she adores you, Harry. We're all going to be praying for you. Remember to go to Mass every chance you get, and keep your rosary with you in your pocket. Introduce yourself to the chaplain. You're going to be just fine. Just do what you're told. Make sure you eat enough." There's nothing else she can think of, and he isn't leaving until Monday, so she takes both of his hands in hers and looks down at his long fingers. Her eyes are welling up, and she doesn't want him to see. "Okay, off to bed, you. Go get some sleep."[21] She reaches up and pats him on the head. "Good night, Mom," he says as he kisses her on the cheek. "Go on!" she says.

Harry lies in his bed, thoughts racing through his head. With his head on the pillow, he rolls left to look at the small framed picture of his girl. Dorothy's right, he thinks. He's going to do it; he'll marry her tomorrow. They'll go to the courthouse and get married. No one even needs to know. People do it all the time, especially fellows going off to the war. They still have a few days. He'll go to war a man, a husband. He likes how that sounds and how it makes him feel: bigger and older.

Harry wakes up early the next morning and runs to the corner market. Then, back home, he hops into his mother's car and takes off. He drives down Center Street, takes a left, and goes down the road to Dorothy's small house by the train station. His heart is pounding, he is so full of plans. He rings the bell, holding the flowers behind his back. Dorothy opens the door. Her hair is in a tiny ponytail, and her jeans are rolled up on top of her white sneakers. It is the first time he has seen her without her red lipstick on, and Harry thinks how young she looks without it. How wonderful it would be to wake up next to that soft, young face. "What are you up to?" she asks, turning her head to the side and leaning, arms crossed, in the open door.

He gives her the flowers and takes her hand. "Let's get married today, Dot. You're right about everything. Let's just do it, let's do it today. It will be our secret!"

Dorothy's eyes light up. "And you won't go? You'll stay here and not go?"

"No, Dorothy. I have to go. I'm going to get drafted if I stay. And I've already signed up. It's the right thing, and I want to go. My mother says we are too young. But she's wrong. I've never been more sure of anything in my life. But if we don't tell her and we go find a justice of the peace in Boston, no one will have to know. It will be the secret we can keep the whole time while I'm gone. If I know we are married, Dorothy, I will make sure I come home. I promise!"

Dorothy's smile droops. "Harry. No. We can't get married like that. I was carried away last night. I want a nice wedding and music and a dress. Harry, I won't go against your mother's wishes. You were right last night. I was wrong." She touches his cheek with her hand. "But don't you worry, Harry Gray. I will be right here waiting for you, when you come home."

※

Frank Bowes is in his green chair in the living room at 55 Welcher Avenue with the radio on. His pipe in his hand, he takes tobacco out of the fold-over bag from the drugstore and packs it in just right. He sets the pipe in his teeth, cups his hand around the bowl, and lights the match down low over it, taking a deep drag. The radio crackles.

A voice intones, "The Supreme Commander, Allied Expeditionary Force, General Dwight David Eisenhower."

This is the moment the country has been waiting for, and Frank settles in to listen closely. Helen and his sister-in-law, Jane, come in from the kitchen. Each sits in the chair she always sits in, just across from Frank and next to each other, facing the radio. Betts slides onto the edge of Helen's chair and pulls in close. After she settles in, it is perfectly quiet. General Eisenhower begins:

> People of Western Europe: A landing was made this morning on the coast of France by troops of the Allied Expeditionary Force. This landing is part of the concerted United Nations' plan for the liberation of Europe, made in conjunction with our great Russian allies.
>
> I have this message for all of you. Although the initial assault may not have been made in your own country, the hour of your liberation is approaching.

The world has been waiting for five anxious years for this announcement, often wondering if it will ever come. Can this be the beginning of the end of this war? The firm, calm voice of General Eisenhower continues:

All patriots, men and women, young and old, have a part to play in the achievement of final victory. To members of resistance movements, I say, "Follow the instructions you have received." To patriots who are not members of organized resistance groups, I say, "Continue your passive resistance, but do not needlessly endanger your lives until I give you the signal to rise and strike the enemy. The day will come when I shall need your united strength." Until that day, I call on you for the hard task of discipline and restraint.[22]

Later that night they all gather again, like other families across the United States, to hear President Roosevelt's address to the nation, a national prayer. It is 10:00 p.m., but few have gone to bed.

Almighty God: Our sons, pride of our Nation, this day have set upon a mighty endeavor, a struggle to preserve our Republic, our religion, and our civilization, and to set free a suffering humanity.

Frank, Helen, Jane, and Betts hang on every word. They say a silent prayer for Harry, who will be leaving soon. In Arlington, Anne, Harry, and Nancy listen at their radio. Anne sits up straight in her chair, as do Harry and Nancy—all silent, listening, feeling the weight of the president's words as he goes on:

Lead them straight and true; give strength to their arms, stoutness to their hearts, steadfastness in their faith.

They will need Thy blessings. Their road will be long and hard. For the enemy is strong. He may hurl back our forces. Success may not come with rushing speed, but we shall return again and again; and we know that by Thy grace, and by the righteousness of our cause, our sons will triumph.[23]

The next morning, Frank pores over the *New York Times*, featuring a prominent photo of General Eisenhower surrounded by paratroopers with blackened faces. The picture was snapped just prior to their being loaded on C-47s that will carry them across the English Channel to their airborne assault into France. The headlines blare:

HITLER'S SEA WALL BREACHED; INVADERS FIGHTING WAY INLAND; NEW ALLIED LANDINGS MADE[24]

The articles below report that in Philadelphia, the Liberty Bell was rung, and at Lexington and Boston's Old North Church, services are being held to pray for "our boys."

On June 15, 1944, Dominick Grossi, having been through Officer Candidates School in Quantico, Virginia, and graduating with a character assessment of "Excellent," is preparing to "shove off." He writes home to his girlfriend, Ruth, and his mother, Lena, on stationery that is embossed at the top: LIEUT. D. J. GROSSI. He tells his mom that he is headed to where his sister Marie is (San Diego). Her husband, Jim, who is also in the service, is Dom's closest buddy, and he hopes he will meet up with him when he gets there. He writes, "My outfit is all equipped and ready. I have 55 men. It certainly feels good to have an outfit of your own and look after them."

✕

Warren Holloway Graham is the son of Jennie and Augustus Graham of Salisbury, North Carolina. He has a BS in chemistry from Virginia Polytechnic Institute in Blacksburg, and has just begun his training at Ashland Oil and Refining Company in Kentucky. That June, Graham, who according to his enlistment records is Methodist, five foot nine, and 164 pounds and has a slight speech defect, is about to shove off; he is headed to Parris Island.

✳

At the same time, across the Pacific, the Marines of V Amphibious Corps have just smashed ashore on the island of Saipan in the Marianas. The landings of the 2nd and 4th Divisions are hotly contested by the dug-in Japanese defenders following the rigid principles of the "Tamura Doctrine," which calls for engaging the attackers at the water's edge and hurling them back into the sea.

― 10 ―

D-Day: From Normandy to Saipan

They will be sore tried, by night and by day, without rest—until the victory is won. The darkness will be rent by noise and flame. Men's souls will be shaken with the violences of war.

—"Franklin Roosevelt's D-Day Prayer," June 6, 1944

As Task Force 58 readies for the long trek into the Marianas, General Vandegrift is back home speaking at a veterans' hall. The Medal of Honor recipient from Guadalcanal had become the eighteenth commandant of the United States Marine Corps. His audience includes men recovering from recent wounds and older vets from World War I.

The general begins, "Mr. Mayor, veterans, guests and friends—it is indeed a pleasure for me to be here tonight to do honor to those men from this community who have gone forth to fight for our country. They are here in spirit. They would appreciate your turning out to do them honor."[1]

It stirred the general's heart to hear the band play the same martial music he had heard on the docks in 1942 as his Marines boarded the ships that took them to the South Pacific. Now he looks into the eyes of men in the honor guard, and he recognizes some of them. They share the unspoken language of common experience. They know the jungle, the heat, the bodies, the deafening explosions, the darkness "rent by noise and flame," as FDR had so eloquently put it in his radio address. They know the awful cost but also the deep pride of victory together. The general continued:

> It is a special pleasure to talk to veterans, and to talk in the halls of the veterans of tomorrow. You veterans are graduates of the armed forces; we meet on common ground; we speak the same language.
>
> You, along with all Americans at home and overseas, are charged with the privilege of showing the Axis how far they underestimated us when they began this war—just as you did when Germany drew us into the last one.
>
> The Japanese in particular looked upon us Americans as constitutional weaklings. They were convinced our manpower had grown soft, spoiled by the luxury of the highest living standards in the world. I can assure you they are wrong![2]

><

In late 1943, an interview with a Japanese fighter pilot somehow dodged the censors and found its way into *Fuji* magazine. Major Jiro Tsukushi revealed his prescient concerns about the enemy and the battles to come:

> If the mastery of the air is in enemy hands, it will be impossible to ship the necessary material to the island, and after about a week, the soldiers on the island will find it impossible to keep themselves alive from lack of foodstuffs. Then when the island falls, the enemy immediately builds an airbase there. The next island also meets the same fate . . . and the next . . .[3]

On the afternoon of June 11, 1944, at first they appear as thousands of specks, dots along the horizon; then, coming into view, they become clear: the ships of Task Force 58's massive armada are moving into the waters of the Marianas. There they will pummel the islands with unrelenting bombardment for three days. Overhead, the roar and rumble of the engines of hundreds of US planes fill the skies.

They swoop and dive on the Japanese targets, bombing and strafing, pounding at the island's defenses. It is like an orchestra of instruments with deadly aim. The battleships shell the islands with such force that the hulls and the men who stand on the decks of these ships rumble from within with each enormous explosion from the big guns.

The stunned Japanese watch from their bunkers. "All we could do was watch helplessly," wrote one who was on Saipan.

Another wrote from Tinian, "The planes which cover the sky are all the enemy's. They are far and away more skillful than Japanese planes. Now begins our cave life. Enemy planes overhead all day long—some 230 in number. They completely plaster our airfields. Where are our planes? Not one is sent up. Our AA [antiaircraft] guns spread black smoke where the enemy planes weren't. Not one hit out of a thousand shots."[4]

In two theaters of battle, ordinary American men—teachers, coaches, high schoolers, bookkeepers, and firemen, most between the ages of eighteen and twenty-four—who left their hometowns and traveled across the ocean, are now turning the tide against the evil that has paralyzed so much of the world. One week ago, the largest armada ever assembled in the history of man, nearly seven thousand vessels, landed on the beaches of Normandy, France, and now in June 1944 the "Normandy Invasion of the Pacific" is under way.

Since the devastation at Pearl Harbor, US forces have moved along the central Pacific Japanese perimeter. Under the direction of Admiral Nimitz, they have won at Midway, then secured the Gilbert and Marshall Islands, and moving up from the region just north of Australia, they ousted the Japanese from Port Moresby in New Guinea and Tulagi in the Solomon Islands. General MacArthur's forces are the secondary line, moving up the western sweep with the Philippines in their sights, but Guam and the Northern Marianas are the next priority. Guam, a US territory, had been captured by the Japanese in the days just after Pearl Harbor. The westernmost reach of US influence and central to the United States' access to the entire region, it must be liberated. Tinian and Saipan have essential airstrips on the path to the Japanese homeland, and then there are Iwo Jima and Okinawa, the doorstep of imperial territory. So it is the Marianas that the men of the US Navy must reclaim now.

On the ships, nervous, sweaty sailors and Marines try to stay loose. They huddle in the tight, dank spaces on the deck between the racks, dealing rounds of cards. The air smells of men and metal and sea salt. Faces light up as one Marine hangs his upper body down from his rack. In his hand is a pinup picture from his wallet. The others laugh and pass it around, whooping and hollering as they take turns looking. One corpsman lingers a bit too long, and another snatches it to get a look. Another young man, with the face of a boy, looks at a picture of his sweetheart and shares it so the guys can gaze at her for a moment, too.

Benny Goodman plays on the scratchy radio, which is bolted down like everything else on the ship. As the song ends, a young woman with perky English, whom they call Tokyo Rose—she calls herself Orphan Ann—taunts them with sweetly delivered jabs as she lures them in with music that takes them home, if only for a moment. How did she get her hands on all those records? they wonder.

"This is your favorite playmate and enemy, Ann. How are all you orphans in the Pacific? Are you enjoying yourselves while your wives and sweethearts are running around with 4Fs in the States? Here's another record to remind you of home."

She pokes at their homesick eighteen- or nineteen-year-old armor, she tugs at the strings in their hearts, she tries to scare them, warning them that their enemy is ready and waiting for them. But she barters music for her badgering, and they are willing to take the trade. Home is such a long way away.

Eventually fatigue conquers nerves, and they drift into a light sleep, the waves rolling beneath.

In the morning, their vessels churn through the salty sea under bright cerulean skies, heading to the Marianas, the islands that came under Japanese control under the terms of the Treaty of Versailles after World War I. Now Marines of the 2nd and 4th Divisions squint their eyes in the sun for a first look at the four-thousand-yard stretch of beach on Saipan.

The 2nd Division will land on the left, on the Red and Green beaches. The 4th Division will land on the right, on the Yellow and Blue beaches. Dividing the beaches is the old sugar dock that sticks prominently into the lagoon and the tall smokestack of the destroyed sugar mill just behind. North of the sugar dock and between the two divisions is Afetna Point. A shallow lagoon separates the deep blue water from the invasion beaches, just as on Tarawa. Here, thankfully, there is enough water to float the landing craft.

Private First Class James Russell received the Navy Cross at Tarawa for his deadly bazooka shot into the key Japanese bunker that opened the back door of the Japanese defensive line. Here he is in the first wave of attackers. As his LVT plows the water, he notices little colored flags that seem to be on floats scattered throughout the lagoon.[5]

Lieutenant General Yoshitsugu Saito, the commander of the Northern Marianas Army Group, knows the Americans will land on these two beaches. He has expertly placed his observation post on a spot the Americans have designated as Hill 500. His guns sit on the reverse slope, out of view from the air. His position puts him out of the line of fire during the US bombing runs.

He is the mastermind behind the little markers that sprinkle the blue waters and indicate target areas. His gunners know them by heart.

As a lieutenant colonel with the 4th Division later noted, "Wall diagrams in observation posts marked registration points on the reefs, the channels, the beach lines, roads and intersections adjacent to the beach."[6]

As the LVTs pass the bobbing tattletales, it is as if they trip a wire. Suddenly geysers of water shoot into the air as Japanese mortars hit. Russell and the others duck instinctively, staring at the floor of their rocking boats. They coil themselves into position, ready to vault over the sides, while all around them, landing craft are being blown to bits.

Sixty-eight armored amphibian tanks are in the 2nd Division's first wave, and thirty-one are knocked out in the lagoon or as they hit the beaches.[7] James Russell fears he has reentered Tarawa-hell.

In the first hour, the four battalion commanders of the 2nd Division's assault force are all wounded and out of action. Murderous flanking fire rakes the Marine lines; the 2nd Battalion, 6th Marines, goes through four battalion commanders.[8] Eight thousand Marines cram ashore during the first hour as enemy gunners continually rain fire down on them.

Afetna Point juts out into the lagoon between Green beaches 2 and 3. From this deadly post, antiboat guns fire down the shoreline as the landing craft approach the beaches. As the boats come in, the gunners wait until they pass in front of their muzzles, then blast away. The barrage of naval gunfire that had targeted the point in the days prior to the landing had been unable to take out this crucial firing line position.

Company G immediately turns south to attack Afetna Point, but the Japanese protecting the guns answer with a hail of rifle and machine-gun fire. The Marines are armed with Winchester Model 97 shotguns in addition to their regular arms. Since the point protrudes into the lagoon, regular rifle fire directed into the point could miss, continue down the beach, and hit the 4th Division Marines, just a few hundred yards away.

The shotgun-wielding Marines blast their way through the Japanese defensive lines, slowly clearing the bunkers and disabling nine antiboat guns. "Attached combat engineers, with their flamethrowers, bazookas and demolitions, were invaluable in destroying enemy pillboxes."[9]

Despite their progress, more enemy antiboat gunners refuse to abandon their guns and train them on the next wave of LVTs. They keep firing away, ready to die at their posts.

The Marine assault line slowly advances through the position with engineers brandishing twenty-pound satchel charges with high-velocity explosives. Any enemy who attempts to charge the Marine line is cut down by shotgun blasts with double-0 buckshot containing

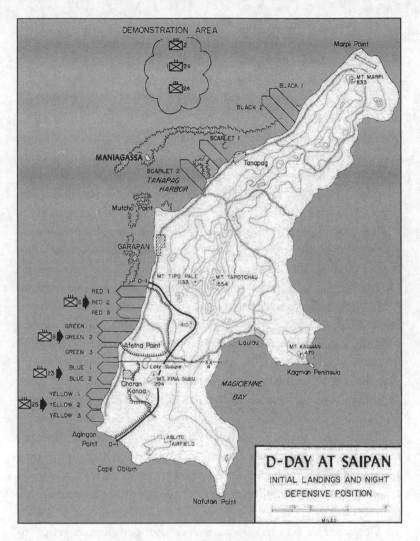

nine .33-caliber lead balls. The point is finally cleared during the late morning of the following day.[10]

On the other side of Afetna Point and the sugar dock, the 4th Division is pinned down. Some are dug in barely twelve yards off the water's edge. Only four of the fourteen medium tanks make it to the beach.

First Lieutenant John C. Chapin: "All around us was the chaotic debris of bitter combat: Jap and Marine bodies lying in mangled and grotesque positions; blasted and burnt-out pillboxes; the burning wrecks of LVTs . . . knocked out by Jap high velocity fire; the acrid smell of high explosives; the shattered trees; and the churned-up sand littered with discarded equipment."[11]

As the day winds down, the casualties are high: more than 2,000 killed, wounded, or missing.[12] The 2nd Division is hit the hardest—238 dead, 1,022 wounded, 355 missing—most of whom are later added to the dead.[13]

That night, 20,000 Marines cling to their toehold on the beach, while the Japanese light the dark night skies with tracers. They probe for targets. Their mortar rounds fall along the Marine line. Is a night attack coming?

These Japanese fighters are not like the abandoned defenders of earlier island battles, who had no hope of reinforcements. These defenders have been informed that their great fleet, including 9 carriers with 222 fighters and 200 dive- and torpedo bombers, has weighed anchor from their harbor at Tawi-Tawi Island, southwest of the Philippines. Help is on its way.

That morning, at 8:55 a.m., as the Americans conduct their amphibious operations, Admiral Soemu Toyoda, commander of the Japanese Combined Fleet, signals from his headquarters on the Inland Sea to all naval commanders: "The Combined Fleet will attack the enemy in the Marianas area and annihilate the invasion force."[14]

Back on May 3, 1944, Emperor Hirohito appointed Admiral Toyoda to command the Combined Fleet, and the next day, Toyoda messaged all commanders, "The war is drawing close to the lines vital to our national defense. The issue of our national existence is unprecedentedly serious; an unprecedented opportunity exists for deciding who shall be victorious and who defeated. . . . We will make this task our responsibility."[15]

His plan to strike this major blow is called Operation A-Go. When the time comes, detailed orders will be issued. "We must achieve our objectives by crushing with one stroke the nucleus of the great enemy concentration of forces, reversing the war situation . . . and shifting directly to the offensive."[16]

Toyoda's naval fantasy is rooted in Japan's great victories over the Chinese in 1895 and the Russians in 1905 and at Pearl Harbor. All were triumphant one-strike blows. He is determined to please the emperor by turning the tide with a stunning reversal sparked by a "divine wind," a climactic stroke.

While the Japanese fleet is on the move, darkness falls on the first night of battle on Saipan. Japanese attack forces form up in the town of Garapan, just to the north of the Marine invasion beaches, and begin moving south toward an assault line. The approach begins two miles north of the 6th Marines' positions, hastily dug in just off the Red beaches. This time, the Japanese make no attempt at stealth. They are coming in columns, some 2,000 strong; some ride trucks and tanks, some come on foot, "with the customary clamor of a traveling circus."[17]

Their swords flash in the moonlight; battle flags flutter in the night breeze; the clipped voices of the leaders can be heard as they make impassioned speeches, firing up their fighters. A bugle blares, and the massed force presses forward; first at a trot and then with increasing speed, it builds to a full charge.

US naval guns fire star shells that roll back the darkness, lighting the sky and revealing the pulsing, screaming Japanese attack columns streaming down from Garapan. Fire from the Marines pours into their ranks, shattering their momentum. It first slows the charge and then stops it cold. Mortar, bazooka, rifle, and machine-gun fire tear into the charging ranks, ripping them to pieces.

Staggering, the Japanese attackers fall back, perhaps to gather for another charge. But before they can regroup, land-based artillery and naval gunfire from offshore blanket them in pulverizing explosions.

Just before dawn, there is a second attack; this one comes from the east, accompanied by three tanks. Emerging from the gloom of the marshes around Lake Susupe, 200 Japanese slam into the lines of the 4th Division. Private First Class James Russell empties his Browning automatic rifle as fast as he can into the charging line, and then reloads. The weapon's barrel glows cherry red. He worries that it may melt down completely.[18]

Like the attack from Garapan, this one evaporates under withering Marine fire. When the sun rises in the morning, the bodies of 700 Japanese soldiers litter the road and the beaches down the coastline. Naval warships aim their guns onto Garapan and flatten the source of the attack.[19]

At 4:30 a.m. on the morning of June 16, a submarine lieutenant commander, Robert Risser, has his right eye glued to the lens of the periscope of his sub, the *Flying Fish*. He is looking for any sign of the Japanese offensive, and now he can barely believe his eyes: ship after ship, battleships, carriers, cruisers, silhouetted against the island's landmass, steam out of the San Bernardino Strait into the open waters of the Philippine Sea moving due east.

Risser's natural instinct is to launch all his torpedoes against the seemingly endless naval parade and then dive to the bottom, but his mission is not to attack; he is to watch and report. At this moment, he is the eyes of Task Force 58.

Finally the great parade passes him, and he surfaces the *Flying Fish*. He taps out a message to Admiral Raymond Spruance, the commander in chief of the Pacific Fleet: "The Japanese Fleet is heading for the Marianas."[20]

Emperor Hirohito has made clear that defeat is not an option. His empire is shrinking, and he has demanded the course that is now under way. He has told his admiral in no uncertain terms, "Rise to the challenge; make a tremendous effort; achieve a splendid victory." With Prime Minister Tojo, the man he elevated over the protestations of so many of his advisers, he has been even more direct: "If we ever lose Saipan, repeated air attacks on Tokyo will follow. No matter what it takes, we have to hold there." Tojo has filled the emperor's head with promises of "balloon bombs," a weapons program he is readying for the fall. Hirohito is buoyed by the knowledge that there is still a way to take the fight to the ever-encroaching Americans.[21]

Back on Saipan, on D + 1, artillery duels rage up and down the line. At nightfall, the order is to dig in. The Marine line has now advanced inland almost twice as far as on the first day.

Japanese general Saito has a bold plan for the night of D + 1. Confident that the naval Operation A-Go will soon be pummeling the US fleet and providing aerial support, he plans a large-scale attack against the 6th Marines—again against its left flank, facing Garapan. This will be an even greater, all-out effort than the attack of the previous night, which left 700 of his men dead. Saito will crush the enemy with tanks and infantry.[22]

On the southern outskirts of Garapan, Colonel Hideki Goto forms up the remaining thirty-seven tanks from his 9th Tank Regiment. He lost seven during the first night's abortive attack and certainly must have wondered why this all-out attack was not delivered then. He stands tall in the turret of his command tank and flourishes his saber overhead. Other commanders, steeling their courage, take their cue from him. Down the line, turrets pop open and warriors stand to face what is to come. Like Goto, they brandish their sabers aloft.[23]

The Japanese tanks are small, almost toylike, compared to the American Shermans. But they are fast, highly maneuverable, and well armed. Against other armor, they would be outmatched, but against infantry they are formidable. Three men squeeze into each tiny crew compartment.

The driver crouches down low on the right-hand side. Rubbing shoulders with him on the left, the machine gunner operates a .30-caliber gun with almost 1,200 rounds of ammunition. A second gun, operated by the tank commander in the turret and armed with another 1,800 rounds, faces almost to the rear. The 37 mm cannon with 130 rounds, also operated by the tank commander, is the main battle gun.[24]

At 3:30 a.m. on June 17, Saito's attack begins. Colonel Goto, like a cavalry leader of the Light Brigade at Balaclava, gives the side of his tank a slap with his saber, and at the sound of that metallic clank, the driver inches the vehicle forward. The other tank commanders clank the sides of their tanks to set them into motion, as if digging their spurs into their horses' sides. They are off, moving slowly forward in a cacophony of squeaks and rattles.

The Marines have nicknamed the Japanese tanks "kitchen sinks."[25]

As they approach some fifteen minutes later, the 6th Marines is waiting for them. With the Navy lighting the early-morning darkness, one Marine describes the furious firefight: "The battle evolved itself into a madhouse of noise, tracers, and flashing lights. As tanks were hit and set afire, they silhouetted other tanks coming out of the flickering shadows to the front or already on top of the squads."[26]

Amid the chaos and the blare of bugles, the Marine bazooka men take careful aim and send their rockets into the thin-skinned tanks with devastating results. Two privates first class, Herbert Hodges and Bob Reed, take out twelve tanks with eleven rockets and a grenade. As the Japanese attack disintegrates, Marine half-tracks move in. They scour the blazing battlefield like hyenas, finishing off Goto's wounded tanks. Twenty-four of the thirty-seven become smoldering, blackened hulks.[27]

The two night attacks have cost the Japanese dearly, but the Marines have also paid a Tarawa-like toll. By the morning of the third day, their casualty list tops 3,500, and the attacks that day that press the Japanese line farther back add 500 more.[28]

On D + 3, June 18, the Marine and Army infantrymen awaken to a sobering sight: the eight hundred ships that had their back are gone. The loneliness of the calm blue ocean and the gentle waves breaking in the lagoon tell them they are now on their own.[29] For some, it brings back memories of the dark days at Guadalcanal when the Japanese routinely drove the US Navy off, allowing them to blast away at the isolated Marines at will.

But this time, the Navy has not been driven away; it has gone out to prepare for a showdown with the advancing Japanese fleet. The support is still there; it is just out of sight, over the horizon.

The fifteen carriers, five hundred fighters, and four hundred bombers of Admiral Mitscher's Task Force 58 raced to an intercept point in the west. The battleships shield the island from their patrol positions twenty-five miles to the west. The smaller escort carriers are on call for aerial support for the invasion force—out of sight.[30]

But there is much more; in addition to the fifteen carriers and seven battleships, ten cruisers and fifty-eight destroyers complete the naval phalanx of ninety ships facing the approaching Japanese fleet.[31]

All this is unknown to the men ashore, who anxiously ask, "Where the hell are our ships? What about food and ammunition? Will we get back the supporting naval gunfire and the star shell illumination?"[32]

The supply transports have been moved out of harm's way to the vacant seas to the south and east. There they join the ships containing the men and materiel destined to assault Guam in the next phase of Operation Forager as soon as Saipan is secured.

At 5:42 a.m. on June 19, the sun rises over the Philippine Sea west of the Marianas. The first sign of enemy action isn't until 8:00 a.m. To the south over Guam, a large group of enemy planes approaches the island. Carrier planes from Task Force 58 vector out to intercept, and by 9:30 a.m., the F6F Hellcats have shot down thirty-five of them.[33]

At 10:04, the general alarm sounds throughout the carrier task force. Enemy planes are detected in great numbers all around the horizon. Admiral Mitscher rigs his carriers for combat, clearing his decks of all bombers and torpedo planes that are in the way, sending them to rendezvous to the east. This is to be a day for fighters, and fighters only. The decks are prepared for the task of launching, recovering, rearming, and servicing fighters in steady rotation. Mitscher anticipates a long battle.[34]

The first wave of Japanese attackers zeroes in on the battleships, but they are doomed from the start. Expert fighter-director officers on key US ships, especially on Admiral Mitscher's flagship, USS *Lexington*, analyze all aspects of the attack and guide the Hellcat fighters by radar to precise points in the sky to intercept the attackers.[35]

Part of the analysis includes some less-than-sophisticated eavesdropping. The coordination of the Japanese attacks is dependent on a senior squadron commander who takes a position flying high above the battlefield. The American fighter directors nickname him "Coordinator Joe."

On board *Lexington*, a team of officers, including a translator, listens intently for "Joe's" first transmission. When his voice comes up on the frequency, within moments, they know precisely every detail of the oncoming strike: location, numbers, direction, and tactics.[36]

Japanese pilots, poised to swoop down and fire, are blindsided by streaking, diving US fighters, which outnumber them and blast them from all sides. Japanese bombers are hit, catch fire, and free-fall from the skies. The Americans lose only one plane in that first wave, while thirty Japanese aircraft plunge to the sea.

The rest of the first wave tries to reverse course, but they run up against fierce antiaircraft fire thrown up by the US battle fleet. The wall of steel becomes so dense that more than a dozen more Japanese planes plunge into the ocean. The second wave sees nearly 125 Japanese planes rain down from the sky.

The third wave circles around to the north to try to avoid the US defensive battle line and make a run at one of Mitscher's carriers. Some forty enemy planes penetrate the defense. One scores a direct hit on the *South Dakota* with a 210-kilogram (462-pound) bomb; one crashes into the side of *Indiana*. There are near misses on a heavy cruiser and several carriers, doing slight damage and causing small personnel casualties.[37]

The fourth and final wave of Japanese planes is a chaotic last gasp. Many of the Japanese pilots never even sight the US carriers, much less attack them. Trying to escape, they fly toward Guam to attempt to land, but they are overtaken and shot down by avenging Hellcats. Of the 373 Japanese planes that attack that day, fewer than 100 are able to even attempt a return to their carriers. The Americans lose just 29 planes in the Battle of the Philippine Sea, which is quickly and forevermore nicknamed "the Great Marianas Turkey Shoot."[38]

The few Japanese planes that survive the "shoot" fly west. When they arrive at the spot where their carriers should be, the sea below them is empty. The pilots search in vain for the sunken carriers, *Taibo* and *Shokaku*, and then, with nowhere to land and no gas left in their tanks, they sputter, glide, and finally nose-dive into the ocean.

The 33,000-ton *Taibo* was the largest carrier in the Japanese fleet; it was torpedoed and sent to the bottom with its remaining planes and its entire crew compliments of the US submarine *Albacore*. The 22,000-ton *Shokaku* is also now at rest on the ocean floor, sunk by four torpedoes from the submarine *Cavalla*.[39]

The following day, June 20, Mitscher's task force detects what is left of the Japanese fleet fleeing south, already 250 miles away. Despite the waning light, the admiral makes the call to launch 216 planes to run down the enemy fleet and finish it off.

The pilots who fly the 216 planes know well that even if they catch up to the fleeing Japanese and attack, many will not have the fuel to make it back. Still, as has happened again and again, no one asks, "Why me?" No one seeks exemption. The squadron commander of USS *Yorktown*, Lieutenant Commander Bernard "Smoke" Strean, simply says, "Okay, gentlemen, we have our orders. I'll lead the entire strike. We'll be the first in to find the targets."[40]

They fly off and finally catch up to the enemy fleet in the waning light of the last rays of the sun. They sink another carrier, *Hiyo*, damage three others, and sink two oilers at the cost of twenty planes. The return flight is as predicted. Eighty planes are lost as they exhaust their fuel. Thirty-eight crew members perish; the rest are rescued. It might have been worse had Admiral Mitscher not ordered all the ships to turn on their lights to serve as beacons for the aircraft struggling home.[41]

For the Japanese, the defeat is devastating. They lost three aircraft carriers, one fewer than at Midway, and although the fleet escaped total annihilation, it is severely crippled. As the Navy reported, "The important result, Japanese carrier aviation was substantially finished as a naval force in the war."[42] Prime Minister Hideki Tojo no longer has the confidence of his government or the emperor and is forced to resign.

Ж

Back in Arlington, Massachusetts, Harry Gray is packing his small duffel bag. His mom, Anne, is next to him. She has lovingly washed and folded his underwear, T-shirts, and socks. She stacks it all neatly in his bag, even though he insists he can do it himself. She wants to touch his things, make sure they are just right. She presses it all down, leaving the scent of her hands on it all. Harry zips it up.

Nancy is on the bed, watching and swinging her feet. She doesn't want him to go. She worries that it will be lonely in the house with just her mom and grandma. She knows she will long for him to poke his head into her room and ask her if she has a couple of bucks he can borrow or if she wants to play some touch football.

Last night he said his good-byes to Dorothy. She slid her hand over the pocket of his shirt, where her picture was tucked inside. She kissed him and wrapped her arms around his back, burying her face in him, trying to imprint in her memory how his broad shoulders felt and the scent of his shirt, so she could summon him to her senses later. "Let's pretend we are already married," he whispered. She wished they had not listened to his mother, that they had just run off to the town hall and exchanged vows. But there is no going back now. She will have to wait, and when he comes back, their life will begin.

On that hot July morning at South Station, Harry kisses his mom and Nancy and hugs them tight. He tells them not to worry, he will be home soon. He shakes hands with Uncle Frank, who has come up to see him off. They stare hard into each other's eyes for a few seconds. "Take care of yourself, son," Frank says.

There isn't much for anyone to say now, so they stand for a moment, hearts in their throats. Anne breaks the tension by smiling up at her boy and giving him one more squeeze. "Off you go now, my boy. Don't forget to write. And we will see you when you get leave." Harry turns, beams back at them, and hops onto the train, flashing his million-dollar smile. He looks so young in his trousers and shirt, his sandy hair flopped over his forehead, as he looks back and then watches them through the windows as he takes his seat. They all keep watching and waving until they can't see each other anymore. Then, like other families all across the United States, Harry's family turns away from the departing train as it slips away, headed ultimately for boot camp at the Marine Corps Recruit Depot, Parris Island, South Carolina.

※

Miles away in Pennsylvania, Charlie Gubish is also packing his bag. His wife, Ethel, folds his things, and Charlie is lost in thought, hoping he made the right decision. Three-year-old Charlie Jr. is at his feet, playing with a wooden truck on the floor, and Richard, the baby, just four months old, naps on the hot summer night in the next room of their small farmhouse in Wassergass. Charlie thinks back to when he met Ethel. He and his dad took their produce to sell at a farm stand in South Bethlehem, where she lived. From town and the Bethlehem Steel Mill and back to the farm, that's all he ever knew. Here he knows or is related to just about everybody.

But there's a war on, and he feels he should go. Truth be told, he'd about had it working at the steel mill as a lieutenant fireman. The women who worked under him were always after him, asking if they could take breaks. The higher-ups kept giving him a hard time for taking pity on them once in a while. That was the kind of stuff he had to put up with and the kind of stuff that had made him "join the damn service."

One day, one of his buddies said he'd signed up and was heading to the Navy. He said it didn't matter that they were exempt because of their work at the steel mill, that you could go sign up anyway, and that was what Charlie decided to do. But when he got there, he saw the pictures of the uniforms and decided he would rather be a Marine. And that's why he's now packing his bag and leaving Bethlehem. He worked all his young life on the farm and then at the mill, like most everyone else.[43] But now life is changing. Bethlehem Steel built the rails on which he will soon be rattling off to Parris Island to become a Marine.

Between 1941 and 1945, 205,000 civilians were turned into Marines at Parris Island. In July 1944, each man went through eight weeks of basic training and eight weeks of basic field training, including 147.5 hours of rifle training.[44] When those young men stepped off their trains in South Carolina, they stepped into another world.

χ

Harry's train pulls into the station near Parris Island the next morning. The whistle and the brakes shake the slumber off the young men in the cars. They are shuffled onto a bus that lumbers down the dusty road and past the sign at the gate. A drill instructor steps onto the bus and faces them. "Get off my bus!" he yells. "Say 'Yessir!' Louder!" Harry and the others stand and shout "Yessir" as loud as they can. The hot July sun pours through the windows, and the idle bus grows hotter by the second. A bead of sweat drips down Harry's back as he stares straight ahead. "Yessir!" he shouts again, as loud as his vocal cords can muster.

By the end of that day, his sandy blond hair is completely gone; he has a number—565110—a uniform, boots, and a rifle. He has been yelled at within an inch of his face to sit and stand and line up and pay attention. The process has begun; he is being transformed from a boy into a Marine. He has left behind all the trappings of his life at home. He has emptied his pockets and been told there is no "I"; he is to refer to himself only as "this recruit."

Warren Graham, the chemist from North Carolina, did not have as far to travel; he arrives at Parris Island on June 27, 1944. The military likes to do things alphabetically, so Gray, Graham, and another young man from Dayton, Ohio, named Herman Graeter are next to one another just about every time they line up or eat or run or scramble over a wall carrying a bucket of cement.

Herman Robert Graeter is the only son of Golda Marie and Herman Graeter, Sr., of Dayton. He was born in January 1926, so he is eighteen like Harry but six months older. Graeter played varsity football and basketball at Dayton High School. Under "Occupation" on his registration form, Graeter wrote in blue pen block letters "Part-time mail clerk and student" and said that he could type thirty-five words per minute. Under "Duty Desired" Herman requested "Radar Technician."

Charlie Gubish, the married father of two, has only just arrived at Parris Island when he starts thinking that his problems back at the mill look pretty darn manageable. His face, his uniform, his boots, and his rifle are caked in mud, and his drill instructor, a policeman from New York, is staring down into his face and calling him a "shit bird." When it is time for bed, he is exhausted and humiliated from being knocked around and cursed at, and pain racks his body from head to toe. He hears the guys near him say that one of the other guys tried to kill himself last night. He is so desperate for relief that he thinks to himself, I'd take my life, too, if it would save me from one more day of facing that New York drill instructor. But I can't, he realizes as he drifts off. They are watching all the time.[45]

By the end of week four, though, things are looking up. He and his fellow "shit birds" just beat the college boys on the obstacle course, carrying a bucket of cement the whole way. Something in Charlie is changing. It turns out that he can endure pain and punishment he never dreamed existed. They tell him they are going to turn him and the other "shit birds" into Marines, and Charlie nods to himself, thinking, I guess they are right.[46]

In Peekskill, New York, three weeks later, Frank Bowes sees a letter in the small pile of mail that has been pushed through the slot in the porch screen door. Under a couple of bills, the corner of a handwritten letter has this return address:

PVT H. E. Gray #565110 USMC
Platoon 409 6th BU
Marine Barracks
Parris Island, South Carolina

It is dated Sunday, Summer 1944.

Dear Uncle Frank,

Well here I am at Parris Island and everything is fine. I am in perfect health and have gained weight. I have had two shots and a blood test. Tomorrow we have 2 more.

We do calisthenics every morning until we almost collapse but try to keep on going. Yesterday we drilled in the sun at 120 degrees wearing full combat gear. We kept this up until 3 fellows collapsed, this place is so nerve wracking that one fellow from another platoon tried to commit suicide last night by cutting his throat. Just by chance they found him before he died.

Every morning we are up at 4:30 and between this time and 6:00 we sweep and wash the barracks, clean the windows, make our bunks, wash, shave, disassemble our rifle and clean it. At 6:00 we eat chow.

Next week our platoon has to appear for Colonel Inspection. We have to know many facts such as, "General Orders, all officers of rank, all parts of our rifle and many other items."

Well that's all my troubles. How is everyone in Peekskill? Fine I hope. Tell Betsy, Aunt Helen, Jane and Mr. Walsh I was asking for them.

I don't have much time to write, please thank Aunt Helen for her gift and Betsy's card. I appreciated them very much.

I have to go and study now so I will try and write later.

> *Lots of Love to All,*
> *Harry*

P.S. Tell Betsy I would love to receive a letter from her.

Frank reads it over several times, then tucks it carefully back into the envelope. He will show it to Helen and the family and will make sure Betts, now nine years old, sends off a letter of her own. He thinks Harry sounds pretty good, all things considered, and it's a load off his mind just to get the letter. He relaxes in his chair, opens the newspaper, and lights his pipe.

That night in Arlington, Nancy Gray lies in her brother's bed, about to fall asleep. Ever since her father died and her grandmother moved in, she's had to sleep in a twin bed in her mother's room, but since Harry left, she sleeps in his room. She feels so cozy, surrounded by his warm blanket, which still smells like him. She looks up at the stuffed gray owl on his dresser and wonders what he likes about that ugly thing. He thinks it's wonderful. She can't for the life of her imagine why, but he is a boy, so . . . She says her prayers and drifts off to sleep.[47]

11

Japan's Doorstep

I'll be seeing you in all the old familiar places / That this heart of mine embraces all day through. / In that small café, the park across the way.

—Bing Crosby singing "I'll Be Seeing You" in 1944

In hometowns across the United States, families were missing their boys abroad and factories were buzzing overtime, building weapons to win the war and bring them back home.

Ford, General Motors, and Packard factories hummed around the clock, building parts, engines, aircraft, and tanks. The shipbuilder Bath Iron Works in Bath, Maine, was turning out destroyers for the Navy at a blistering pace of one every seventeen days.

The Boeing factory in Seattle rumbled day and night, turning out the B-17 bombers that were the workhorses of the European war. However, the Department of War had put out a call for a new bomber, one that could fly higher and faster and carry more bombs. The top secret project, at a cost of $3 billion, was by far the most expensive program of the war. It was known as the XB-29.

Ninety-eight feet long and metal from nose to tail, the aircraft that would become known as the Boeing B-29 Superfortress could fly at speeds of up to 350 miles per hour and at an altitude of 30,000 feet. It had a 4,000-mile range, making the stretch between the islands in the Pacific and mainland Japan attainable, even loaded down with 10,000 pounds of bombs and equipment. It was a flying silver dragon of cutting-edge technology that boasted the first-ever pressurized cabin. Dual-wheeled tricycle landing gear added stability on landing even for battle-damaged aircraft. The B-29's five General Electric–built remote-controlled machine guns, which were an early use of computer technology, ultimately made it the dominant, game-changing aircraft of the Pacific.[1]

But the endeavor to build the "plane that took down an empire" came at great cost. On February 18, 1943, during a secret test flight to measure climb and engine cooling, the XB-29's number one engine on the left wing caught fire. The highly regarded Chief Test Pilot Edmund P. Allen shut the engine down, and the fire extinguishers were activated. He began his descent and headed toward Boeing Field in Seattle. Then there was an explosion, and radio operator Harry Ralston said, "Allen, better get this thing down in a hurry, the wing spar is burning badly." In moments, the prototype burst into flames, metal was peeling and flying off, leaving a trail along the ground as Allen successfully avoided the buildings downtown. At 12:26 p.m., the plane crashed into the side of the Frye & Company meatpacking plant. Three crewmembers bailed out moments before impact, but they, along with Allen, seven crewmembers, and twenty employees at Frye, as well as a local fireman, all perished in one of the worst aviation disasters of the time.[2]

Around the same time in New Rochelle, New York, the Rex Manufacturing Company could barely keep up with the demand driven by the war. Under tremendous pressure and with a shortage of skilled workers and metal, Rex was a year late in delivery on its 1943 contract for the Navy. It took until 1944 to complete the order to the exact quality specifications, a measure of utmost importance. When the crate was ready for delivery, its precious cargo was intact: 135,000 Purple Hearts ready to be bestowed on those who had shed blood for our country and given to the families of those who were never coming home. The Navy was glad to receive them. Certain that a naval blockade of Japan was going to be the strategy, they were confident they would not be needing another shipment before the end of the war.[3]

After the Great Marianas Turkey Shoot, Fast Carrier Task Force 58, the indomitable strike force of the Pacific, sets its sights on its next mission: the Bonins, a chain of volcano islands stretching from five hundred to eight hundred miles directly south of Tokyo.

This is not just another stepping-stone. This is Japanese homeland. Sacred ground. Hirohito has pulled entire divisions out of China and Korea and rushed them to these islands to hold them. The United States and Great Britain have been quite successful in cracking the code of Japanese radio transmissions in order to gauge their next movements, but the Japanese have failed to do the same with the US transmissions. They can never be sure where their enemy is headed next.[4]

Navy pilots are the first to gaze down at the tiny pork chop–shaped island with the menacing volcano. Iwo Jima is an island of almost nothing, really, except a small fishing village, called Nishi, which would soon be evacuated. *Iwo* means "sulfur," and the foul element is the island's only "fruit." Nothing grows on the brown, moon-like, ash-covered stretch of rock. There is no water, barely any trees, and not a blade of grass. It is either scorchingly hot or bone-chillingly damp as the deep ocean surrounding it sends a cold wind across its shelterless rocks. Mount Suribachi's vents puff foul vapor into the air at the outer edge of Iwo's tiny eight-square-mile area. It is one of the most isolated places on Earth. The southern watchtower of Japan. The Americans have been inching closer, and Iwo's two precious airstrips are just the right distance to service B-29s coming from and going to bombing routes over mainland Japan, the ultimate target to end the war. The Japanese cannot lose this island, but the United States is determined to win it.[5]

But now, in mid-June 1944, the island is getting its first glimpses of battle. For two straight days, Task Force 58's seven carriers, and the aircraft that line their decks, take to the skies over Iwo. Thirty-plus Japanese pilots get airborne to guard the hundred planes parked on the island. US fighters sweep most of the Zeros from the sky and take out almost all of those parked on the runways. When the strike force pulls out of the area after this initial pass, Iwo is wounded but far from dead.[6]

On June 24, Task Force 58 is back and takes another pass over the island. It is clear that the enemy has resupplied. Enemy planes meet the US fighters in the skies and launch attacks on the carriers themselves. But again they are outmatched. One hundred fourteen Japanese fighter planes are shot out of the sky or blown up on the island. Only nine US planes are lost.

On July 3, another fighter sweep of sixty-three aircraft sorties to Iwo. Again, Iwo staggers under the assault but stands.

)(

On July 18, 1944, Imperial General Headquarters issues a report. The delusional propaganda describes wild imaginary successes.

Since the enemy task force came attacking the Marianas on June 11, the Japanese Air and Sea units gained the following war results:

1. Sank . . . Two aircraft carriers, three battleships, four cruisers, three destroyers, and one submarine, two warships of an unknown type, two transports.

2. Sank or damaged more than five aircraft carriers and over one battleship.

3. Damaged five or six aircraft carriers, one battleship, three cruisers, three destroyers, one warship of unknown type, seven transports.

4. Airplanes . . . shot down. More than 863.[7]

These are all fantastic lies, since during the Marianas campaign to date, Japan has managed to damage only one aircraft carrier, *Bunker Hill*; and a few other ships are in need of repair. The rest of the US fleet is intact.

The Japanese report ends with this oxymoronic conclusion: "It is indeed regrettable that despite such brilliant war results, we were unable to frustrate the enemy's malicious attempts."[8]

)(

Guam is the second target of Operation Forager. Five hundred US servicemen have been imprisoned there for three years, since the day after the Pearl Harbor attack. Back when the smoke was still rising in Hawaii, Japanese bombers turned their sights to the other targets, including Guam. The Japanese swept the island almost effortlessly and began forcing the native Chamorro people into unpaid labor. Elvina Reyes Rios was thirteen years old. She worked in the rice fields. She was forced to walk four hours to be at work by 6:00 a.m. If she paused for a moment, she was slapped or hit with rocks. They were not paid or fed for their work. They complied because they feared they would be killed or put into prison camps if they did not. As the Americans got closer, the Japanese soldiers became nervous, and the abuse turned deadly. Barbara Dela Cruz saw three Chamorro men beheaded after they were accused of spying and assisting the one American holdout, George Tweed. The Japanese told Barbara and the others not to turn away during the killing, or they would be next. Days before the US invasion, forty-six men and women were massacred at Tinta and Faha, and that was the last straw for the Chamorros. They fought back, using whatever they could get their hands on, and killed every Japanese soldier they could find.[9]

On July 21, the island is awakened by earthshaking noise. Explosions are resounding from the beach, and this time it is a welcome violence coming from six battleships, nine cruisers, and destroyers and rocket ships of the US Navy.[10]

But the 19,000 Japanese defenders of Guam are ready. They have imposing defensive positions overlooking the invasion beaches to the north and south of the Orote Peninsula.

Lieutenant General Kiyoshi Shigematsu tells his men, "The enemy, overconfident because of his successful landing on Saipan, is planning a reckless and insufficiently prepared landing on Guam. We have an excellent opportunity to annihilate him on the beaches."[11]

The landings are hard; dug-in Japanese fire away as Americans hit the beaches and the hills. The labor of the enslaved Chamorros has created heavily fortified cave positions. Gunfire lights their apertures and shells rain down on the water and sand, some missing and throwing earth into the air, others exploding the amtracs and killing Marines fighting their way onto the beaches of Guam.

But during those first five days of battle, the Japanese play all their cards at once and launch two devastating banzai charges. The enormous casualties in these ill-fated attacks hasten the island's fate. The suicidal charges cost the lives of 3,500 men of the estimated 19,000-man force. But more critically, 95 percent of the Japanese officers are killed.[12]

Now the Marine and Army divisions are on the move, up the long axis of the island, chasing the remaining Japanese forces as they retreat deeper and deeper to the north.

Their commander, Lieutenant General Hideyoshi Obata, is living for the time being in a cave near Mount Mataguac. He is well hidden from planes above, but he hears the Americans getting closer. He knows his time is running out. He sends a message to Hirohito, one the emperor is growing weary of receiving: "We are continuing a desperate battle. We have only our hands to fight with. The holding of Guam has become hopeless. Our souls will defend the island to the very end. . . . I pray for the prosperity of the Empire."[13]

His final transmission before taking his own life: "I shall be the bulwark of the Pacific Ocean."[14]

Sixteen hundred Marines are killed on Guam, 5,000 wounded. More than 18,000 Japanese have made the final sacrifice for their emperor.

Operation Forager's focus now moves to the last of the Northern Marianas, Tinian. The veteran 2nd and 4th Marine Divisions, worn out from the grueling Saipan campaign, are "skinny" at only two-thirds strength.[15] Looking across the three miles of water to Tinian, they wonder, "Don't they have anyone else to fight this war?"[16]

Tinian is essentially a cane field. Mostly flat, it is 12 miles long and 6 miles at its widest. The boys from New York see a shape not unlike that of Manhattan, some 7,500 miles to the east.

On the island there are about 9,000 Japanese defenders, many of them hardened veterans of the war in Manchuria.

Tinian has only one real beach for landing, and it is on the southern end of the island in the harbor of Tinian Town. Every Japanese gun will have its sights squarely on that beach, ready and waiting for the Americans.

Admiral Harry W. Hill, the commander of the Northern Landing Force, will later note, "The more we looked at the Tinian Town beaches, the less we liked them."[17]

On the north side they find the only alternative: a small beach that is made up of more craggy sharp coral than sand.[18] It is divided by a protrusion of jagged coral, and each side has only about sixty-five yards clear enough for a vehicle to land. The rest is biting, skin-ripping rock and coral. Maybe four to eight men abreast can go ashore at a time. On Saipan they landed ninety-six across.[19]

Admiral Hill concludes, "My staff was of one mind: land on the northern end of the island."[20] Marine General Holland "Howlin' Mad" Smith recognizes the possible surprise factor of landing where it seems folly to try. Based on the reconnaissance reports showing that the area is almost undefended and only a few small defensive positions exist, he casts his vote with Hill.

However, Hill's superior, Admiral Richmond Turner, nixes the idea, saying it is impossible. He orders Hill to work on another plan. Hill does as he was told but lets some on his staff keep working on the northern landing.

A second attempt by Hill and Smith to convince Turner to land in the north turns the admiral testy. "You are not going to land on the White Beaches," he snaps at Holland Smith. "I won't land you there!"

Smith is not to be outdone. "Oh, yes, you will. You'll land me any goddamned place I tell you to," he booms back.

But Turner is unmoved. "I'm telling you now, it can't be done. It's absolutely impossible."

"How do you know it's impossible? You haven't studied the beaches thoroughly," Smith howls back. "You're just so goddamned scared that some of your boats will get hurt!"[21]

The matter is kicked upstairs to Admiral Raymond Spruance, the commander of the Fifth Fleet, who calls a meeting of all concerned, where all agree that they favor the northern beaches. Turner gives in.[22]

Indeed, Colonel Kiyoshi Ogata, commanding the Japanese 50th Infantry Regiment, confirmed Smith's hunch: "The enemy on Saipan . . . can be expected to be planning a landing on Tinian. The area of that landing is estimated to be either Tinian Harbor or Asiga (northeast coast) Harbor."[23]

As there has been no hint that the Marines will land in the north, the Japanese defenders have put just one 37 mm antitank gun into a covered position and two 7.7 mm machine guns into pillboxes.[24]

The newly acquired air base in Saipan has eased the way for preliminary aerial, artillery, and naval bombardment. Everything is moved from shore to shore across the less-than-three-mile stretch between the two islands. July is typhoon season in the Pacific, and they need a three-day window of good weather. Most of the reconnaissance and minesweeping go off without a hitch, except for the night before the attack, when Demolition Team 5 heads in on rubber boats to clear mines off the northern beaches and blast away some of the underwater rock formations. A squall moves in after the swimmers among them get into the water, and the visibility suddenly goes down to zero and the mission turns back.[25]

Jig Day, July 24: It's "go day," and the 2nd Marine Division is on the move. Plowing through the water in the direction of Tinian Town, they attempt to trick the Japanese gunners lodged in the hills just above the harbor into thinking they are coming in for the attack.

The coxswains gun their engines and head full bore toward the shore. The Japanese gunners immediately open up on the waves of incoming LVTs. Fountains of water shoot into the air as the LVTs hit the gas. But about two thousand yards from shore, the coxswains bank hard to the left and turn back. Another fifteen hundred yards, and they hit the brakes, hovering offshore. The Japanese try to figure out what's going on as they keep pummeling the Marines nonstop from the harbor. Water and shrapnel are flying everywhere, but no one has been hit.

Up in the hills, though, the 6-inch guns are blasting the battleship *Colorado* and the destroyer *Norman Scott*. *Colorado* is hit twenty-two times. Forty-five sailors lie dead on her decks, and 198 are injured. *Norman Scott* is hit six times. The captain is dead, along with 18 others; 47 others are wounded.[26]

It is now almost 8:00 a.m., and the first LVTs carrying Marines from the 4th Division are hitting the rocky White beaches, just a few abreast, firing back at the weak Japanese defense. The gunner and the pillbox fall silent.

They then begin their day's work, moving supporting arms and equipment onto this part of the island. By nightfall, 15,000 men have set up and dug into the sugarcane, creating foxholes wherever they can. They tip their helmets forward over their eyes to attempt to sleep in the cool breeze coming off the water. There has been steady progress so far, but no advance comes without a cost: 15 Marines are dead. Medics tend to the 225 wounded; those who won't mend here are being loaded onto the hospital ship.[27] Some wish they were headed there; a bit of relief it might be to get off these hot, thorny islands and rest in a hospital cot.

Night sets in, and a stinging, burning smell hangs over Tinian. It is rising off the charred Japanese bodies in the trenches and the singed palm trees. There is something about the preinvasion bombardment here that is eerily different.

In the past few months, Army Air Corps researchers at Eglin Air Force Base in Florida have been experimenting with a new weapon concoction. They have mixed diesel oil, gasoline, and a metallic salt

UNKNOWN VALOR

from naphtha that is used in the manufacture of soap. They have discovered that this sticky, thick, jellylike substance is highly flammable, sticks to surfaces, and burns with high intensity. They call it napalm.[28]

Admiral Hill has seen a film demonstrating its use and was impressed with its potential. Five days before the Marianas invasion, he signaled to Admiral Nimitz that they would need more. As the Marines tested its efficacy, they were awestruck. They watched as each firebomb released from their low-flying planes tumbled end over end to the ground and erupted in a rolling wave of fire, engulfing everything in a seventy-five-foot-wide-by-two-hundred-foot-long inferno.[29]

Those who fought in Saipan saw it in action first. Without the napalm gel, the emanating fire billowed and could be blown by the wind; with it, the tanks fired a virtual fire hose of flame speeding straight and steady toward the target.

The Marines establish a main line of resistance. They assign sectors of fire and ensure that all Marines know their jobs. Those who are to man the perimeter dig in. Experience has taught them that after nightfall, the desperate Japanese fighters will gather to die and will use whatever they have—guns, knives, and fists—to take out as many of them as they can. They will go down in the banzai charge attack, attempting to push the Marines back into the sea.

The Japanese forces are scrambling to catch up to the unexpected attack in the north. A thousand troops are shifted from the airfield to the new front. They head to the left of the Marine line. Fifteen hundred more converge on the center. To the right, 900 men, a battalion of the Japanese Mobile Counterattack Force, assemble. Marine intelligence reports lots of "Japanese chatter" along the front.[30]

At 2:00 a.m., a tightly formed group of Japanese appears a hundred yards in front of the 24th Marines' lines.

As the first Marine bullets and shells find their targets, the enemy bursts into a screaming, forward-thrusting mass. The shadows come alive as 600 leaping Japanese naval troops respond to the command "Banzai!"[31]

Tracers suddenly light the battlefield, and every Marine weapon is now ablaze as the massed enemy hurls toward them. The Japanese attackers move to within a hundred yards of the 1st Battalion's Company A. Six tanks join in the defense, and two 81 mm mortars fire more than fifteen hundred rounds. Company A is down to 30 men with usable weapons. Within a hundred yards of the Marines' lines, 476 Japanese bodies lay entangled on the battlefield.[32]

In the center, the first probes in the early-morning darkness are quickly repulsed but the banzai attackers reorganize and smash into the lines between the 24th and 25th Marines. Several hundred attackers find a "weak" point and pour through, threatening the Marine artillery on the beach and the rear area of the 25th Marines.

A reserve company of the 25th quickly moves in to clear them out, killing 91. The second group presses on to attack the artillery units near the beach as they start their direct fire missions to the front. All the rear-area Marines rush in to suppress the attack. The Japanese continue to push, but now they are the targets of two .50-caliber machine-gun teams laying down a devastating volume of fire, highlighted by streams of red tracers, tearing the Japanese to pieces.[33]

The remaining enemy troops regroup and advance again, this time with tanks. Personnel on the ships offshore see them and send up illumination rounds.

Lieutenant Jim G. Lucas recalls:

The three lead tanks broke through our wall of fire. One began to glow blood-red, turned crazily on its tracks, and careened into a ditch. A second, mortally wounded, turned its machine guns on its tormentors, firing into the ditches in a last desperate effort to fight its way free. One hundred yards more and it stopped dead in its tracks. The third tried frantically to turn and then retreat, but our men closed in, literally blasting it apart. . . . Bazookas knocked out the fourth tank with a direct hit which killed the driver. The rest of the crew piled out of the turret, screaming. The fifth tank, completely surrounded, attempted to flee. Bazookas made short work of it. Another hit set it afire, and its crew was cremated.[34]

Five tanks are destroyed and 267 men die in beating down the attack.

The operation grinds on for another eight days. The Japanese defending forces are basically broken. But the repetitive grisly sequence of securing the island is in motion. There is a final banzai charge, but then the Marines witness something they did not see before Saipan and now see on Tinian: the ritual suicide jump of desperate Japanese villagers.

They choose to die for the emperor and to avoid what they have been told will be brutal treatment if they fall into the hands of the enemy. *Time* reporter Robert Sherrod was embedded with the Marines on Saipan. He had heard of the mass ritual suicides and went to the cliffs to see for himself. A Marine had told him, "You wouldn't believe it, unless you saw it, hundreds of Jap civilians—men, women and children—up here on this cliff. In the most routine way, they would jump off, or climb down and wade into the sea. I saw a father throw his three children off, and then jump himself." Sherrod watched with them as a fifteen-year-old boy paced on the beach. "He swung his arms as if getting ready to dive; then he sat down at the edge and let the water play over his feet. Finally he eased himself slowly into the water."

"There he goes," the Marine shouted.[35]

Later they will be revered in Japan. A correspondent from the *Yomiuri Shimbun* praises the women who committed suicide with their children, writing that they were "the pride of Japanese women" and calling it "the finest act of the Showa period."[36]

The operation on tiny Tinian is dubbed the "perfect amphibious operation." General Clifton Cates, the commanding officer of the 4th Division, will later note:

The enemy, although long alerted to our intentions to attack Tinian, was tactically surprised when we avoided his prepared defenses and landed on two small beaches totaling in width only about 220 yards. Before he could recover from the shock, he was out-numbered and out-equipped on his own island. His subsequent effort to throw us into the water resulted in complete failure. We then pushed the length of the island in nine days, while suffering light casualties in comparison with those of most other island conquests.[37]

⋇

While the battle is still being fought, the Seabees are already at work, rolling out onto the old Japanese runways and converting them into what will be the largest airfield in the world.

Around the clock in scorching heat, they lay down six runways, each 8,500 feet long, ready for the B-29 bomber. Hundreds of the planes begin arriving in October. On November 24, 110 B-29s take off from Saipan for their initial strikes against Japan. Shortly after, B-29s from Tinian join in, softening up the mainland of Japan for the invasion that is to come. The perch on the Marianas has brought them that much closer. Before the war is over, 19,000 combat missions against Japan will take off from Tinian.[38] One of them will be piloted by Colonel Paul Tibbets in a B-29 named for his mother, *Enola Gay*. It will carry the heaviest payload of all: the atomic bomb headed for Hiroshima.

⋇

As the B-29s begin their routes from Tinian in January 1945, the Marine Corps Recruit Depot on Parris Island is turning out fresh recruits. The newly minted Marines are lean and muscled from sixteen weeks of intense training. Private Harry Gray is in that proud number; like Charlie Gubish, Warren Graham, Herman Graeter, and George Colburn, he has his photograph taken in uniform. Anne Gray frames the photo and places it on the center table in her living room. The glimmer in her boy's eyes brings a tear to hers. She is glad that he looks happy and handsome, so she smiles back at him. She hopes that he is praying his rosary, the gift from his grandmother that Anne tucked into the leather pouch and put inside his bag. Prayer will give him support and strength. Work has been a good distraction for Anne. At night in bed, all she can think about is boot camp and the stories she hears about what it's like. Harry has spared her some of what he put into his letters to Uncle Frank, about the "nerve wracking" intensity and the suicide attempt by one of the guys.

The new Marines are given the customary weeklong leave after boot camp, and Harry heads for home on a hot September day. Riding the trolley from the train station down to the Linwood Street stop, he breathes in the crisp air and gazes at the people on the streets and the blue sky over Arlington. It is like a dream after the rigors of Parris Island, and he can't wait to walk through the front door, hug Mom and Nancy, and then sleep in his own bed.

As he walks the final steps to the house, his little sister, fourteen-year-old Nancy, is watching for him from the upstairs window. Since she got home from school that day, she has been there watching for Harry. Finally she sees a fellow walking up the street. She squints past the curtain. It looks like Harry, maybe, but his hair is practically gone and he is in uniform. She knows it is her big brother and her heart leaps as she runs down the stairs, but still, she can't get over it; he is like a different person.

That week, Harry spends most of his time with Dorothy. They are eighteen and sixteen, and they are in love and he is heading off to the war, so Anne and Nancy relish the moments they have with him and let them have their time together.[39]

Dominick Grossi, the broad-shouldered twenty-two-year-old from Lockport, New York, with the warm smile, was a football star back home. In fact, he turned down an offer to play for the New York Giants. In the military, he is enjoying his increasing responsibilities as a second lieutenant. Maybe the Giants will still be interested when he gets back. He doesn't plan to be gone too long. After all, the war is almost over.[40]

That fall of 1944, he writes home several times as he makes his way

Harry Eugene Gray and his little sister, Nancy, pictured in a friend's garden in Arlington, Massachusetts. Months later, Nancy recalls, "everything changed." (Nancy Gray Shade Family Archive)

"Uncle Frank" holds his "only boy," nephew Harry Gray, age two, at Horseneck Beach in Massachusetts. Frank Bowes would become "like a father" to Harry after his dad died. Frank urged Harry not to enlist. "The war is almost over," he told his seventeen-year-old nephew. (Nancy Gray Shade Family Archive)

Harry Gray waves the American flag as a Boy Scout. A few years later and 7,300 miles away, he would see it in the distance, raised on Mount Surihachi. (Nancy Gray Shade Family Archive)

The Grossi family of Lockport, New York. The parents, Pasquale ("Patsy") and Lena, are in the center, while Dominick (back row, second from the left) *is* surrounded by Rose, Marie, Elizabeth ("Betty"), Patrina, and Patsy Junior.

Lena and Patsy ran an Italian restaurant in town. Marie's husband, Jim, also served in the South Pacific and was Dom's "best buddy." While they were both overseas, on different islands, Dom wrote to him, "Keep plugging and the day will soon be when we are standing elbow to elbow over a bar, talking family troubles, instead of war." (Grossi Family Archive)

Anne Gray takes Nancy, Harry, and their cousin "Betts" Bowes (the author's mother) to the World's Fair in the spring of 1939. Called the "World of Tomorrow," the $135 million spectacular showcased the "Modern Electric Era." That year, on September 1, Hitler invaded Poland, beginning World War II. (Nancy Gray Shade Family Archive)

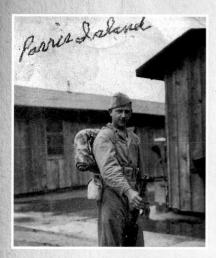

Private Charles Gubish, USMC, 968165. Charlie endured the grueling sixteen-week boot camp and the severe commands of his staff sergeant, a former New York City policeman. In the end, he says, "they made me a Marine." (Gubish Family Archive)

Marine on Iwo

MARINE PVT. GEORGE J. COLBURN, of 38 Grant ave., Medford, who has just written his parents from an Iwo Jima foxhole that "things were pretty hot." Pvt. Colburn, son of Mr. and Mrs. George W. Colburn is with the Third Division. He was graduated from Medford High in 1944.

Private George J. Colburn, of Medford, Massachusetts, played football against Harry Gray. Their mothers shared their boys' letters over the phone. (Colburn Family Archive)

Jefferson J. Rebstock, Jr. (Drez archives)

Private Harry Gray, USMC, 565110. (Nancy Gray Shade Family Archive)

Lieutenant Dominick Grossi, USMC, 395929. (Grossi Family Archive)

James C. Russell, in the middle. (Drez archives)

D-Day, Iwo Jima, February 19, 1945. As amtracs grind and falter in the volcanic ash, Marines in the first wave are forced out of their vehicles and have to climb the terraces on foot; with each step they take, the ash claws them in, like quicksand. At first they encounter little Japanese resistance on the beach, but then all hell breaks loose. (US Marine Corps)

Harry Gray writes: "I am in what they call 'Beach unloading party #3.' This means I am in the 3rd wave and unload supplies from Higgins boats. It is a very heavy job but not too much so for me. I think it will be ammunition, but don't know when. After the unloading is completed, we shall take our places in the lines or be held in reserve." (US Coast Guard)

February 23, 1945. The 2nd Battalion, 28th Marines, plant the first flag atop Mount Suribachi. The photograph was taken by Staff Sergeant Louis Lowery of Leatherneck *magazine. When Secretary of the Navy James Forrestal saw the flag go up, he said to General Holland Smith, "The raising of that flag means a Marine Corps for the next five hundred years."* (Louis R. Lowery)

The second flag raising, seen in AP photographer Joe Rosenthal's Pulitzer Prize–winning photo, is perhaps the most iconic image of World War II. As of October 2019, the correct names of the six flag raisers are, left to right, Ira Hayes, Harold Schultz, Michael Strank, Franklin Sousley, Harold Keller, and Harlon Block. Of those who raised the two flags on Mount Suribachi, six were killed in the coming weeks of the battle. (Associated Press)

Dominick Grossi's last letter home. "Remember I love you all so much. The Lord will see me through. Your son Dom, xxx (Grossi Family Archive)

To Mrs. Lena Grossi
438 West Ave
Lockport, N.Y.

Dearest Mother,
I'm still on Iwo Jima and am well. Our leave from here has been delayed a couple of days. I'll write again as soon as I hit my base. Give my love to all. Remember I love you all so much. Don't worry. The Lord will see me through.
Your Son
Don. XXX

V-MAIL

WESTERN UNION

BU27 70 GOVT=WASHINGTONDC 26 1001A
MRS ANNE GRAY=
17 LINWOOD ST ARLINGTON MASS=

DEEPLY REGRET TO INFORM YOU THAT YOUR SON PRIVATE HARRY
E GRAY USMCR WAS KILLED IN ACTION 13 MARCH 1945 AT IWO
JIMA VOLCANO ISLANDS IN THE PERFORMANCE OF HIS DUTY AND
SERVICE OF HIS COUNTRY. WHEN INFORMATION IS RECEIVED
REGARDING BURIAL YOU WILL BE NOTIFIED. TO PREVENT POSSIBLE
AID TO OUR ENEMIES DO NOT DIVULGE THE NAME OF HIS SHIP OR
STATION. PLEASE ACCEPT MY HEARTFELT SYMPATHY. LETTER
FOLLOWS=
    A A VANDEGRIFT LT GENERAL USMC COMMANDANT OF THE
    MARINE CORPS.

Telegram sent to Anne Gray, 17 Linwood St, Arlington, Massachusetts:
"DEEPLY REGRET TO INFORM YOU THAT YOUR SON PRIVATE HARRY E. GRAY USMCR WAS
KILLED IN ACTION 13 MARCH 1945 AT IWO JIMA VOLCANO ISLANDS IN THE PERFORMANCE
OF HIS DUTY AND THE SERVICE OF HIS COUNTRY. A.A. VANDEGRIFT, LT GENERAL USMC
COMMANDANT OF THE UNITED STATES MARINE CORPS." (Dean Laubach)

Harry Gray wrote on the back page of his wallet prayer book before boarding the ship for Iwo Jima, "Treasurers, I beseech thee to bring this matter to a happy end, if it be for the glory of God and the good of my soul. Amen." The wallet, stained in his blood, was later returned to his mother. (Dean Laubach)

In Tokyo Bay, on September 2, 1945, US military personnel, photographers, and onlookers cram into every inch of the USS Missouri *to witness the official surrender of Japan.* (Department of Defense)

Below: Grave site, 3rd Marine Division Cemetery, Iwo Jima. (Nancy Gray Shade Family Archive)

Japanese dignitaries take their turns signing the Instrument of Surrender. After the ceremony, General MacArthur addresses the people of the United States: "Today the guns are silent. A great tragedy has ended. A great victory has been won. The skies no longer rain death—the seas bear only commerce, men everywhere walk upright in the sunlight. The entire world is quietly at peace." (Carl Mydans)

Martha MacCallum meets Charlie Gubish, age 100, for the first time. (Lori Frye)

The author at the US Memorial and site of the iconic flag raising on Mount Suribachi. (Briana Vota)

to San Diego and then sets out to sea. He writes to his mother, Lena, and she reads his letters to her husband, Patsy. Dom, now a second lieutenant, shares his thoughts about leadership and what lies ahead:

At times I'm tough but that is only when we have got work to do and do it fast. When I give orders they all cooperate and jump to. I'm sort of glad that I'm starting. I'm tired of standing by and waiting. I think I'm going to enjoy the coming adventure. The only thing that bothers me is you. I want you to promise that you will not cry and break down. I know you're going to worry, but please be strong. . . . Time does fly and in only a short while I'll be with you all again. Love to all, God Bless you xxxxx

Your devoted son, Dom

In another letter on November 28:

Dearest Mother,
I am still at sea and still going strong. This beautiful morning I attended mass aboard the ship and received holy communion. The Chaplain who served the mass once taught at Niagara University.

Dom goes on to send a note to each of his siblings. This one is to the youngest, his brother, Junior.

HiYa Junior,
How's your arm coming along? I haven't forgotten about the boxing gloves. You had better get in good shape because when I get back, you and I are going to box. One word of advice brother, I want you to stay away from the Canal Banks. I've heard that you have been there, but I don't want to hear of it again. Do you understand?

God Bless you, Goodnight xxxxx
Love, Dom[41]

12

"A Ghastly Relentlessness"

In late July, as Operation Forager ground on in the Marianas, the military brain trust of the United States was poring over maps and pondering its next steps. FDR and his admirals and generals were flush with victory. General Eisenhower and the Allied army in Normandy had broken out of the confined pocket that had hemmed them in since June 6. The German Army had fought furiously to keep them contained, but on July 25, the dam had finally broken.

Following a massive bombardment by 1,800 bombers from the Eighth Air Force, the German line at Saint-Lô was pulverized and the US Army poured through the gap. The American war correspondent Ernie Pyle wrote of the sheer force of the air attack, "Their march across the sky was slow and studied. I've never known anything that had about it the aura of such a ghastly relentlessness."[1]

A ghastly relentlessness! In the Pacific, the Marines stormed the beaches, clawed through the jungles, and clung to their gains, killing and moving, moving and killing, breaking the will of the Japanese with that same kind of "ghastly relentlessness."

By the end of the Marianas battles, the Marines had triumphed in seven major amphibious assaults across the stepping-stones of the central Pacific. The campaign had begun in August 1942 at Guadalcanal, and with the exception of a few surviving soldiers there, whom the emperor had deigned to rescue, the rest of the island defenders had chosen death over dishonor.

War Plan Orange, hatched thirty-seven years earlier, had for the most part been remarkably forward thinking and imaginative in an age when aviation was in its infancy and the range of airplanes was measured in a few hundred miles. The vision of future aerial capabilities had anticipated long-range bombers to bring about the defeat of Japan and detailed just how that plan should unfold. Despite interservice rivalries, arguments, and harangues, US forces were now poised on the inner ring of Japan's defenses to start the beginning of the end.

The capture and occupation of the Marianas had brought about significant events envisioned in War Plan Orange. The great climactic naval battle, anticipated by each side for forty years, had been fought in the Philippine Sea. The Japanese had joined battle with their Navy, risking everything in a winner-take-all showdown. And the Great Marianas Turkey Shoot had settled the question of naval supremacy once and for all.

Though early planners had envisioned China as the home base for the aerial assault against Japan, they had been wrong only as to the location. But as early as 1924, one of those visionaries had actually recognized that the Marianas were a great possibility.

General Billy Mitchell, the great Air Service hero of World War I, had said, "If we ever use a southern line of operations against Japan, Guam is a point of tremendous importance. It can hold any size air force."[2]

In 1944, Mitchell's prediction became reality and the Twentieth Air Force was in a position to conduct unrelenting war against what Mitchell had called the "vital centers" of the enemy. "The entire nation is, or should be considered, a combatant force," he said.[3]

Mitchell dismissed as folly the idea that war could be waged by detached armies on some romantic field of battle where the winner dictated a settlement and the loser lived to fight another day. He felt that waging war against an opposing army necessarily led to annihilation.

The Great War had been proof of that. The materiel of war would have to be stopped at the vital centers of production, before it got to the battlefield. Once it arrived, the battle area would become "a slaughterhouse from beginning to end . . . one side makes a few yards, or maybe a mile and thousands of men are killed."[4]

Although "humanitarians" shunned the thought of war against vital centers (always ensconced within the civilian population) and routinely opted for "more gentlemanly" battlefield slaughterhouses, US military planners had no such illusions. They knew that war is not a game played with a human chessboard laid out on some distant, remote battlefield.

The authors of War Plan Orange had, from the time of its original draft in 1906, defined the strategy for victory against Japan as "the destruction of Japanese capacity to resist."[5]

In January, at the Casablanca Conference, President Franklin Roosevelt had expressed his same understanding of the total capitulation of Japan when he called for the empire's "unconditional surrender." "Japan was to be occupied, disarmed, and stripped of all overseas possessions and its leaders unseated and prosecuted."[6]

Now, on July 26, the president had arrived in Pearl Harbor on the cruiser *Baltimore*, accompanied only by Admiral William Leahy, his personal chief of staff and closest confidant. Conspicuously missing were the rest of the Joint Chiefs. This meeting was to be with General MacArthur and Admiral Nimitz to settle upon the next military step against Japan. The gist of the argument was whether to advance against Luzon in the northern Philippines or to bypass it and attack Formosa to the north along the coast of China.

Admiral William "Bull" Halsey, commanding the part of Fast Carrier Task Force known as Task Force 38, had radioed Nimitz that he should cancel any cautious, deliberate approach to the Philippines. Halsey's recommendation was not just speculative. He was on the scene, and his carriers were hard at work blasting the enemy. His fleet stood within sight of land in the central Philippines, and there were no Japanese aircraft to challenge him. He had ordered 2,400 sorties and destroyed hundreds of Japanese planes, and still there was no reaction from the enemy.

The Fast Carrier Task Force was prowling the Philippine waters like an alpha dog spoiling for a fight, and there were no takers even as it continued to sink ships and bomb installations. As far as Halsey was concerned, attacking Yap, Palau, Morotai, and Mindanao would be a waste of effort. He argued for a leap forward to the north, a strike directly at Leyte.[7]

Nimitz concurred with Halsey's assessment, except that he nixed the bypassing of Palau. MacArthur was opposed to anything that would threaten his advance on Luzon, from which he had retreated in 1942, vowing, "I shall return." Luzon was not to be left out.

Now at Pearl Harbor, meeting with the president and Admiral Nimitz, MacArthur urged the president to side with him on the question of Luzon. He browbeat Roosevelt until he submitted, and the president left the three-hour ordeal feeling irritated and exhausted. "Give me an aspirin," he demanded. "In fact, give me another aspirin to take in the morning. In all my life, nobody has ever talked to me the way MacArthur did."[8]

Roosevelt put his irritation aside and agreed with MacArthur that the next military moves should be first against Leyte in October and then against Luzon in December. But a preliminary to the attacks on Leyte and Luzon was to secure Palau, 550 miles east of MacArthur's flank. Palau was a massive atoll 77 miles long by 20 miles wide. The military focus was not on the entire atoll but on the tiny island of Peleliu on the extreme southern tip, which contained its vital airfield.

There had been significant controversy as to the importance of Peleliu, and many thought it should be bypassed; but MacArthur and Nimitz wanted it to secure the right flank of the Philippine invasion, and D-Day was set for September 15, 1944. The attackers would be the veteran Marines of the 1st Division, together with the Army's 81st Infantry Division, with the Marines making the initial landings.

To many veterans of Guadalcanal and Cape Gloucester, the tiny islet of Peleliu eerily resembled Betio, which was located similarly on Tarawa Atoll. Everybody knew about the bloodbath at Tarawa. "Old salts" and "new guys" alike knew of the long wade-in across the fire-swept Betio lagoon; the Higgins boats that couldn't cross the reef; the rock-ribbed Japanese defenses; the deadly coconut wall; and the more than one thousand casualties a day. Before they had died, the Japanese defenders at Betio had decimated the 2nd Division.

The thin silver lining to Tarawa's terrible cloud had been that the battle had been short. The burning question now about Peleliu was: Would it be deadly but short, as Saipan and Guam had been? Or would it drag on, testing the limits of their endurance?

The 1st Division's commanding officer, General William Rupertus, was confident that the operation would be quick. Addressing his Marines four days before their ships weighed anchor at Pavuvu in the Russell Islands for the two-thousand-mile trek to Peleliu, he told them, "We're going to have some casualties. But let me assure you this is going to be a short one, a quickie. Rough but fast. We'll be through in three days. It might take only two."[9]

The general's optimistic assessment to his officers and senior NCOs was infectious. They returned to their ships' anchorage, sixty miles northwest of Guadalcanal, and happily repeated Rupertus's assessment to the Marines: "Three days, maybe two. It's gonna be in-again-out-again-Finnigan!"[10]

The word spread to the news correspondents, and many decided not to stick around for an operation that would be over so quickly.

But there was a lurking reality of which they were not aware. Captured enemy documents from Saipan revealed a significant difference from Tarawa: "Betio had been garrisoned by 4,836 Japanese, with no other substantial enemy forces within reach. . . . Early estimates placed 9,000 Japanese on Peleliu, and . . . upward of 25,000 additional troops posted on islands within practicable reinforcing distance."[11]

There had also been a change in the mind-set of the Japanese defenders. The traditional call of "Banzai!" would no longer be used.

Emotionalism and bombast were to be replaced with pragmatism. The *bushido* bravado of "Eat three of the American devils with each morning's bowl of rice"[12] was substituted with cold strategic reality. The Americans must be hammered with firepower, not flesh and bone.

"We must preserve personnel. . . . We must detect the opportunity for opening up accurate fire," declared Lieutenant General Sadae Inoue. "It is certain that if we repay the Americans with material power it will shock them beyond imagination."[13]

Aerial bombs were not to be feared. "The only fearful thing . . . is the psychological effect upon ignorant and inexperienced personnel. By observing very carefully the activity of enemy planes and the bombs while they are falling, avoiding thereby instantaneous explosions, and by taking advantage of gaps in bombardment in order to advance, it can cause no great damage."[14]

Concerning naval gunfire, Inoue was most optimistic: "The object of naval guns was to sink ships. . . . Their physical power is not very great against men who are advancing at a crawl, utilizing terrain, natural objects, and shell holes."[15]

General Rupertus had drummed into those attending the training exercises that commanders should be prepared for, and expect, a banzai charge during the first night after landing. Digging in for that attack should commence during daylight.

But there would be no banzai charge on Peleliu. Whereas the Marines had come to realize that those human-wave attacks actually shortened the battle by exposing the major part of a Japanese force to certain destruction in one climactic action, the new philosophy was designed to extract a fearsome toll on the attacking Marines. They would now have to dig each defender out of a hardened position.

Peleliu was six miles long and only two miles at its widest point. The airfield of hard-packed coral was located on the southern end. Rising above the airfield was a low, five-hundred-yard-wide, wooded ridge covered in greenery that ran from southwest to northeast for about two miles.

The Japanese had renamed the ridgeline Momiji Plateau after they had taken over the island as a result of the League of Nations mandate. The original Micronesians had called it Umurbrogol Mountain. Soon the Marines would rename it a third time: Bloody Nose Ridge.[16]

Intelligence revealed that the defenders were crack troops, mostly the 14th Division of the Imperial Japanese Army. They had been a part of the fierce Kwantung Army that had fought in China and had recently been rushed to the Pacific after the Japanese defeat in the Marshall Islands.[17]

Commanding all of Palau was Lieutenant General Sadae Inoue, who headquartered himself on the northern island of Babelthuap. His subordinate, Colonel Kunio Nakagawa, commanded at Peleliu.

In March 1944, General Inoue had met with then Japanese premier Hideki Tojo on a dire subject. Tojo saw that the continuing advance of the Americans meant that sooner or later they would attack Palau and that continued possession of the island was no longer possible. He urged a strong defense of the island to make its capture a lesson in blood for the Marines.

Inoue took command of the Japanese forces there and set about converting the island into a killing field. He would block, for as long as possible, its capture and use by the Americans. He concluded that Peleliu was the key to all of Palau.

The previous commander had built numerous blockhouses, reinforced-concrete structures, pillboxes, bunkers, and fighting positions, all above ground, and had also begun expanding the defensive positions by improving the existing caves and tunnels. Some of that excavation was the result of previous mining operations on Umurbrogol. Much of it was camouflaged under a canopy of overgrowing scrub and secondary growth.[18]

In March, the carriers of Task Force 58 had visited Peleliu, bombing and smashing the airfield and turning it into a junkyard. But the Japanese there, hunkered down in their underground tunnels and shelters, had escaped unscathed.[19]

Nakagawa knew how to convert Peleliu into a formidable fortress. In addition to registering artillery and mortar fire to cover every inch

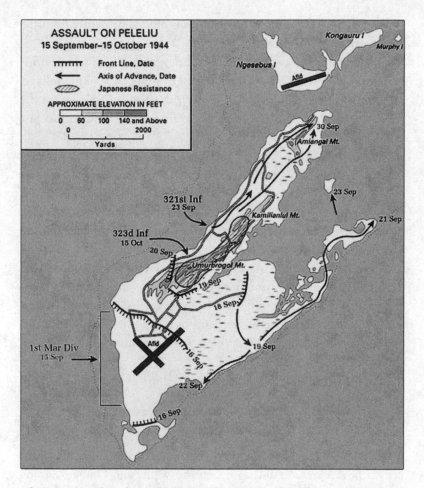

of all landing beaches and the reef immediately offshore, he had his
men plant five hundred wire-controlled mines in the shallow waters.
Seven hundred yards farther offshore, he registered massive concentrations at the edge of the reef, where he anticipated that the transfer
operations would occur to embark the assault forces into the attacking LVTs.[20]

But most important, he set all his forces to the task of digging,
tunneling, blasting, and boring into the most hostile collection of up-
thrusting, razor-sharp coral mutations that formed the myriad mazes

of Umurbrogol. Those badlands had been hidden by nature from the prying lenses of US aircraft.

The reconnaissance cameras had photographed a simple, continuous ridge covered with a lush, thin veil of innocent-looking foliage. But in fact, it was not lush at all but scrub growth surviving on the minuscule amount of moisture extracted from the coral and rocks just below its surface.

When Nakagawa had finished his unprecedented engineering project, he ordered his army into the interior of Umurbrogol's natural fortress. Except for a few battalions of infantry left to man positions along the western beaches and airfield, the massif swallowed soldiers, tanks, mortars, and artillery into its coral honeycomb of five hundred caves and tunnels.

"The tunnels were designed for . . . barracks, command centers, hospitals, storage and ammunition magazines, cooking areas complete with fresh water springs and seepage basins, and firing embrasures with elaborate concealment and protective devices, including a few sliding steel doors."[21] Everything was interconnected by horizontal and vertical tunnels.

Umurbrogol had been transformed into a "thousand-eyed"[22] mountain.

)(

On September 15, the assault waves of the 1st Marine Division churn across the shallow reef and approach the White and Orange landing beaches on the southwestern tip of Peleliu. It is a blistering hot summer day: the temperature at Peleliu rarely dips below 100 degrees F.

There is an air of confidence among the Marines in the advancing first wave. Some hum the tunes they heard Tokyo Rose play on the radio last night; others smoke a cigarette and look out at the sea. One catches the eye of a pal and holds up four fingers: "In again, out again, buddy!" He hopes it will be true.

In no time, the tenor changes and tension creeps back into their bodies. The game is forever changing and moving, and expectations are thwarted by reality over and over again.

As soon as they hit the beach, it is on fire. Amtracs no sooner touch down than they are engulfed, turned into burning hulks by Japanese high-velocity antitank guns. Within an hour of the morning landing, sixty landing tractors are destroyed or disabled by the deadly guns firing relentlessly down the long axis of the beaches.[23]

The eighteen tanks landing to support the 1st Marines on the northern end of White Beach are also under fire. Seventeen of them are hit in the first hours. Nine are completely destroyed.[24]

All along the congested beaches is a sea of appalling human destruction. Fire from the dug-in Japanese beach defenders, as well as heavy mortar and artillery fire now unleashed from Umurbrogol, rake the pinned-down Marines: "Limbs, and heads, and pieces of flesh flying through the air; . . . men staggering about in the last throes of death, their lives spouting crimson from severed faces or stumps of arms."[25]

For eight hours, the savagery drags on, and then the Japanese make their only mistake of the day: they mount a massed tank assault across the northern portion of the airfield with infantry following closely behind. But once on the airstrip, the tankers rev their engines and leave the infantry in their dust, barreling forward to where the 1st and 5th Marines' lines join.

That thrust is short lived. All available Marine weapons, including three Sherman tanks and even a Navy dive-bomber, turn to meet the onslaught, raking the thirteen onrushing smaller tanks and blowing them apart. The Marines call them "tankettes." The fight is over almost before it starts.[26] It isn't a banzai charge, but except for a few probes of the Marine lines that first night, it is the only time that Colonel Nakagawa will expose his troops to the superior US firepower.

By nightfall, it is clear that "in again, out again" is not even a remote possibility. The 1st Marine Division carves out a beachhead three thousand yards long but only five hundred yards deep. It runs from the 1st Marines' positions on White Beach in the north to the 7th Marines on the southern Orange beaches, the 5th Marines sandwiched between.

They have run the gauntlet of devastating interlocking beach defensive fires, fought off an armored attack, and endured the first saturating salvos of dug-in Japanese artillery. There are 1,100 casualties, and 200 Marines are dead.[27]

The second day, the 1st Marines advance toward Umurbrogol. Whereas previously the features of that devastating defensive position had been shrouded, air strikes and naval gunfire have stripped away its disguise and reveal it to be a three-headed monster. The regimental narrative describes it:

> The ground of Peleliu's western peninsula was the worst . . . the rocky spine was heaved up in a contorted mass of decayed coral, strewn with rubble, crags, ridges and gulches thrown together in a confusing maze. There were no roads, scarcely any trails. The pock-marked surface offered no secure footing even in the few level places. It was impossible to dig in: the best the men could do was pile a little coral or wood debris around their positions. The jagged rock slashed their shoes and clothes, and tore their bodies. . . . It was impossible to get under the ground away from the Japanese mortar barrages. Each blast hurled chunks of coral in all directions, multiplying many times the fragmentation effect of every shell. Into this the enemy dug and tunneled like moles; and there they stayed to fight to the death.[28]

The 1st Marines' probe of the rugged coral ridges is an attack for which these veterans never prepared: a frontal assault against a dug-in, invisible enemy while scaling the steep slope of Umurbrogol. This first slope juts up two hundred feet.

The attacking Marines of the 2nd Battalion are constantly raked by small-arms and machine-gun fire as they claw their way up, but that is not the worst. Blasting them from close range are mountain guns and dual-purpose guns that appear and disappear as the Japanese gunners run them into and out of covered positions.[29]

The tanks and armed LVTs supporting the assault are blasted into flaming hulks. Nothing escapes the thousand-eyed mountain's observation. When at last the attacking Marines gain the top of Hill 200, there is still no respite or decrease in the enemy's fire. Just to the west of Hill 200 are the taller, steep-sided Hill 210 and yet another army of defenders and mountain guns.

The sole surviving company commander on Hill 200 reports, "We're up here, but we're knee-deep in Purple Hearts."[30] A *Time* magazine reporter describes the nightmare as "the incarnate evil of this war."[31]

The men of the 1st Marines continue cliff climbing, peak scaling, and cave clearing across boulders and rubble in the stifling heat through September 21, when they are finally forced by loss of men to grind to a halt.

Adding to the misery is a severe lack of water. When water finally arrives in fifty-five-gallon drums, the thirsty men drink it down quickly, ignoring its faint diesel taste from the poorly cleaned drums, leaving many of them very sick. The regiment's casualties climb to over 1,700.

They kill almost 4,000 enemy soldiers and overrun ten defended coral ridges, three large blockhouses, twenty-two pillboxes. They destroy thirteen antitank guns and clear or seal off 144 defended caves.[32] The enemy, worn out, is no longer a tactical fighting force.

After a solid week of the most tenacious fighting, the 1st Marine Division, with its 1st, 5th, and 7th Regiments, is in total control of the southern end of Peleliu. But the cost of that conquest has been severe: 4,000 Marine casualties, the equivalent of the loss of one entire regiment and the severe thinning of the other two.[33] The Army's 81st Infantry Division relieves the Marines.

MacArthur's flank for his attack in the Philippines is secure. The

Japanese have no means to threaten him. Critics say the Peleliu battle should not have happened at all; the forces should have been withdrawn and the Japanese defenders left "to die on the vine." But the battle grinds on.

"Finnegan" will hang around; he is not "out again" but rather dug in through the end of September and then October. The fighting continues on the godforsaken island for seventy-three days, until the days are indistinguishable, hellishly long, and seemingly endless.

On November 24, the same day that B-29s take off from Saipan for their first mission to Tokyo, Colonel Nakagawa acknowledges to his men, "Our sword is broken and we have run out of spears."[34] Nevertheless, he issues orders to his few remaining men to continue to attack and inflict casualties. His final message follows the pattern of those who have gone before him: accepting that his men are on the verge of annihilation, he has the 2nd Infantry Regiment flag destroyed, so as not to become a souvenir. The burning of all the documents follows, and then he sends his final message, telling its recipient that it will be the last he will hear from him.[35]

Colonel Nakagawa retires to a secluded section of his final command post and, like General Saito on Saipan, commits ritual seppuku. The act generally involved leaving behind a "death poem" and then stabbing oneself with a sword in the torso and grinding it upward to ensure death. Three days later, on November 27, the ghastly ordeal is over. Peleliu is secured.

The Japanese have inflicted 6,526 casualties on the 1st Marine Division and an additional 1,393 on the Army's 81st Infantry Division.[36] Of the reported 10,900 Japanese defenders, only 19 soldiers are captured. With no banzai attack option remaining, the Japanese soldiers are told to dig in, wait, and, when their moment comes, kill as many "invaders" as they can, before dying themselves for the emperor.

In Tokyo, Emperor Hirohito is having a tougher time selling the notion that his Imperial Army is prevailing, when the opposite is true. Day after day, US planes rain bombs down on the mainland, softening targets for the coming invasion into the "heart of the Empire."[37]

)(

During those long days at Bloody Nose Ridge, Americans hope and pray that the war is almost over. But for Harry Gray, Charlie Gubish, Herman Graeter, George Colburn, and Warren Graham, it is just beginning. After a week at home, each boards a bus or train and makes his way to Marine Corps Base Camp Lejeune in North Carolina. At some point along their separate journeys, each presses his forehead against the cool window, watching America go by. Toughened by their long weeks at Parris Island, they are not the boys they were before, but now they venture a bit farther from home than any of them has been before.

In the morning heat, on the bus or the train, they move through the tall grasses and the farms of North Carolina. Dew beads on the outside of the window, and bugs stick smushed to the glass, their legs sometimes sticking some distance away from their flattened bodies. It is hotter down here than at home in September. Beyond these bits of information, they have little idea of what will come next. They do not know one another or that they are all ultimately headed to a tiny island in the middle of nowhere, a place they cannot imagine. The place they are in, rolling along through the tall grass, is different enough for now.

Harry is the youngest of them, having just turned eighteen that June. These are the answers he gave on his enlistment forms in Boston, days after his eighteenth birthday: "S" for his marital status and "2" for dependents, his mom and Nancy. He didn't support them, but they did depend on him, so that was how he answered the question. Under academics, he noted his diploma from Arlington High School and that he completed "Math thru Trig." Under "Sports in which qualified," he checked baseball, football, tennis. Under "School or Team," he put "Sandlot." Under "Talent for Furnishing Public Entertainment": "Piano." He could have written "Artist." He loved to draw Revolutionary War and biblical scenes in his large sketchbooks. His buddies found his sketches of pinup girls entertaining; his mother, on the other hand, did not. Under "Work experience":

"General Ice Cream Corp, Cambridge, Truck driver." "What did you do?" "Loaded up truck with ice cream, drove to various stores to deliver it. Some days drove from town to town. Drove days only, could make a few minor repairs." When the interviewer asked him "Duty desired?," Harry had written "AVN, Aerial Gun."

Herman Graeter, also eighteen and just a few months older than Harry, was from Cincinnati. He was the only son of Mr. and Mrs. Graeter of Melrose Avenue, Dayton, Ohio. Herman wrote on his enlistment form under "Employment" that he had been a "Duplication machine operator," a copy boy, at the local printer after school and in the summer.

Like Harry, he arrives at Camp Lejeune on September 13, 1944. In the next six months, they will go halfway around the world together, although neither knows it now.

13

"An Island of Sulphur: No Water, No Sparrow, and No Swallow"[1]

Five months before, as the assault waves of the 2nd and 4th Marine Divisions had hit the beaches of Saipan, Admiral Marc Mitscher's Fast Carrier Task Force had reached its long arm far to the north to destroy any Japanese air forces that might intrude into the battle. In doing so, they had swept over the Bonin island of Iwo Jima, 760 miles south of Tokyo.

The 7,000 Japanese defenders dug in frantically, scampering toward bomb shelters as sirens blared. Japanese aircraft hurried into the sky to meet the threat, engaging in a desperate dogfight. On the island below, the defenders watched the action above, as the Americans gained control. One discouraged defender wrote in his diary, "Somehow, my faith in our Navy air groups has been somewhat shaken."[2]

Four days later, on June 19, the Americans were back. This time, 101 Japanese fighters took off from Motoyama 1 airfield. "There was an air battle for about fifteen minutes, 5,000 meters south of Iwo Jima," said First Lieutenant Musashino. "Those who had been watching the battle felt very sad when none of our planes returned. After, some ten to twenty planes came to Iwo Jima from Japan . . . but all of them were destroyed. . . . There was now no Japanese planes and no vessels."[3]

Major Yoshitaka Horie, the officer in charge of the supply and communication base at Chichi Jima, lamented, "Now we have no fleet and no air forces. If American forces will assault this island it will fall into their hands in one month. Therefore, it is absolutely necessary not to let the enemy use this island. The best plan is to sink this island into the sea or cut the island in half. At least we must endeavour to sink the first airfield."[4]

)(

On October 20, 1944, the US battle line faces the remnants of Japan's "Absolute National Defense Line."[5] That line's right flank is rock solid, with the Marines and Task Force 58 of the Fifth Fleet in total control of both the Marianas and the Palau islands. Nine hundred miles to the west, General Douglas MacArthur begins his long-anticipated return to the Philippines with his invasion of Leyte. The fall of the Philippines would mean the loss of all of Hirohito's expanded empire. His dreams of domination have shrunk to a desire simply to hold his own homeland. The loss of the Philippines would sever the few lines still open for industrial and oil supplies.

From October 23 to 26, Japan pours every last measure of its air and sea capability into an offensive that precipitates the biggest naval clash in history: the Battle of Leyte Gulf. Waves of kamikaze pilots dive out of the blue sky, spiraling down to attack enemy ships below. The human-guided suicide missiles bore full throttle into the US ships, crashing and detonating in their final heroic mission for the emperor.

Admiral Soemu Toyoda, the commander in chief of the Japanese Combined Fleet, fights with his back to the wall, knowing that for him, there is no tomorrow. He commanded the fleet during the disastrous Great Marianas Turkey Shoot and now faces his fleet's most desperate moment. His 69 ships face off against 166 of the US Navy. His 716 aircraft attempt to match the power of 1,280 US carrier-based aircraft.[6] Toyoda puts all of his chips in the center of the table. As he will later say:

Without the participation of the Combined Fleet, there was no possibility of the land-based forces in the Philippines having a chance. . . . It was decided to send the whole fleet, taking the gamble. If things went well, we might obtain unexpectedly good results; if the worst would happen, there was a chance we would lose the entire fleet; but I felt that chance had to be taken.[7]

The outcome is catastrophic: Japan loses 26 ships, the United States only 6. From October to December, Japan will lose 7,000 aircraft, including 722 kamikazes; during those months, the United States will lose 967.[8]

As 1944 grinds to an end, the strategic situation in the Pacific resembles a giant triangle. At the apex stands Japan. Forming the base angle on the left are MacArthur's forces in the Philippines; on the

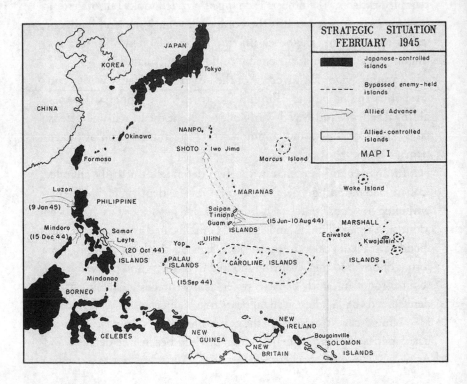

base angle on the right, Nimitz's forces are poised at Palau and the Marianas.

⚹

In May 1944, on Iwo Jima, Major General Kotau Osuga had directed his men to dig in at a frantic pace to the elevated, barren, rocky terrain to create an in-depth defense. But their work had been interrupted by the arrival of two of the highest-ranking Japanese general officers in the Pacific, Lieutenant General Yoshitomi Tamura and Lieutenant General Hideyoshi Obata, on an inspection tour. Tamura was the assistant chief of staff, and Obata commanded the newly created 21,000-man Thirty-first Army, responsible for the inner line of Japanese defenses protecting the homeland.

"What is the meaning of a beach line?" Tamura asked the assembled officers. The officers exchanged puzzled looks but offered no answer to the question. It is the border between water and land, and allowing for tides, "the beach line has to be defended," Tamura told them. It was there that the enemy could be annihilated.[9]

Tamura's vigorous advocacy of the beach-line defense was legendary; thus the name the "Tamura Doctrine." The Imperial Japanese Army Academy and Naval War College taught the beach-line defense as a matter of course and common sense; the annihilation of the enemy at the beach was key.

In answer to his demand, the Iwo defenders dutifully changed course; abandoning their work on the "in-depth defense," they switched to construct beach-line defensive positions, as had been done at Saipan, Tinian, and Guam. Guns located to the north, embedded and concealed in the rocky ridges on the high ground, were brought down to the beach and moored in bunkers and pillboxes. The Umurbrogol in-depth defense system constructed at Peleliu, which had served the Japanese well, appears to have been a lesson ignored.

A huge caveat existed in the teachings of the *Sakusen Yomurei*, the Japanese operations manual, that advised beach-line defense, and

it somehow escaped the attention of General Tamura. In 1939, in a border clash with the Soviet Union—the Nomonhan Incident—the Japanese Army had been outgunned, outsupplied, and overwhelmed by the Soviets, who were armed with five hundred tanks, more than three hundred armored cars and five hundred aircraft.[10] Against those staggering numbers, the Japanese had fielded a pitiful fraction that had been humiliatingly defeated.

From then on, the *Sakusen Yomurei*, though continuing to teach the beach-line defense, added the proviso that "against an overwhelmingly armored enemy, a series of position groups must be made in depth."[11]

Generals Tamura and Obata then left the island, going their separate ways to Saipan and Guam to watch their beach-line defenses swept away in the first hours of battle by overwhelming US firepower. On Saipan, in the first two days, the Americans landed and cut to the opposite side of the island. In fourteen days, they pivoted to the north and succeeded in grinding the Japanese defenders underfoot. For two weeks the Japanese fought and fell back. Although they inflicted many casualties on the attacking Americans, they died by the thousands in the effort. On Guam, the story was similar. Ultimately, facing total defeat, Tamura and Obata chose to end their separate ordeals with the rite of seppuku—for their own honor and that of the emperor.

In Tokyo, Prime Minister Tojo had watched it all with dismay. The Americans had swept aside much of the inner defensive ring protecting the homeland and were poised for a final advance and potential invasion.

As they crept closer, all eyes turned to Iwo Jima. Just 760 miles from Tokyo, it was the obvious next target. A US conquest of the tiny volcanic island would be an invasion of Japan itself.

The "imperial decision" was to fight a bloody war of attrition, a war that would make the conquest of Japan so painful that the Americans would opt for negotiation, rather than Roosevelt's stated

"unconditional surrender" and occupation. The final defensive efforts were to fortify Iwo Jima and Okinawa and turn them into massive killing fields.

Iwo Jima's barren, bleak, hostile terrain would be first. According to the historian and Marine Joseph Alexander:

Mount Suribachi dominated the narrow southern end, overlooking the only potential landing beaches. To the north, the land rose unevenly onto the Motoyama Plateau, falling off sharply along the coasts into steep cliffs and canyons. The terrain in the north represented a defender's dream: broken, convoluted, cave-dotted, a "jungle of stone." Wreathed by volcanic steam, the twisted landscape appeared ungodly, almost moon-like . . . something out of Dante's Inferno.[12]

To command the defense of Iwo, before Tojo resigned, he had selected the fifty-three-year-old Lieutenant General Tadamichi Kuribayashi, a distinguished descendent of a samurai warrior family that had served in the Army under six emperors. Tojo told him, "Only you among all the generals are qualified and capable of holding this post. The entire army, and the nation, will depend on you."[13]

Kuribayashi's orders were perfectly clear, and he revealed his understanding of them in a letter to his brother: "I may not return alive from this assignment . . . but I shall fight to the best of my ability, so that no disgrace will be brought upon our family. I will fight as a son of Kuribayashi, the Samurai."

Kuribayashi had served as a military attaché in the United States from 1928 to 1930. He had written letters to his young son and drawn pictures of America for him. His son Taro later wrote:

While visiting Boston, he was lying sprawled on the gardens of Harvard University watching a clock tower, in another he is taking a walk in Buffalo, in another, playing with some American children and being invited to the house of Medical Doctor Furukohchi, etc.

Throughout his letters, it is clear that my father used to drive in many directions in the United States, studied very hard late at night, and tried to be a gentleman. Also, he used to have many friends in foreign countries.[14]

On June 13, one month after Generals Tamura and Obata had inspected the defense preparations, General Kuribayashi arrived on Iwo Jima, although he was not to take command until the end of the month. A dilapidated car picked him up from his seaplane at the east boat basin and took him to a run-down headquarters. For two weeks he examined the progress made on the defenses, and on June 29, he met with Major Horie and told him, "The enemy will come to Iwo Jima without fail. When the enemy comes, we could contain him and our Combined Fleet would come from the homeland or Okinawa and slap his face. Our role could be a great containing operation."

Major Horie sat in stunned silence for a moment. Obviously the details of the great defeat of the fleet in the Philippine Sea had been kept from the general just as it had been concealed from most of the population. He finally spoke up in a low tone. "General, we have no more Combined Fleet in Japan. Some tiny naval forces still remain, but there are no more striking powers."

The general scoffed at Horie. "What a stupid man you are! This island belongs to Tokyo City."

Horie pressed on. "General, Japan died ten days ago on 19 June 1944."

"You must be drunk," said Kuribayashi.

The following day, the general and the major took the old car to the southern beaches to examine the land. Kuribayashi lay prone on the black sand as if he were an invading soldier. For the next two hours, they drove around the airfield, stopping often while the general examined the fields of fire. He ordered Major Horie to "stand here" and "lie down there" while he detailed places of concealment. As the inspection concluded, Kuribayashi lamented, "I had not known the facts."[15]

Now that he knew he must defend the island without any help from the homeland, he set about his task. He scrapped most of the work on the beach-line defenses but allowed some of it to continue for political reasons. The adversarial Navy headquarters, always at odds with the Army, had offered to deliver three hundred machine guns and the materials for building pillboxes for them, but only if they would be employed in a beach-line defense.

Major Horie objected in no uncertain terms: "I would like to know how long the seaside guns lasted at Saipan and Guam? Please teach me how the seaside pillboxes at Tarawa were effective? This is baby play. . . . The 40-centimeter naval guns of the enemy will blow up any pillbox."[16]

The Navy brass balked at Horie's rebuff, threatening to cancel the whole deal and provide nothing. Kuribayashi smoothed the ruffled feathers and offered to use half the Navy resources for the beach defense; he would provide, he said, 1,000 men a day for the pillbox construction if the rest of the guns and resources could be used in his defensive line. The Navy agreed and offered to send a total of 350 guns.

So 135 pillboxes were constructed for the beach defense, none of which would survive the initial US bombardment; the other 175 guns went into the cave and bunker defensive line.

Kuribayashi evacuated all the civilians from the island and received his final reinforcements, bringing his army's strength up to 21,000. Arriving with the last soldiers were the mining engineers who would convert Iwo Jima into a Pacific Gibraltar.

Digging and tunneling were grueling, backbreaking work, and many of the soldiers collapsed on the job. "Using an army pick, I continued digging the rock, and found that an average person could not continue work for ten minutes," said Major Horie. "Sulphur came up and it made our breathing hard. The key point of position construction was to make a cave from which we could snipe, and to link these caves with underground paths. Everybody, including the general, staff officers, and men made his position, and his tomb, by himself."[17]

They dug the underground tunnels sixty to ninety feet deep, creating side rooms, sleeping quarters, dining rooms, resting areas, and fighting positions, all connected to vertical and horizontal tunnels.[18]

General Kuribayashi even published his "Cave-Digging Discipline," whereby everyone was to accomplish his share—no exceptions. Some of the older men, knowing their final fate was ultimately death, grumbled about the digging: "Regardless of this cave-digging work," they said, "our deaths will be inevitable. Better to die without making this hard work."[19]

Colonel Takeichi Nishi, a tank commander and individual show jumping gold medalist in the 1932 Los Angeles Olympics, wrote, "We are going to dig the land 20 meters deep and make underground streets; then we won't worry about the enemy's one-ton bombs."[20]

Lieutenant Colonel Nakane cheerfully wrote home to his wife, "The enemy air raids come more than 10 times a day. Now we have saved enough water, and yesterday we made baths. Everybody was happy. We can get some fish because whenever the enemy makes air-raids, many fish come to the beach, being killed by their bombs. . . . So if they do not come, we miss them. . . . We're gladly waiting for the enemy."[21]

The 21,000 defenders on the surface of the island slowly disappeared one by one, gun by gun, into the island; 361 artillery pieces, 65 mortars, 33 large naval guns, and scores of large-caliber antiaircraft guns were swallowed into the earth. Kuribayashi's own command post, in the extreme badlands in the northern sector of the island, was seventy-five feet deep and connected with more than five hundred feet of tunnels.[22] "One installation inside Mount Suribachi ran seven stories deep."[23]

To a newcomer, the island would look completely deserted, just as the rock-ribbed Japanese defenses dug into Umurbrogol on Peleliu seemed to be nothing more than a peaceful, green forest landscape.

As the Japanese Army disappeared into the island, each fighting position prominently displayed Kuribayashi's "Courageous Battle Vows":

1. *We shall defend with all-out effort.*
2. *We shall run over enemy tanks with explosives.*
3. *We shall infiltrate and annihilate.*
4. *We shall kill the enemy with one-shot, one-kill system.*
5. *We shall not die until [each] has killed ten men.*
6. *We shall harass the enemy even though only one man remains.*[24]

✕

To the Japanese, it was a foregone conclusion that Iwo Jima was an eventual target; the Americans were slower to come to that conclusion. It was not until the first launchings of the B-29 aerial offensive against Japan in early 1944 that Iwo Jima came clearly into focus.

There was a problem that stemmed from "a vexing little spit of volcanic rock lying halfway along the direct path from Saipan to Tokyo."[25] Iwo Jima's position directly in the path of the northbound bombers flying out of the Marianas gave mainland Japan a two-hour advance notice of the approaching strike.

It also gave the Japanese fighters on Iwo an opportunity to strike at the northbound B-29 Superfortresses, which had no fighter escort—and a second one on their way back, especially when some of the planes were shot up and crippled. Without escorts, the bombers were most vulnerable; and without possession of Iwo Jima, there was no possibility to stage escorting fighters.

Over the target areas on the Japanese mainland, enemy fighters forced the bombers to fly higher, and bombing from higher altitudes was most ineffective. Therefore the Joint Chiefs of Staff in Washington targeted Iwo Jima for attack; in October, they ordered Admiral Nimitz to plan to seize the island.[26] The Marine Corps was tasked to do the job.

For the first time in its long history, the Marine Corps would fight as a corps—three divisions—forming V Amphibious Corps. The newly created 5th Marine Division would join the veteran 3rd and 4th Divisions in the attack. The landings would storm ashore on the southern beaches of the rocky island—the 4th across the Yellow and

Blue beaches and the 5th across the Green and Red beaches. The 3rd Division would remain offshore as a ready reserve.

The Iwo Jima operation (code-named Detachment) consisted of almost five hundred ships, ten times the size of the 1942 Guadalcanal task force. US intelligence expected that the detachment would encounter 13,000 to 14,000 enemy and that the enemy would concentrate on "repelling or destroying our forces in the water and on the beach" and "counterattack our beachhead with all available reserve strength under the cover of darkness."[27]

General Kuribayashi's plans for his 21,000 defenders included none of those things.

)(

On October 23, 1944, Harry Gray of Arlington, Massachusetts; George Colburn of neighboring Medford; Charles Gubish of Hellertown, Pennsylvania; Warren Graham of Salisbury, North Carolina; and Herman Graeter of Dayton, Ohio, are all assigned to the thirty-fourth replacement draft of the 3rd Marine Division and prepare to enter the war in the Pacific. Two days later, Harry writes:

Dear Uncle Frank,

I am sorry I haven't written you before but I have been terribly busy and haven't had much time to write. I am fine and in the best of health. The past two weeks, I have lived in a tent. I got very little food as I survived on K rations and one canteen of water per day. This was for drinking, washing and shaving purposes. We had actual combat fighting from 5:30 pm until 1:00 am with a half hour for [other] chores.

The first week was rugged being 10 and 1/2 miles from camp and carrying field transport packs weighing 60–80 lbs. The second week we spent on the combat range. I was there during the hurricane and many of the boys got soaked because their tents blew down but I was okay. I didn't change my clothes for two weeks.

I have been using all types of weapons, including BAR Browning

*Automatic Rifle, M-1, Carbine, Flame thrower, Grenade launch-
ers, TNT, Bangalore Torpedoes, rifle grenades, machine guns and
bayonets. I have learned bayonet fighting, knife fighting, club fighting and hand to hand combat which is Judo.*

*I have had street fighting which is preparing me for the very near
future. I have just received word that our 9th [unit] has become the
34th Replacement Draft. I also have been given word that we will
be going overseas by Nov. 3. So this is it, all the furloughs have been
cancelled along with 12 hour passes.*

*How is Betty, and Aunt Helen? I hope they are fine. Well I guess
that's the highlights for now and hope this letter finds you all in
good health.*

> *Lots of love your Nephew,*
> *Harry*

He packs his bag in his barrack at Camp Lejeune. His name and
number, 565110, are stenciled in black on the side. It is a methodical
job for him now, arranging his clothes and gear tightly in his duffel.
He feels years older than when he watched Nancy, Mom, and Uncle
Frank disappear on the train platform, but it has actually been only a
few short months since then.

As Harry gathers his belongings, he rolls his rosary beads in his
palm, a gift from Grandma Bowes. Back home in Arlington, he dutifully went to Mass with his family. But most of the time, truth be
known, he was staring at the stained-glass windows in Saint Agnes
Church, thinking about Dorothy. But now he looks forward to the
quiet of the Mass and the words that make him feel less alone. He is
scared, and praying makes him feel as though God is watching over
him and all the other men who kneel next to him at Mass each week
at Camp Lejeune.

He holds the beads in his hand, silently prays an "Our Father,"
and safely tucks them deep inside. He glances at the signet ring Uncle Frank gave him for graduation and then opens the wallet from

his mother and flips through its contents: photographs of Dorothy smiling at him in front, Nancy and Mom close behind. A tiny leather-bound prayer book fits perfectly inside, and a strap closes the folded wallet. With HEG embossed in gold letters across the front, it is a real man's wallet, and he likes the feel of it in his hand. He puts it deep into his front pants pocket. His most precious possessions accounted for, he yanks the strap through the metal-rimmed holes and hooks it to the handle. As he slings the bag over his shoulder, he glances down at the shiny object on his wrist, taking a longer second look and feeling the now-familiar pang of missing home.

The last night of leave, he and Dorothy went for a walk. They stopped in Robbins Park near the *Menotomy Indian Hunter* statue. He opened the small box wrapped in gold paper that she handed to him, and a smile broke out all over his face when he saw his name engraved on an ID bracelet, along with his number, 565110, and U.S.M.C. "Turn it over, Harry," Dorothy said. With his thumb and forefinger, he turned it over; on the back it was engraved LOVE, DOT. "Never take it off," she said, closing the clasp on his wrist and noticing the thick muscles that had grown in his forearms. Pressing the face of it onto his wrist, she said, "I will be right there with you, every time you look at this, no matter where you are."

To Harry, it was the closest thing to being married. It was the vow between them, the promise. He could not explain to her how much it meant to him, and tears were in his eyes that he did not want her to see. He kissed her. She looked up at him, staring straight into his now-glistening eyes, and it was a look that pained him: her wet, sparkling eyes.

The next day he proudly showed the bracelet to Anne and Nancy just before he got onto the trolley to head to South Station in Boston. Anne saw how deeply he cared for this girl she barely knew. He's so young, she thought. But his look of love was ageless, unmistakable. She had known it herself, she missed his dad so. She had dated in recent years. She had an offer of marriage, but passed on it. At age forty-five, she wondered if she would ever again feel what she saw in young

Harry's eyes. She was happy that he felt it now, that he knew that kind of love. Nancy, now fourteen, was tall and slender, with lovely brown curls. She turned the bracelet on her brother's wrist a bit to get a closer look. The giving of an ID bracelet was serious business. She wished she had someone to give one to, but most of the boys in town were off at war these days, like Harry. Certainly all the good ones. She reached up and put her arm around Harry's neck, teased him a bit about it, hugged him, and then waved good-bye.

After their final training in California, Harry and the rest of the draft board the troop carrier USS *Rochambeau* (AP-63), and on November 12, they sail from San Diego.

Their first stop is the Eniwetok Atoll in the Marshall Islands. A chain of forty coral islands, to Harry it is like pages in *National Geographic* come to life. Palms rustle against each other in the wind, making a dry, scratchy noise. The beach is like pink cake flour, and the water is crystal-clear blue, nothing like the thick deep sea green of the Atlantic with its seaweed scent, where he sailed with his dad a lifetime ago.

Back in February, Eniwetok was secured in a fierce battle. Abandoned machines lie along the beach, some half submerged and washed daily by the waves; the men who operated them have moved on to other islands or to God. He tries to picture the fighting, the noise of it all, in this now-blissful place. The atoll's spell is broken only by the bustling on the transport of the arriving Marines, moving and talking around him as they take it in.

They spend the morning in "work parties" on the ship and beach. On *Rochambeau*, Harry has reconnected with a football acquaintance from Medford, Massachusetts, George Colburn. Medford is right next to Arlington, and it warms Harry's heart to hear his familiar Boston accent in the rack below. George signed up for the Marines with his two buddies from Medford High: "Chubby" Cramer, who was no longer chubby after his weeks at Parris Island, and "Red" Francis, whom all the girls liked because of his russet head of hair.

(Back home, George's mother, Mary Ellen Colburn, and Anne Gray learned through the grapevine that their boys were both in the 34th Replacement Draft. They called each other every time one or the other heard from her son, to share their letters and any bits of information they could glean from them.)

It was so cramped for so many weeks on the ship, and so hot, they often slept out on the deck under the stars. In Eniwetok, one of the officers wisely decides it would be a good idea to get the men off the ship and let them run around and have a bit of fun. Everybody needed to let off some steam. There was too much young energy in too-tight quarters, and before it combusted, it was time to let the boys loose for a while. The officers let down a raft from the ship, and as soon as Harry gets wind of what's afoot, he smiles at George. "C'mon, buddy, no time like the present. This is paradise. C'mon, let's go!"

Suddenly, in a heartbeat, hundreds of them are out of their uniforms, tripping over their pants legs to be free, climbing onto the rafts, paddling into the beach. Harry jumps off the raft, disappearing into the cool blue-green silky water. He pops up smiling and laughing. "George! It feels so good. Have you ever felt anything this good?"

Then George jumps and disappears under the cool water, comes up smiling, shaking the water off his eyes, howling and laughing. "I think we must be dead, Harry."

"This is heaven, right?"

"We've died and gone to heaven. It was a hell of a battle, and you're a hero, my friend!"

All the men, most of them just teenagers, are having a ball! They splash water at each other, so happy just to be happy. There are even beers for them on the beach, like a party. "We were like boys that day. We were brothers, we would have done anything for each other," remembers George.[28]

In mid-December, *Rochambeau* docks at Naval Operations Base Guam. Harry writes to his uncle:

Dear Uncle Frank,

I have received your two v mail letters and was very pleased to hear from you. We have had mail twice since we left the States. Both were in Port, but I'm sorry to say I can't tell you where. I received 18 letters the first time and 12 the second.

I was sick at the beginning of the trip, but after a fashion I didn't mind it too much. It is very hot here and I sleep on the weather deck every night. Usually rains sometime during the night, but it never lasts.

We had a fair Thanksgiving, but of course couldn't compare with home. We had turkey, dressing, celery, squash, candy and a cigar. Now we are planning Christmas on board ship.

I think I will see George Smith, if I do he will be quite surprised.

I have been to confession three times since we left. To Mass every Sunday and some weekdays. The Chaplain comes from Jamaica Plain and knows the Priests at St. Agnes. I had quite a chat with him the other night. Bob, the boy from Newton is with me and there are many fellows from my section. I chum around with a fellow from Medford. Will write later. Hope everyone is fine.

Love, Harry[29]

Harry takes out his tiny wallet prayer book and reads the prayer he wrote there after his talk with the chaplain. In blue pen on the blank back page he has written in all caps, "HOLY ST. JOSEPH, SPOUSE OF MARY, BE MINDFUL OF ME, PRAY FOR ME, WATCH OVER ME. GUARDIAN OF THE PARADISE OF THE NEW ADAM, PROVIDE FOR MY SPIRITUAL AND TEMPORAL WANTS. FAITHFUL GUARDIAN OF THE MOST PRECIOUS OF ALL TREASURERS, I BESEECH THEE TO BRING THIS MATTER TO A HAPPY END IF IT BE FOR THE GLORY OF GOD AND THE GOOD OF MY SOUL. AMEN."

※

Charlie Gubish's wife back in Bethlehem waits faithfully in their home near the mill for his letters. Golda and Herman Graeter, Sr., in Dayton also keep an eye out for the mailman each day, hoping for word that their only child is safe. Like Harry's family, they have received the standard postcards with their names filled in by their sons at the top: "Dear _____, I have been transferred overseas and have arrived safely at my destination." The cards were prepared prior to their departure and are sent home after they arrive. They include a San Francisco address to send mail to but of course no indication of where they are now.

The same is true on the ship. Mail call is, for the men who get handfuls of letters at a time, the most uplifting moment of the day or week or weeks, since so much time can go by without any word at all. For those who do not receive any letters, mail drop is a morale killer. The men go their separate ways, to their bunk or any place else where they can take a moment to pore over the good wishes and news from home. It is what keeps them going. They read the letters over and over, sometimes sharing them with one another and talking about the people who sent them. They fill in some of the missing pieces about their families and life back home. Sometimes the letters make them miss home even more. They all try not to let on in their letters how homesick and uneasy they are. Harry, Warren, Charlie, Herman, and George lie in their bunks at night, talking, sometimes hiding tears from one another as they drift off to sleep.

One morning after they have settled in on Guam, Charlie wakes up and nudges "Gray," as he calls him, as they scramble out to line up for work party assignments. "What's up, Pop?" Harry always calls him that since he's twenty-four and Harry is only eighteen. "We never did get the 'beer-a-day' they promised us on the ship." "Yeah, so what are we going to do about it here?" "We are going to ask for it," says Charlie. A smile creeps across Harry's face; he just shakes his head at Pop.

Sure enough, on Saturday, someone takes pity on them and sneaks them a whole case. They down a few beers apiece and share some with their buddies. Harry never really had much beer back in Arlington, and it hits them both pretty fast. They are both leaner and stronger than when they left home and worn down from a week of heavy work rebuilding a church in the hills with the Seabees. With each beer the laughter comes easier, the stories spill out, and Harry is doubled over at Pop's tales of growing up on the farm in Pennsylvania. Harry passes around his picture of Dorothy, which all the guys look at longingly. Warren whistles and says, "Gray, you are a lucky man, my friend." But after a while, the laughter turns to melancholy. Charlie and Harry start talking about home. Charlie tells Harry about his wife and boys and wonders why he signed up for all this. Harry is homesick and hot and tired. Somehow they end up ambling over to the first officer's office. Both are now teary; they tell the officer their woes and say that they just want to go home. He gets their platoon sergeant, who's having none of it and yells, "Get these two goddamn guys out of here or throw 'em in the brig!" But the first officer is kind; he just takes away their guns and knives for the night, so they don't hurt themselves, and makes them get into their sacks. They are asleep in no time, exhausted from drinking and talking and crying and getting into trouble. In the morning, they decide it was all worth it. That spit-warm beer was the best thing they'd had in months.[30]

Warren Graham, the organic chemist from North Carolina, also tempts trouble. He watches the guard near the supplies and studies his pattern of movements. He waits for the perfect moment when the guard is on the opposite side, then gets down onto his belly, crawls over to where the crates of orange and grapefruit juice are kept, and steals a can. He dodges his way back to the guys, and they peel back the top of the can and pass it around, pleased that Graham has pulled it off. Pop chastises him, though. "If they catch you, they're going to kill you, you know," he says as he takes a big gulp.[31] He keeps at it, though he did get written up for something he did on October 17, back at Camp Lejeune. The guys don't know for what, though.[32]

Second Lieutenant Dominick Grossi, 18th Replacement Draft of the 3rd Marine Division, has been in Guam a few weeks already. His parents, at home in Lockport, New York, have received the yellow postcard in the mail that tells them he has safely reached his destination. That is all that Lena and Pasquale Grossi know, and their imaginations fill in the rest on many a night as they toss and turn in bed after their long nights working at their restaurant.

For the first time in years, this fall Dom is not spending the crisp afternoons at football practice. The all-state football star is now preparing for a very different kind of game. He lies in his rack and thinks back to the big send-off he and the other players received. The townspeople turned out in droves to wave their team, now in military uniforms, good-bye as they headed to Parris Island. Dom was always well thought of in Lockport. His earnest face had been splashed across the local sports page, showing him down on one knee, talking to the coach, preparing for Saturday's game. In the Sunday paper, a photo is titled "The Look Back," as Dom is shown running for a touchdown and glancing back over his shoulder to make sure no one is on his tail.

Like so many sailors and Marines, he has been at sea for Thanksgiving, and now Christmas is coming on Guam. In the heat and between rainstorms, he tries to imagine the kitchen at home: his mother stirring pots on the stove, his brother and sisters helping as always. He thinks of his girlfriend, Ruth, and tells his mother that they have been writing to each other; he confides that he has "told her how I feel." He asks his parents to "be good to her." In another letter, he writes:

Tuesday Dec 12, 1944
"12 more shopping days 'til Christmas"

Dearest Mother,
Have finally reached an island and am half settled, but not for long. Am standing by for new orders now. I may move to another part of this island, or move to another island. I'll give you more dope later.
On this particular island it rains eight to twelve times a day. The rainy season is just finishing so it won't be like this all the time.
I'm living in a large tent with six other officers and we have folding cots like those you use for camping. I am washing with rain water that we catch in barrels. We also have an improvised shower made up of a barrel with a pipe attachment that also catches water.

Today we took a ride to the other side of the island to get paid. I drew $100 and paid back $65 that I owed. (Gambling again.) We went about 20 miles and saw quite a bit of the island. We went through areas where a lot of fighting was done and saw many caves in which the Japs fortified themselves. I passed through a town and it was bombed flat. Some of the natives have returned to their shambles and rebuilt small shacks from the lumber they could salvage. The natives are half Korean and half Chamorro. They have American missionaries and all the children go to school every day.

We have movies every night and this evening we had a 15-piece orchestra that played some damn good music.

I received Patrina's letter dated Nov 28, but that was the only one from home. Evidently, some of my mail hasn't caught up with me. Glad to hear everyone is well, especially Junior.

Love Dom

On Christmas Day 1944, the 5th Marine Division begins loading its combat troops on the Big Island of Hawaii. The 4th Marine Division follows suit on December 27 on Maui. As Private Jay Rebstock of the 5th Division, Company E, 27th Marines, loads onto his troop transport, his destination is unknown. The scuttlebutt among the men of the 27th Marines, who are always second-guessing their destination, is that the target is either China or Formosa, which would be just a warm-up for the final target of Okinawa.

The final liberty call in Honolulu is jammed with Marines trying to enjoy the last bit of civilization. "There were ten men for every girl, hamburgers sold out, and the bars were loaded to capacity."[33]

On board the *Haskell*-class attack transports, Marines gear up for battle, cleaning and recleaning weapons; sharpening and resharpening knives. Rebstock loads machine-gun belts and magazines for his Browning automatic rifle. Belowdecks, they sleep five high in cramped quarters, and during the day there is nothing to see but the endless ocean.[34]

A week into the trip, company commanders assemble their men

wherever they can crowd together and crane to see, showing them their first look at where they are headed: Iwo Jima. The men of Company E look at one another and ask, "Where the hell is that?"[35]

When the convoy gets to Saipan, Rebstock reloads onto a landing ship tank (LST) and, after some practice assault runs, waits for D-Day. Briefings are held every day, and the men study the maps and terrain models. They figure that the 13,000 Japanese have to be sick and disoriented from the seventy days of bombardment. The fight should last four, maybe five, days, and once Suribachi is taken, that will be it. In the evenings, they listen to Tokyo Rose tell them that the Imperial Japanese forces are lying in wait for them on Iwo.[36]

The men of the 4th Marine Division sail from Maui on January 8, 1945, to begin their 3,700-mile trek to Iwo Jima. Eniwetok is their first stop, and then they will go on to Saipan and Tinian. In the eyes of the veterans of those previous invasions, the two islands have dramatically changed. Now endless white runways for B-29s replace the battlefield that was once littered with the rotting enemy dead.[37] On January 27, after final rehearsals, they are Iwo Jima bound and sail into the rendezvous area on February 11.

On February 8, 1945, the 3rd Division, now complete with its thirty-fourth replacement draft, begins combat loading in Guam.[38] "Marines write their last letters home. They are allowed to say they are at sea, going into combat—nothing more, except general statements about the weather."[39]

Harry Gray writes:

Jan 16, 1945
Central Pacific

Dear Uncle Frank and family,
*   How is everyone? I have been going to write you many times but something always seemed to come up and I had to put it off. I want to thank you very much for your swell package. It was very delicious and sure came at the right time.*

It was in swell shape. I looked for your friend George to give him some fruit cake but couldn't find him.

I had a letter written to you on the boat but was unable to mail it because many of our activities on the ship which I included were barred. I received your two magazines and Omni book, and thanks from the fellows too as everyone is enjoying them besides me. I also received your v mail of which the last one came yesterday.

I am fine and in good health. During the trip my medical records were lost and upon arrival had to have another physical. Everything is perfect except my teeth and had to have a tooth filled. The only thing I minded then was the two needles before they filled it. Novocain of course.

In our training we have been assigned to our duty when the beachhead is made, I am in what they call "Beach unloading party #3" this means I am in the 3rd wave and unload supplies from Higgins boats. It is a very heavy job but not too much so for me. I think it will be ammunition, but don't know when. After the unloading is completed we shall take our places in the lines or be held in reserve.

It is very warm here but the breeze is very pleasant and keeps the heat down. It usually rains once or twice in 24 hours mostly at night.

Yesterday we went on a twelve mile hike and it was pretty tough. We left camp at 7:20 and were back at 1:00. We made very good time considering the rough terrain.

We have quite a few recreational facilities but not much time. In the first place it is too hot and when the day is over I like to take it easy.

Well I guess that's the news for now. I'll sign off.

With love to everyone
Harry

The 34th Replacement Draft is now attached to the 3rd Pioneer Battalion as part of the division's shore party.[40] That means hitting the beach and handling the massive jobs of unloading and transporting supplies and ammunition, in addition to serving as replacements for the attacking regiments.

On February 17, Transport Squadron 11 weighs anchor in Guam to carry the 3rd Division to the battle area. Harry Gray, Charlie Gubish, George Colburn, Herman Graeter, and Warren Graham are on board USS *President Adams*. Two days later, the ship anchors eighty miles off the volcanic island of Iwo Jima.

14

"Hell with the Fire Out"

Put on the whole armour of God, that ye may be able to stand
against the wiles of the devil.

—Ephesians 6:11, read by a Protestant chaplain on board
the *Bunker Hill*[1]

For four months, air strikes pummel Iwo Jima. On December 8, the
horses of the Seventh Air Force join the hounds of the Navy to again
pound away at its defenses. In the greatest aerial attack of all the battles
of the Pacific theater, B-24 Liberators from the Marianas rain bombs
and explosives on the Bonin Islands for seventy-four straight days.[2]

General Kuribayashi writes letters to his wife; he warns her not
to expect him to return and to get her affairs in order. "Are you still
in Tokyo? Believe me, the bombings will get steadily worse, so I wish
that you'd go to a safe place."[3]

February 11 is the 2,605th anniversary of the founding of the nation of Japan. For the occasion, "Song for the Defense of Iwo," is
played on the radio. The battered men, huddled in their caves and
surviving on water and small vegetables, listen to the children sing.[4]

> *Down south from the imperial city*
> *a small lonely island floats.*
> *The fate of our imperial country*
> *lies in the hands of this island,*
> *Iwo Jima.*

Before D-Day, the Navy carries out three days of heavy bombardment at Iwo Jima. The Marines had requested ten days, but the Navy
insists that its plan "would accomplish all the desired objectives."[5] At
the end of day one, only seventeen targets were destroyed, with seven
hundred more to go.[6]

Despite the Marines' frustration, they put on a good face. Major
General Harry Schmidt, commanding V Amphibious Corps, says,
"The landing force is ready for combat. . . . We expect to get on their
tails and keep on their tails until we chop them off."[7]

For the old salts of the Corps, in combat in the Pacific for more
than two years now, "life boil[s] down to a very simple formula: training for combat, combat, more training, followed by more combat . . .
[and] the certainty that 'another rock' had to be taken."[8]

February 17 is a day of reconnaissance. Iwo Jima is unlike Tarawa,
Saipan, and Roi-Namur with their reefs and lagoons. The landing
vehicles will slam directly from deep water onto a steep black volcanic
ash beach.

No one knows if the beaches or the land beyond will be mined. Will
the tractors hit hard-packed sand, or will they sink in? Answering these
questions is the work of the Underwater Demolitions Team (UDT).

Under gray skies, three battleships and the cruiser *Pensacola* ease
in close to shore as protectors for the men of the UDT operation.
The island is quiet, as it has been in all the reconnaissance photos
and during all the flyovers. Minesweepers move into position just offshore; the battleships fire from three thousand yards at suspected enemy areas to deter any Japanese gunners who might be tempted to fire
at the vulnerable minesweepers. *Pensacola* is just eight hundred yards
off the sheer face of Suribachi, delivering its own cover fire.

At 9:00 a.m., an enemy shell explodes on *Tennessee*. It is just one
and does little damage, but it stuns everyone on board and sets anxious eyes into motion, scanning with binoculars across every crevice
on land, hoping to spot where the gun is that fired the shot. But the
island gives nothing away. *Tennessee* continues its bombardment.

Inside Suribachi, the Japanese soldier behind the 6-inch gun tracks the cruiser *Pensacola*'s every move. The ship is so close to Suribachi that the gunner and his men are shocked that the US cruiser is such a clear target.

For a few moments, the battery's officer resists the temptation to open fire, which he knows will give away his position. But as *Pensacola* stares back at him, he knows that such a moment will not come again. "Fire!" he yells. The first 6-inch shell impacts just fifty yards off target, but in quick succession, the excited Japanese crew sends six more, and they smash into *Pensacola*, sending its men flying and igniting fires on the ship.[9]

The cruiser maneuvers farther offshore, trailed by columns of thick smoke and fire; the men of *Pensacola* frantically scramble onto the deck to extinguish the flames. But *Pensacola* is wounded: when the smoke clears, seventeen men are dead, including the executive officer, and ninety-eight others are wounded.[10]

Watching the smoke rise from *Pensacola*, the other bombardment ships back off their positions close to the island. But ten landing craft, infantry (guns), or LCI(G)s, move in to take their places. These 160-foot gunboats are like floating porcupines, sporting weapons rarely found together on one platform. Each has three 40 mm guns and four 20 mm guns to complement the firepower of its six .50-caliber machine guns. But their most impressive firepower comes from twelve rocket launchers positioned on each of their decks that can deliver rocket fire to support the beach landing.

They move in to within a thousand yards of Iwo Jima's eastern beaches to support the UDT frogmen and unleash a combined seven hundred rockets to flail the three-thousand-yard landing area; 40 mm cannons probe possible enemy concealed positions.

Watching all this through his binoculars, General Kuribayashi is sure that the landing is now under way, and he gives the order to unleash his barrage against the gunboats. It is a devastating bombardment, like a knockout punch.

All the LCI(G)s are hit, as if by volley fire, and in the twelve gunboats, 170 crewmen are killed. The first Japanese shell that slams into

Gunboat 449 wipes out the 40 mm gun mount and its 5-man crew. The second kills 12 more men stationed at the base of the conning tower, and the third hits the bridge, blowing out one side of it and slamming the commander to the deck, killing him.[11] All the other officers are killed or fatally wounded; the quieted gunboat is dead in the water, with no one at its helm.

Lieutenant (Junior Grade) Rufus Herring, hit three times and bleeding, barks over the intercom to the engine room to get the ship moving again as he drags himself to the helm. But he is too weak to stand, so he props himself up among some empty shell casings nearby and gives orders to his men, steering the ship out of the melee and thereby avoiding its destruction.[12] Lieutenant Herring will become the first recipient of the Medal of Honor at Iwo Jima. Before the bloody battle is over, for their extraordinary heroism, twenty-six others will qualify for the Medal of Honor; only half will survive to receive it. Ten valorous men will receive the Navy Cross.[13]

But the Japanese gunners pay a price for this initial victory. The guns that fired on the flotilla have exposed themselves to the searching eyes of the Navy spotters. The battleship *Nevada* trains its 14-inch guns on the discovered targets and pounds away at them. Then she, along with the battleships *Tennessee* and *Idaho*, lays down a thick smokescreen to cover the returning UDT frogmen.

"Swimmers reported beach and surf conditions suitable for a landing. No underwater or beach obstacles existed and the single mine found was destroyed."[14] The divers bring back a sample of sand and have left behind a small sign, WELCOME TO IWO JIMA. The path for invasion is clear.[15]

General Holland "Howlin' Mad" Smith will later say of the fight for the "stone fortress of the sea," "I was not afraid of the outcome of the battle. I knew we would win. We always had. But contemplation of the cost in lives caused me many sleepless nights."[16]

It became clear from reconnaissance before the battle that the sand would pose a problem and that Kuribayashi's defenses, guns, and blockhouses were disappearing underground.

Those who did the planning for the invasion seem to have a good sense of what lies ahead. Their ominous preparations reveal that for the first time in the Pacific theater, each division has its own hospital. Five thousand beds are readied in Saipan and Guam. A marked photo of the island shows where the cemeteries will be located.

The labeling and loading of supplies for Iwo Jima began four months ago, and the sheer volume of them presages a prolonged stay. The 8th Field Depot is the nucleus of combat logistics support for Operation Detachment. Their commanding officer is Lieutenant Colonel Leland Swindler. The Marines under his command include seven original companies plus four depot companies, which include the largest participation of African American supply personnel in the Pacific theater. They are known as the "Montford Point Marines," for their segregated boot camp in Montford Point, North Carolina. (These men, like all Marines, trained first as riflemen and then in logistics and will be among those pulled into active duty as the ranks on Iwo Jima thin.)[17]

The cargo includes enormous amounts of pencils, matches, toilet paper, gasoline, socks, bullets, prepainted wooden crosses, flares, dog food, holy water, fingerprint ink, cigars, and asphalt-laying machines, among a myriad of other things. "The Fifth Division alone carrie[s] 100 million cigarettes and enough food to feed Columbus, Ohio for thirty days."[18]

ᚷ

At 3:00 a.m. on D-Day, February 19, the landing force is called to chow. Amid the usual clanking of metal trays and utensils as the Marines eat their "warrior's breakfast" of steak and eggs, there is little chatter in the crowded galleys. The weight of what is upon them is sinking in. After the days at sea and the monotonous circling offshore, it is time to go. Some cannot eat; those whose stomachs are not knotted up by nerves happily wolf down what their buddies leave on their plates.

As the call to embark comes, Private First Class Jay Rebstock, in the 5th Division's 2nd Battalion, is in the well deck of an LST where the LVTs are revving their engines. Sergeants hand out extra supplies wherever they can be stashed in the wells: ammo, explosives, land mines, and in Rebstock's case, a five-gallon can of water.[19]

Private Rebstock is rough and ready, sporting a new tattoo. He hunkers in the well deck, glad that he will not have to climb over the side of a troop transport, dangling on a cargo net, where the slightest misstep into a bobbing and pitching Higgins boat can be fatal. Rebstock will ride into battle on the LST; then, when the well deck opens, he'll head down the ramp and splash into the blue Pacific.

Naval gunfire is in full force as the Marines hustle down to the tank deck of the LST, loaded for combat under their heavy packs. They swing over the sides of the tractors, and Rebstock pulls himself up, along with his heavy water can. Once they are in the well deck, the engine noise is deafening, and the men's nostrils burn with a quick intake of suffocating fumes.

A haze hovers above the tractors, and the men begin choking and grabbing for their gas masks, which do no good, because they are designed to filter, not provide fresh air. For thirty excruciating minutes the men sit in this metal tomb, coughing and gagging. The open air of the Higgins boat looks pretty good to Rebstock now as he fears he could die right here, suffocating before he even hits the beach.[20]

With a great bang, the bow doors of the LST open; air and sunlight hit Rebstock's face as the first tractor lurches forward. Like a great hippo, the ungainly tractor waddles down the ramp and into the water, nose first.[21]

It bobs to the surface, rights itself, and churns away just as the second tractor makes its plunge. Rebstock is next, and in seconds he and fifteen other Marines are part of a great swirling circle of tractors, like horses walking in circles before heading to a starting gate. They stay in motion to keep their momentum; they are champing at the bit, their breakfast lying heavily in their stomachs. The LVTs gather, form up, and move to the line of departure. The signal blares, and they are off; the run-in to the beaches has begun. Rebstock feels the sea air on his cheeks; he glances over the side of his tractor, and his chest swells at the sight of the small American flag on each LVT, flapping in the ocean wind.

Four hundred eighty-two amtracs sprawl across the sea, carrying eight assault battalions into combat.[22] All the while, the great bombardment ships are shelling the shoreline with their island-shaking blasts. He smiles as he and his buddies look knowingly at one another. There is no way anyone can survive this pounding. In amazement, they watch the island explode. They know that "when Suribachi falls, it's over."[23]

"We'd listened to Tokyo Rose a lot," Rebstock will later say, "and she told us we were going to Iwo. When we got briefed on the operation we were told it was a real small island with about 13,000 Japs: they were sickly and wounded, and wouldn't put up much of a fight. We'd been bombing them for [seventy-four] days and we were going in there to mop them up in three to five days."[24]

At 8:30 a.m., the assault wave crosses the line of departure, four thousand yards offshore. The run-in will take thirty minutes. Five minutes behind the first wave comes the second, and five minutes behind it, the third starts off.

Rebstock watches the steady, majestic march of the assault waves; he is proud to be part of them as they surge toward Iwo's black sands. He remembers his studies at Gulf Coast Military Academy and a poem by Alfred, Lord Tennyson, who wrote of the advancing cavalry in "The Charge of the Light Brigade":

Half a league, half a league,
Half a league onward,
All in the valley of Death
Rode the six hundred.

"They marched onward under the greatest cannonade of naval gunfire that they could ever imagine."[25] In those thirty minutes, US warships salvo more than eight thousand rounds.[26]

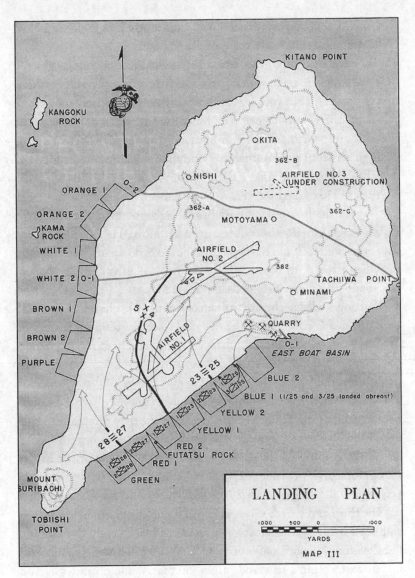

KITANO POINT

KANGOKU
ROCK

OKITA

362-B

NISHI

AIRFIELD NO. 3
(UNDER CONSTRUCTION)

ORANGE 1   O-2

ORANGE 2

362-A

362-C

KAMA
ROCK

MOTOYAMA O

WHITE 1

AIRFIELD
NO. 2

WHITE 2 O-1

382

TACHIIWA POINT

BROWN 1

O MINAMI

5

4

BROWN 2

QUARRY

AIRFIELD
NO. 1

O-1

PURPLE

EAST BOAT BASIN

23 ≡ 25

BLUE 2

BLUE 1 (1/25 and 3/25 landed abreast)

YELLOW 2

YELLOW 1

28 ≡ 27

RED 2

FUTATSU ROCK

RED 1

MOUNT
SURIBACHI

GREEN

LANDING   PLAN

1000   500   0   1000

YARDS

MAP III

TOBIISHI
POINT

Two minutes after 9:00 a.m., the first assault wave of troops (the second wave behind the gunboats) slams onto the three-thousand-yard-long beach. Marines from the 4th and 5th Divisions swarm over the sides of their tracked vehicles "and hit the volcanic sand at a run that slow[s] almost immediately to a laborious walk as their feet s[i]nk ankle deep into soft, loose volcanic ash."²⁷

They feel as though they are being sucked into a strange glue; it feels like a nightmare in which you try to run, move forward, get away from something, but your legs are so heavy they can barely move. But this is real. It is only fifteen feet wide, the first terrace, but some of the men are crawling and reaching hand over hand as if swimming through a viscous pool. Others are upright but leaning so far forward that they are half bent; they gain a few steps, only to slide back down.

Private First Class Rebstock, on Red Beach 1, gasps as he fights halfway up the first terrace. His Browning automatic rifle and extra ammo weigh him down, and he can barely move. He curses the forty days at sea and feels out of shape until he looks down and sees that his right hand is still firmly clutching the five-gallon water can that he was supposed to have dropped on the beach.

Cursing under his breath, he shakes it out of his hand, and it rolls back down. He struggles to the top of the second terrace, finally out of the quicksand; his boots hit firmer ground, and he can now pick up the pace toward the western side.

It is less than a half mile across the narrow neck of Iwo Jima, but to the south of the neck looms Mount Suribachi.

Elements of the 28th Marines break off in that direction to surround the base, while Rebstock's 27th Marines presses on.

So far, gaining the beach itself has been the whole of the battle. Except for a brief fusillade from one blockhouse, their way is relatively easy. Again Rebstock wonders if maybe they are in for a cakewalk.²⁸

The third and fourth waves now pile up on the beach behind them and begin their fight against the grip of the black sand. The 4th and 5th Divisions "[report] only scattered mortar, artillery, and small-arms fire, and excepting a few land mines, no man-made obstacles . . . on the beaches."²⁹ The first thirty minutes on Iwo Jima are passed in a strange, eerie calm, just a *pop-pop* from here and there, a last gasp, perhaps, from the survivors of the hellish bombardment.

From his post, Kuribayashi scans the beach through his binoculars. He is ready. He gives the signal, and the calm explodes into chaos.

The Japanese general's plan is in motion. His strategy: "Let the Marines land against light opposition. Make them lift naval gunfire and halt air support to avoid hitting their own troops. . . . Let the beaches pile up with men and equipment. Then cut off further landings with smothering artillery and mortar fire. . . . Let outfits ashore bleed to death with casualties."[30]

The second half hour is hell on Earth. In a single breath, the Marines' world dissolves into explosions, jettisoned body parts, and death. *Time* correspondent Robert Sherrod is there: "They died with the greatest possible violence. Nowhere in the Pacific have I seen such badly mangled bodies. Many were cut squarely in half. Legs and arms lay 50 feet away from any body."[31]

"The beaches were pulverized with every conceivable type of fire, and waves of raining shells swept back and forth like a giant scythe. Marine bodies were crushed, and landing crafts exploded. . . . Men from the first waves, already wounded and awaiting evacuation, were annihilated, along with the medical personnel attending them."[32]

One hour into the fight, Company B, including Private First Class Charles Tatum, is pinned down between the second and third terraces by the sudden enemy barrage.

"I could feel the hard concussions from nearby hits," Tatum will later say. "Fear was now a stark reality, as real as the hideous death and carnage occurring on all sides of us. . . . We moved out, crawling. It was the only option that seemed open to us."[33]

An explosion detonates in front of him, then another in the same place. He thinks the enemy gunners have him zeroed. Then two more come in the same place. As he burrows down into the sand, the concussions force grit into his eyes and mouth; he gags on it and spits it out.

A hand whacks him powerfully on the helmet. He looks up and sees the familiar snarling face of Marine Corps Gunnery Sergeant John Basilone staring down at him. The Medal of Honor recipient from Guadalcanal is shaking him and frantically pointing at the swirling sand, where the enemy mortars continue to land.

Tatum squints to see through the blinding sand and only then makes out the shape of a blockhouse. The explosions he thought were impacting mortar rounds were not mortars at all but concussions from the muzzle blasts of a Japanese gun.

Tatum brings his machine gun into action and pulls the trigger, but nothing happens. Sand and grit jam the breech. The Japanese gun continues to fire as Tatum rolls onto his side. "Why did this have to happen now?" he yells as he fumbles for a brush to clean the breech.[34]

He rolls back over, sets the gun in the tripod, and reloads. He instinctively pulls back on the bolt and lets it slam forward, chambering a .30-caliber round. Half expecting the gun not to fire again, he is relieved to hear it spring to life and watches as his tracer rounds bounce harmlessly off the wall of the blockhouse.

Basilone nudges him to move to the right, to face the blockhouse aperture at an angle. Tatum's second burst sends a stream of bullets into the enemy position. The Japanese slam the gun port closed.

Now the enemy is blind, and Tatum wants him to stay that way. He fires a few more short bursts. A demolitions man advances just wide of his streaming fire to hurl a satchel charge of composition C-2 at the base of the closed metal door. The explosion sends concrete and metal particles flying.

Before the Japanese can recover, Basilone signals for Tatum to keep firing and directs a flamethrower to advance on the same line, just wide of the covering machine-gun fire. Ignited napalm pours from the nozzle into the now-gaping hole in the bunker.

"There was a loud roar and it looked like a fire-spitting dragon's tongue had erupted," says Tatum. "The unsuspecting and stunned men inside . . . were cast instantly into the jaws of a roaring inferno: an incinerating hell."[35]

The attack is by the book, the way all the Marines have been trained and the way this island's defenses will have to be overcome. Basilone has just shown them how to do it.

Moments later, the hero of Guadalcanal and four members of his platoon, making their way across Motoyama 1, are hit by mortars that kill all of them. Basilone, who was sent home after Guadalcanal and then traveled the United States, telling his heroic story and promoting war bonds, had insisted on rejoining the fight in the Pacific, only to be killed on D-Day at Iwo Jima. When Basilone is hit and dies, the news travels up and down the landing beaches. Everyone realizes that if he didn't make it, they had better start fighting or they won't make it, either. The New Jersey native, who will posthumously receive the Navy Cross, was twenty-eight years old.[36]

In the initial calm on the beaches, eight assault battalions from the two divisions make it ashore. But they are surrounded by hulking, steaming wreckage.

Trucks carrying vital supplies are backed up on the beaches behind them or stuck in the sand. The men of the replacement drafts take on the backbreaking work of carrying them inland from the water while navigating wreckage, sand, and incoming fire. According to the historian Larry Smith, "Tanks and half-tracks lay crippled where they had bogged down in the coarse sand. Amphibian tractors . . . lay flopped on their backs. Cranes, brought ashore to unload cargo, tilted at insane angles, and bulldozers were smashed in their own roadways."[37]

Among the mangled bodies, many of them smashed beyond recognition, is the debris of war. According to a history of the 4th Division, "Packs, gas masks, rifles, and clothing, ripped and shattered by shell fragments, lay scattered across the beach. Toilet articles and even letters were strewn among the debris, as though war insisted on prying into the personal affairs of those it claimed."[38]

As the 5th Division pushes across the neck of the island, the Marines of the 4th Division, on the right, make it to the edge of the Motoyama 2 airfield, but they pay an enormous price for their advance: in taking the imposing ridges of the rock quarry on their right flank, overlooking the east boat basin, they lose 35 percent of their men.[39]

Twelve guns of the 14th Marines (artillery) attempt to land to provide fire for the 4th Division against the Japanese guns, but it proves disastrous. Only four guns make it to shore. Seven others are lost when the crafts transporting them are sunk, and the eighth and final gun lands with defective sights.

According to Lieutenant John Chapin, "There was no cover from enemy fire. Japs deep in reinforced concrete pillboxes laid down interlocking bands of fire that cut whole companies to ribbons."[40]

The Marines crowd onto the narrow beachhead in full view of the Japanese gunners looking down upon them. Protective counterbattery fire from artillery and offshore naval guns is mostly ineffective against the burrowed-in enemy, and any fire meant to impact on an observed enemy position explodes harmlessly on a now-empty position. As soon as the fire sweeps past, the enemy guns and gunners reemerge to hammer the pinned-down Marines.

According to combat correspondent David Dempsey, "The invasion beach of this island is a scene of indescribable wreckage—all of it ours. Japanese artillery, rockets and heavy mortars laid a curtain of fire along the shore. They couldn't miss and they didn't."[41]

The horrific losses experienced during the first two days lead the V Amphibious Corps commander, Major General Schmidt, to call for part of his floating reserves.

The 3rd Marine Division is anchored in an ocean corral for ships eighty miles southeast of Iwo Jima. With its three infantry regiments—the 3rd, 9th, and 21st Marines—the 3rd Division is the reserve of the V Amphibious Corps. The status of the two assault divisions, the 4th and 5th, already deep into the island and swamped with casualties, is unknown to the men on the ships offshore. Their job is to wait and, if called upon, to move in and do their part. When and if that call comes, the 21st Marines will be first into action.

The ships—*Cape Johnson, President Adams, Callaway, Frederick Funston*, and *Napa*—steam in like dark shadows. Just before midnight, the last of them arrives.[42] Among the small flotilla are two ships that carry a grim reminder of the reality of battle: *Fayette* and *James O'Hara* are transporting Marines designated as the 28th and 34th Replacement Drafts.

Every man in the invasion force has carefully studied the models and terrain maps of the pork chop–shaped barren rock, which translates from the Japanese name as "Sulfur Island," and sees it as another typical island invasion against strong beach defenses, backed up by a main line of resistance defended by a fanatical Japanese enemy who will, in final desperation, hurl himself at the Marines in a human wave, a banzai charge. There will be few enemy survivors when it is over, and then it will be time to look to the next island, and maybe, just maybe, that one will be the last.

The tactics are simple: There is always a frontal attack. There is no room on these tiny islands for grand maneuvers and flanking. The troops are to cut the island in half, sweep one half clear of all enemy resistance, and then attack the remaining half until the last remnants of the enemy are driven into the sea or left buried in caves. These are the bloody lessons of three years of fighting the Japanese from island to island: the need for close artillery support, the benefits of flame-throwers, demolitions, and tank infantry tactics when dealing with an enemy who will never surrender.[43]

The Japanese have no reinforcements; those days died at Guadalcanal. The banzai charges have been costly, flushing the enemy out into the Marines' field of fire. Despite the savagery and terror of the screaming charges, the Marines pray for them to come. The killing purges in the open fields mean they will not have to dig the enemy out of his caves.

The Japanese now have only the men on the island. There is no navy, and the few remaining aircraft they have cannot do much damage. This is 1945, not 1941, and the Rising Sun is setting, but it sits burning red on the horizon. Bitter fighting lies ahead, but two days into Iwo Jima, there is still the pervasive notion among the Americans that it might take only a few more days.

And then it will be on to the next island and then to Japan. They know that the road home runs through Tokyo. But first, this island, seven hundred miles south of the Japanese mainland, must fall.

The orders for the reserve division are to be ready, from D + 1 onward, to go wherever they are needed. Since the reserves are always called upon to save the day, to plug a gap in the lines, or to relieve a hard-pressed fighting force, they are trained to pass through the lines of a beleaguered force to keep the forward momentum of an attack.[44]

But there is another possible mission: "The division might be required to take up a defensive position to cover a withdrawal."[45]

A withdrawal! The word conjures up visions of defeat, heavy casualties, even capture. The 3rd Division's 21st Marines came into being because of a withdrawal. Formed to replace the lost regiment of the original 3rd Division, the 4th Marines ceased to exist in 1942, losing its colors in the crushing defeat at Corregidor. The Bataan Death March followed, and the specter of the fate of those lost Marines still looms large in the minds of Americans.

The call to action for the Marines of the 3rd Division comes quickly. The reserve flotilla weighs anchor and steams to within fifteen thousand yards of the Iwo invasion beaches. The klaxons and boatswains' pipes call the Marines to their debarkation stations, and all eyes strain to see the island. It is a blur, shrouded in explosions, smoke, and haze. Only the mouth of the volcano Suribachi thrusts above the haze into the blue-gray sky. An artillery observer says that it looks like "Hell with the fire out."[46]

As planned, the 21st Marines is committed first. Its Higgins boats lower into the water, and each of the coxswains maneuvers his forty-foot boat to just touch the sides of the ship. Cargo netting flaps down against the sides, toward the bobbing boats.

It's time to go. Four at a time, the men climb over, their feet finding the first horizontal strand, then searching for the next one as the nets slam against the ship. They must remember not to grip the rope where a buddy might crush their hand. A fall can be, and sometimes is, deadly, as they well know.

According to Private First Class Charles Tatum, "Climbing down rope nets with full gear and weapons require[s] the agility of a monkey, combined with the skill and daring of a trapeze artist, to avoid being slammed against the side of the APA and being crushed by the LCVP as it pitched and rolled."[47]

The regiment completes debarking at noon, and the landing craft move to the rendezvous area to circle, awaiting their time to cross the line of departure. Five minutes will separate the landings of the successive waves.

The circling is interminable: hour after hour of nauseating rocking, rolling, and pitching. The bottoms of the landing craft slosh with seawater and sometimes vomit, and still there is no call to land. Instead, late in the afternoon, the boats are sent back to their ships for the men to reembark. There is congestion on the beach, and waves of Marines are backed up, trying to land on the beach or stuck on it.

The climb back up the nets is even more treacherous. The men's packs and clothing are now sopped in seawater. In their frenzy to climb, dozens of men miss their leap to the cargo nets and fall into the heaving water below. Frantic recovery efforts ensue; some are pulled out, some slip beneath the surface—gone forever.

Several of the boats cannot maneuver back into position for the reembarkation, so they drift off and the men spend a miserable night tossing about, as a twenty-knot gale lashes the invasion area with seven-foot waves.[48]

But the next morning, February 21, the men of the 3rd Division's 21st Marines again load into their crafts, and this time they land on Yellow beaches 1 and 2. They are immediately attached to the 4th Marine Division for operations, and during the next two days, they attack up the terraced slopes while Japanese gunners pound away at them, devastating their ranks.

The men of the 21st Marines struggle to the edge of the Motoyama 2 airfield, where they pause to await the support of twelve tanks. Taking the runways is crucial to the capture of Iwo Jima.

The tanks come under direct large-caliber enemy fire and enemy mines as they hit the southern edge of the airfield. The infantry, without tank support, makes some progress on the western edge of the field, but there are hundreds of pillboxes and the Japanese have all the approaches covered in intersecting fields of fire. For four hours on February 23, the surviving Marines struggle against the hardened positions.

Among them is Corporal Hershel Woodrow "Woody" Williams of Quiet Dell, West Virginia. Woody is the youngest of eleven children, all delivered not by a doctor but by a neighbor of his mother. Williams says of his upbringing, "We were country, country. Dairy farmers." He never had any problem following orders, because his father always said, "I am only going to tell you one time, I'm not going to tell you twice." In 1942, he was too short to enlist, but in 1943, in need of more recruits, the Marines lowered the height requirement to five feet, two inches, and that was when Williams became a Marine.[49]

"We'd been there for two days, we had lost so many people. When we hit the beach, I had six Marines in my unit, flamethrower demolition people that could do either one. But we'd lost all those. So we gathered in a group, and the commanding officer asked me, the last flamethrower left, could I do something about some of these pillboxes that got us stalled? I was told I said, 'I'll try.' I picked four men to protect me while I'm using the flamethrower to try to eliminate the pillboxes. Two of those Marines sacrificed their lives protecting mine."[50]

Carrying the seventy-two-pound weapon on his back and with the cover of four riflemen who fire away and keep the Japanese pinned down or away from the pillbox apertures, Williams charges his first target. With his left hand, he squeezes the handle to light the sparking igniter. He braces himself for the recoil and, with his right hand, squeezes the trigger.

Williams shoots a fiery, seven-second stream of ignited jellied gasoline directly into the pillbox. Everyone inside is incinerated in an instant. "Killing with a rifle or a grenade is different than with a flamethrower. There is nothing like that smell, killing by consuming with fire." A Japanese soldier leaps from his hidden position near another pillbox, and Williams ignites him in his tracks. In quick succession, his four rifleman protectors are all dead or hit. "So then I began

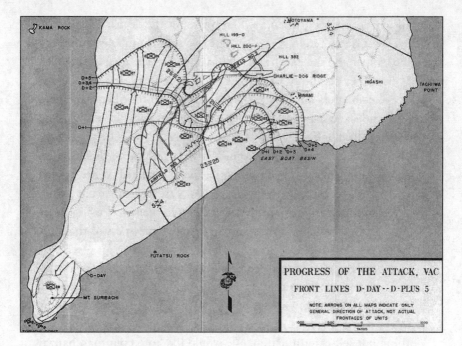

working by myself. I didn't have any more pole charge people. So in the process of four hours, I was able to use up six flamethrowers and eliminate the enemy within seven pillboxes. I have no explanation of how I did it. I don't remember how or when I got the other five flamethrowers. Why they didn't get me, why the mortars didn't get me, why the bullets didn't get me, I have no explanation for that."[51] For his "aggressive fighting spirit and valiant devotion to duty," Hershel Williams received the Medal of Honor for his heroism.[52]

But despite the heroics of the 21st Marines, it is unable to hold its hard-won positions and is forced to retreat to its initial position south of the runway.[53]

On February 22, D + 3, Lieutenant General Keller Rockey throws the entire 5th Division forward in an attempt to dislodge the enemy. Ten officers are killed, joining the ten killed the day before. Thirty-five men are lost in four days of combat.[54] Kuribayashi's killing fields carpet the island. There are no weak points.

The volcano, inert when the first waves hit the beach, roars to life like a beast disturbed in sleep. It is not lava that rumbles within but a hail of sniper and mortar fire that rains down on the men of the 28th Marines. They squint up its dusty, craggy ridges, trying to figure out where the shooters are. Inside, in interlocking rooms and caves, are several thousand Japanese fighters who live in the tunnels, having spent months digging them.

American GIs write letters home as the earth around them shakes with the unrelenting bombardment. Private Richard Wheeler will later say, "It was terrible, the worst [fire] I can remember us taking. The Jap mortarmen seemed to be playing checkers and using us as squares."[55] But on D + 4, February 23, the relentlessness of the 28th Marines pays off and it encircles the base of Suribachi.

Colonel Kanehire Atsuji, commanding the Suribachi sector's defenders, signals his dire situation to General Kuribayashi: "The enemy air, sea, and land attacks are serious. Now the enemy began to burn us with the flame throwers. If we keep ourselves intact, we shall just get nothing but self-extermination. We would like to go out for a banzai charge."[56]

Kuribayashi angrily replies to this challenge to his orders, "I had imagined the fact that the 1st airfield should fall into the enemy's hands. But what is the matter that Mt. Suribachi would fall within only 5 days?"[57]

At 8:00 a.m. on Friday, February 23, a tiny reconnaissance force of four men from Company F begins a slow crawl up the steep face of the mountain high above the invasion beaches. Four soldiers—Sergeant Sherman Watson and Privates Louis Charlo, Theodore White, and George Mercer—climb for forty minutes to the edge of the crater.

At the summit, they see an unattended battery of heavy machine guns with ammunition stacked neatly next to them. There are no Japanese in sight. Watson signals the men back down, and they slide to their starting point among the rocks below to report their findings.[58]

Quickly Lieutenant Colonel Chandler Johnson assigns the task to seize and hold the crest to First Lieutenant Harold G. Schrier of

Company E. He is to lead a forty-man patrol to the top, secure the crater, and raise a small fifty-four-by-forty-six-inch American flag so the whole island can see that the Marines now control the mountain.

The dramatic ascent of Lieutenant Schrier's patrol up the face of Suribachi is witnessed by all. The tiny figures are outlined against the steep, barren slope. One Marine quips, "Those guys ought to get flight pay."

Climbing Mount Suribachi with the Marines that day is Father Charles Suver, S.J., the chaplain of the 5th Marine Division, one of nineteen Catholic priests accompanying the invasion of Iwo Jima. Just days ago, a young lieutenant assured Father Suver that he intended to plant an American flag at the top of Suribachi. The priest told him that if he succeeded, he would say Mass right under that flag. Before they disembarked for the island, the men, many of whom were about to die, asked the priest about duty and courage. He told them, "A courageous man goes on fulfilling his duty despite the fear gnawing away inside. Many men are fearless, for many different reasons, but fewer are courageous." During the first hellish days of the battle, Father Suver, at great personal risk, ministered to the wounded and administered last rites to the dying. On February 23, he follows the men up the mountain and says Mass on the craggy ridges of Suribachi, under the misty skies, amid the chaos of war. He will later say he could hear the Japanese murmuring in their caves nearby.[59]

At 10:15 a.m., the patrol stands high atop the crest, almost six hundred feet above the sea. Sergeant Louis R. Lowery, a photographer from *Leatherneck* magazine, snaps photos all along the way.

Two Marines rummage in the rubble scattered in the crater and find a twenty-foot length of pipe that was part of the cistern to collect rainwater. Lieutenant Schrier and Sergeant Ernest Thomas, Jr., quickly attach the small flag to the pipe. Lowery positions himself slightly on the downslope of the crater wall to snap the picture as the flag goes up.

As the Marines push the pole into the rocky ground, the flag unfurls and snaps high in the wind. Private First Class Tatum is watching from his position with the 27th Marines but at the moment is looking away. His buddy slaps him on the back and points to the crest of Suribachi. "Tatum. Do you see that?"

He turns to see "our *Stars and Stripes* clearly on the peak, waving in the breeze. The 28th Marines . . . now, 'kings of Iwo Jima's hill!'"[60]

Jay Rebstock and his Company E men are preparing to continue their attack along the western coast. Suddenly there is cheering all across the front, and they hear the blasts and whistles from the ships at sea.

"The flag's up," someone says, and they all look to the top of the mountain and holler and yell with joy. Tears fill Rebstock's eyes as his chest swells with pride. Most important, this is the fifth day; all their briefings predicted that it would take five days to gain Suribachi, and when Suribachi falls, the end will be near.[61]

As Lou Lowery's camera shutter snaps the dramatic photo, two Japanese soldiers charge out from concealed positions, hurling grenades in a headlong attack. One heads straight for the flag raisers, brandishing his drawn sword. Private First Class James Robeson, who refused to be in the flag-raising picture, shoots him, and he falls head over heels into the crater below, his sword snapping under him as he careens downward.[62]

The other lobs his grenade toward Lowery, who vaults out of his position in the crater and over the rim to avoid it, but now he's sliding downward, his arms, legs, and hands clawing at the ground to slow down. He lands fifty feet down; his camera is smashed, but the precious film inside is intact.[63] When the photo is developed, he sees that he has captured the moment: the flag raisers planting Old Glory as one Marine looks outward, keeping watch, rifle at the ready.

From far below on the beach, the flag looks tiny, and Lieutenant Colonel Johnson fears that "some son of a bitch is going to want that flag, but he's not going to get it. That's our flag."[64]

So he dispatches a runner to the nearby beached LST 779, and Ensign Alan S. Wood gives him the ship's flag. It is fifty-six by ninety-six inches, twice the size of the one flying now. Johnson sends the large flag to the top and orders his men to "bring ours back." (Others report that Secretary of the Navy James Forrestal came ashore and said that the flag raised on Suribachi ensured that there would be a Marine Corps for another five hundred years, and he wanted it for posterity. That meant they would have to send up another one.)

Associated Press photographer Joe Rosenthal, who is covering the southern beaches that morning, missed the first flag raising and heads up to catch the second one. As he arrives at the top, the first flag is coming down, and six other Marines have already put the new flag on another pipe and are standing ready to place it into the existing hole. He has no chance to get a dual-action shot.

He scrambles to get a good angle, but time is running out. He piles a few lava stones on top of each other, and as he steps upon them, he sees, out of the corner of his eye, that the Marines with the new flag are moving the long pole forward. The first Marine crouches down to place his end of the flagpole into the rocky ground.

All Rosenthal can do is take a quick sight and hope for the best. "I swung my camera around and held it until I could guess that this was the peak of the action," he will later say, "and shot."[65] He continues to prowl the top of the mountain and shoots seventeen other photos. In the evening, he returns to his ship and sends the film off to Guam for development. He dropped the camera in the surf earlier in the day and just hopes that the film is still good.

The historian and former Marine Joseph Alexander will write that Lou Lowery's dramatic photograph "would become a valued collector's item. But Rosenthal's would enthrall the free world."[66] The six Marines whose pictures were hastily snapped as they raised the flag, not facing the camera, were:

Corporal Harlon Block
Corporal Harold Keller[67]
Private First Class Franklin Sousely
Sergeant Michael Strank
Private First Class Harold Schultz[68]
Private First Class Ira Hayes

On this fifth day of the savagery that is the Battle of Iwo Jima, the elation of the flag raising is short lived. In 1942, Winston Churchill spoke words that are so true on day five of this battle: "Now this is not the end. It is not even the beginning of the end, but it is, perhaps, the end of the beginning."[69] In less than a week, three of the flag raisers will be dead, and there is a long and brutal month of fighting yet to come.

As Father Suver will later observe, the most remarkable thing about Iwo Jima was the courage of the ordinary Marines and the care they showed for each other.[70]

15

The Badlands

After the flag raising, it was a horror.[1]

—George J. Colburn, 3rd Division, 9th Infantry Regiment

Bang! The supply crates on the beach rattle as explosions rock the ground up north. The ships offshore hurl 2,500 tons of exploding steel into enemy positions on airfield Motoyama 2. Air strikes quickly follow as the Marines attempt to attack the runway from the other direction.

Off the northern tip of Motoyama 1, two small taxiways connect the two airfields. The plan is to deploy a column of tanks to follow the taxiway from Motoyama 1 to the left flank of Motoyama 2 and attack from there.

It is 9:15 a.m. on Saturday, February 24. As the tanks lumber out onto the western end of the second airfield, Companies I and K of the 3rd Battalion, 21st Marines, will follow three other battalions of tanks across in a coordinated attack.[2]

But the plan implodes. The Japanese have seeded the connecting taxiway with antitank mines. The first tank in the column hits a mine and grinds to a halt. The column presses forward, but now the second tank is hit and explodes in a burst of scorching flame, triggered by a tremendous five-hundred-pound aerial torpedo rigged as a mine.[3]

Again the staggered column lurches forward, straight into the teeth of Japanese antitank fire coming from the fifty-foot ridge at the intersection of the northeast–southwest runway and the east–west runway eight hundred yards to the east. In minutes, three more tanks are hit and disabled. The remaining tanks, blocked by the five smoldering hulks to their front and outgunned by the Japanese high-velocity antitank weapons, abandon the attack and withdraw to the first airfield under cover of smoke grenades. Fifteen tank crewmen are killed or wounded.[4]

Major Holly Evans, commanding the 3rd Tank Battalion, will later say, "On the second day of fighting for Motoyama 2, only 19 of my original 46 tanks were operative. We were hit by anti-tank weapons, machine gun cannon, five-inch guns, and 150mm mortars, as well as mines of all descriptions. Most of our men and equipment were lost on the airfield—ten tanks were knocked out on the strip within a few hours."[5]

With no tank support for the Americans, the advantage shifts to the Japanese. The 21st Marines, poised to attack from the southern tip of the airfield as part of the tank and infantry assault, now have no choice but to go forward without support. Going forward is a bad idea, but it's the only idea available. Waiting is not an option on Iwo Jima.

As long as the Japanese can hold fast to their perch on Motoyama Plateau, they have eyes everywhere. The dirt-brown, barren island slopes downward and away from them. It is a near-perfect shooting gallery. Every bit of beach, every makeshift medical station, every foxhole and crater stretches out below. Bullets rain down on the advancing Marines and the already wounded men waiting for evacuation. They blow apart supplies, ignite crates of ammo, and keep every nerve on edge, every minute of every hour. They are ready and waiting for the next armored column that comes along to try again on Motoyama 1.

The two companies of the 3rd Battalion, 21st Marines, about to attack from just off the southern tip of the airfield, will be the first to test Kuribayashi's main line of resistance for the defense of Iwo Jima. After the fall of Suribachi, the general's plan left the south of the island passive and the beaches with a strong defense. The core of

The Badlands

his resistance is a line across the middle, extending from northwest to southeast through Motoyama 2 airfield, with its flanks anchored on the opposite coasts. A final defensive line has been installed to the north in the vicinity of the unfinished airfield number 3.[6]

The V Amphibious Corps's commander, Major General Schmidt, knows there can be no pause while Kuribayashi relentlessly pounds the Marines from the plateau. He tells his aides, "We'll keep hitting them. They can't take it forever. We've got to keep pressing until they break."[7]

He has already committed one regiment of his reserve 3rd Division—the 21st—to the battle, and now he calls for a second regiment, the 9th. The battle is only five days old, and he is already reduced to a single reserve regiment, the 3rd.

The 21st Marines prepare to attack down the center of the Motoyama Plateau to seize the second airfield. It is wedged between the 5th Division, attacking on its left, and the 4th Division, to which it is attached, on its right.

Lieutenant Colonel Wendell H. Duplantis, commanding the 3rd Battalion, having observed the destruction of his supporting armored column, curses loudly and races to a foxhole near the southern tip of the airfield. Two of his company commanders are dug in, staring across the concrete flatland; they will have to negotiate under fire to seize the dominating high ground half a mile distant.

"We're in one sonuvabitchin' mess," he barks to twenty-two-year-old Captain Clayton Rockmore, the commander of Company I, and twenty-four-year-old Captain Rodney Heinze, commanding Company K. "But we've got to have the goddamned airstrip today."[8] At 9:10 a.m., Duplantis is ordered to "jump off on time, tanks or no tanks."[9]

At 9:30 a.m., fifteen minutes past the attack hour, Duplantis receives another order that there will not be three battalions of tanks, but there will be one company, six tanks from the 4th Marine Division, to support Company I against attacks from the pillboxes.[10]

The assault against the commanding heights to the north of the

[237]

two airstrips is a daunting task with little to no tank support. Japanese artillery and high-velocity guns fire straight down the runways; their 47 mm antitank gun can penetrate up to four inches of tank armor.[11] To get to the high ground, the Marines will have to run the gauntlet of the long axis of the runway shooting alley.

It will be a frontal attack across an open field. If there is any silver lining at all, it is that with Suribachi quiet, they will not be shot at from behind. Ahead, it is a straight lunge into the line of fire. First Lieutenant Raoul Archambault, the Company K executive officer, looks out over the flat runways and thinks, "This is fighting on a pool table."[12]

The two companies of the 21st Marines move out thirty minutes late, with Company K advancing mostly on the mile-long northeast–southwest runway and Company I paralleling it on the right. The objective is eight hundred yards away.

As they set off, the eight hundred Japanese pillboxes that ring the field and the high ground to the north spring to life, and the Marines quicken their pace. The two captains are everywhere, shouting orders, pointing out targets, encouraging their men, and the green line surges forward. Captain Rockmore, at the head of Company I, leads his storming Marines toward the pillboxes on the right. He is shouting to his men, running crouched and moving forward, and then, in an instant, the twenty-two-year-old officer, who left Cornell University to enlist, is shot in the throat and falls dead on the airfield. Captain Heinze is also down. Two grenades thrown from a hidden spider trap blast his legs out from under him. Three lieutenants fall one after the other in the oncoming haze of bullets, and three sergeants step up to take the place of their fallen leaders without missing a beat.[13] Captain Daniel Marshall moves forward to take command of Company I.

Reeling, the two companies attempt to reorganize under the enemy fire as the lead tank of the six moving with Company I takes a direct hit from a Japanese antitank gun. The other five quickly withdraw until the big gun can be located lest they be picked off one by one.[14]

First Lieutenant Archambault races up to where Captain Heinze has fallen. Close behind him is Second Lieutenant Grossi. With Grossi are just twelve men; the rest of his forty-man platoon are either dead or wounded.[15]

The men take cover where they can, and focus on Archambault, waiting for his order. He is a man to be followed: a Silver Star at Bougainville, a Bronze Star at Guam. In a split second, he is off. He pulls up his Thompson submachine gun and a bag full of grenades and sprints across the runway, yelling back to Grossi, "Let's go, Dom!"[16]

The right-hand platoon of Company K charges across the runway directly toward the fifty-foot hill and into the first line of connected pillboxes and trenches. Nine minutes later, they are across.

With fixed bayonets and hurling grenades in all directions, the Marines begin the climb while howitzers pummel away at the ground above them. The Company I Marines have held their ground and move in with the 4th Marines on their right.[17]

But the friendly fire, smashing the Japanese crest, suddenly goes awry, and rounds begin falling on Archambault's men on the slope. It drives them off the hill, and for a half hour, they pull back and regroup to charge back up again. This time one platoon makes it to the crest, but it meets a hail of Japanese fire from every direction. Mortars rain down on the men on top of the ridge and those still climbing, but they keep going, moving forward despite the crushing onslaught. For fifteen excruciating minutes they battle hammer and tongs, but they cannot hold. The superior enemy firepower finally drives them back down.

Lieutenant Archambault's men scatter and slide to the jagged base of the hill, hunkering down against mortar fire in the enemy trenches, finding space among the dead from both sides. Dom Grossi's whittled-down platoon huddles nearby, and Archambault screams over the radio for more artillery fire. Colonel Duplantis yells that it is on the way and says that when he gets it, he's to "go after the *sonsabitches* again!"

"Will do, Colonel!" the frustrated lieutenant barks back. "But tell the bastard artillery to hit the fuckin' Nips and not us!"[18]

The artillery again smashes the hilltop, and when it lifts, Archambault and Grossi lead the attack back up the fire-streaked, unforgiving slope. But halfway up the hill, the Japanese defenders come down at them, swarming the exhausted Marines and driving them back down again. This time, Company K retreats to the south side of the runway. It is high noon.

Ships offshore and carrier aircraft hammer the hill while the men of Company K try to rearm, reload, evacuate casualties, and consolidate their thinned ranks. It takes them nearly two hours. But Archambault and Grossi are ready. Dominick Grossi's Navy Cross citation reads as follows:

Second Lieutenant Grossi led his unit against the Japanese with dauntless courage, slashing right and left with his bayonet, thrusting grenades into massive emplacements sunk in the sands, dropping them behind rocks, sweeping aside the enemy, holding desperately and fighting furiously in hand-to-hand engagements as he smashed through a sector swarming with Japanese to gain the fifty-foot ridge on the opposite side of the airstrip.[19]

At 2:15, Company I finally crosses the runway and joins in the attack. In two minutes, the attacking Marine line sweeps over the crest against surprisingly light opposition. The surviving Japanese gather on the reverse slope for a final showdown, charging forward into the oncoming fire of the Marines.

The historian Bill Ross will later write, "Japanese officers swung ceremonial swords and were impaled on Marine bayonets. Japanese troops lunged at Marines with bayonetted rifles and were clubbed to death with weapon butts, entrenching picks, even rocks."[20] The official 3rd Marine Division report will call it "one of the most freakish nightmares of the Iwo battle."[21]

This time, it is over in ten minutes. Fifty more Japanese are killed in the final charge. Despite the heavy casualties, Marines are now on the north side of the airfield. The historian Frank Hough will later write of the 3rd Battalion's historic attack to take Motoyama 2, "They fought and died with the same valorous determination as General Pickett's men in the Confederate charge at Gettysburg."[22] But unlike General George Pickett and his men at Gettysburg, the Marines are not hurled back.

The attack gains eight hundred valuable yards from the jump-off point south of the runway to the high ground to the north of the airfield. The drive that began on D + 1, from the black-sand landing beaches to Archambault's hard-won position, cost V Amphibious Corps 5,338 additional casualties to be added to the more than 2,400 lost on D-Day.[23]

First Lieutenant Raoul Archambault's Navy Cross citation reads:

Assuming command after his company sustained heavy casualties and was badly disorganized, First Lieutenant Archambault quickly reorganized the company and, personally leading his men in furious hand-to-hand fighting while under hostile frontal, flanking and enfilade fire, succeeded in seizing a strongly fortified Japanese hill position. Counterattacked and driven from the hill three times, he repeatedly led his men against the enemy and finally regained the position. . . . Archambault was directly instrumental in making possible a break-through of the enemy's main line of defense.[24]

Wounded in the attack on the ridge, Dominick Grossi is taken to a hospital ship offshore from which he writes home. He does not mention his injury or anything about his heroic role in the battle.

February 27, 1945

Dearest Mother,
  I've been doing a little moving lately and that's the reason I haven't written. I know you're worried, but everything is alright. I'm on Iwo Jima and it's really a hot spot. It's just about secured

now and we will move back to Guam in a day or two. There will be another lapse of time before you get another letter, because I'll be aboard ship. Don't worry Mom, I'm in good health and still going strong. I just finished a hot bacon and egg cracker sandwich with a hot cup of coffee. First hot stuff in about five days. I'm busy Mom, so I have to sign off. Give my love to daddy and the children. Your son,

Dom xxx

Don't worry everything is "O.K."

At the same time that Lieutenant Archambault and the 21st Marines crack the Japanese main line of resistance north of the airfield, its sister regiment, the 9th, and the entire division headquarters are landing at Black Beach, a redesignation of the area previously labeled Red Beach 2 and Yellow Beach. By nightfall, the three infantry battalions have moved into an assembly area, ready to join the fight the following day. Major General Graves Erskine sets up his division headquarters just to the north of the first airfield.[25]

Landing with the 9th Marines is the 34th Replacement Draft. Privates Harry Gray, Herman Graeter, Charles Gubish, Warren Graham, and George Colburn land at Black Beach and are immediately attached to the 3rd Shore Party Battalion. It is their first glimpse of the battlefield. Gray and the rest of the unit are immediately thrown in among the scattered supplies and equipment strewn about everywhere at the supply depot on the beach.

The beehive of activity is an all-out effort to get desperately needed supplies to the Marines clinging to the newly captured high ground north of the second airfield. The call has gone out "for volunteers to carry supplies to the front. Seabees cranked up bulldozers and pulled loaded trailers up the terraces, across the first airstrip and to within two hundred yards of the line."[26] Iwo Jima's terrain, with its sliding terraces, boulders, and badlands, means they can shell any vehicle that moves, and that reality has necessitated this resupply technique.

The "human conveyor belt, with hundreds of men packing crates and backpacks, pushing carts of ammo and water,"[27] will become the means of sustaining the attack for the rest of the battle.

But it is not the supplies and the chaos that deliver the rude awakening of war to Private Charles Gubish from Bethlehem, Pennsylvania. He will later say, "There is a pile, four or five feet high, covered with ponchos. And somebody says, 'Look at them Japs, they got boots like we do.' Then they pull the corner of the poncho up, and they aren't dead Japs, they are Marines." Before long Gubish, like so many Marines of his fellow replacements, is assigned the grimmest duty of all. "I was in the 34th Replacement Draft. I wasn't there to be a fighter; they use us where they need us. So my job is picking up the dead, taking off dog tags, carrying supplies to the front lines. That is my job."[28]

By day seven, the men of the 9th Marines have passed through the exhausted men of the 21st Marines and taken up their positions on and around the "pool table." Many more Japanese positions are dug in west and north of the runways, especially two rugged hills labeled "199 Oboe" and "Peter." Though Archambault's attack did indeed crack the defensive line, it is not yet broken.

X

On the northwest side of the island, the 26th and 27th Regiments of the 5th Division continue their attacks up the long axis of the island. They are bound by the water's edge on the left and the 3rd Division zone on the northern edges of the runways on the right. Each day is more of the same: prep fires to the front; attack as far as possible; dig in when pinned down; and continue to fire on the unseen enemy. At the end of each day, it is dig in for the night or fall back to the original position, depending on the progress of the 3rd Division on the right. The flanks of the attacking divisions are never to be left exposed.

Private Richard Wheeler of the 28th Marines, who had attacked around the base of Suribachi, will later say, "This was surely one of the strangest battlefields in history, with one side fighting wholly above the ground and the other side operating almost wholly within it."[29]

Aerial observers flying above the battlefield rarely if ever see Japanese troops moving above ground. To the southern end of the island, they observe thousands of Marines milling around, moving supplies off the beach, attacking along a line of resistance, or down in foxholes. The other side of the battle line seems deserted.

A captain in the 26th Marines will later say it best: "The Japs weren't *on* Iwo Jima, they were *in* Iwo Jima."[30]

On the western side of the island, Company E, 27th Marines, begins its advance again, keeping pace with the 3rd Division on the left. Jay Rebstock says of the advance that it was "strictly by the book: lay down a base of fire, bring up demolitions and the flamethrower, and destroy the positions; move to the next bunker and repeat all the steps."[31]

It becomes a continuous attack against one series of interlocking pillboxes after another. It is a bizarre existence. On Rebstock's right flank, the world is exploding; on his left, peaceful waves break on sandy beaches. His mind drifts over there for a fleeting moment: "What a marvelous spot it would be to spend a lazy afternoon."[32]

The fantasy shatters as Japanese artillery and mortar fire explode to his front. He aims and fires his BAR into the first strongpoint he sees on his right. The weapon bucks into his shoulder. He fires short bursts to drive the defenders away from the apertures. As he pours fire into the position, he sees his team rush to the flanks of the bunker to secure the area for the flame man to deliver the knockout blow.

Before he can close on the bunker, Japanese gunners knock him down. He increases his fire as a second Marine rushes forward to wrestle the seventy-two-pound weapon off another man's back and sling it onto his shoulders. But as soon as he stands to advance, he is gunned down.

Rebstock screams out at the bastards he can never see but who always see him. He changes magazines, pulls the bolt back, and fires a continuous stream into the entire area around the bunker. A third man now picks up the flamethrower, and as Rebstock fires, he suddenly hears the familiar *whoosh* and sees the blistering orange tongue licking at the rocks and boulders, trying to find the seams that will let it inside. Then the third flame man is hit.

The life expectancy of a flame man is brief. The very sight of him strikes fear and terror into the heart of the enemy, who envisions himself immolated in a fiery hell.

The squad moves forward in a rush, past the smoking position, and is immediately driven back by more small-arms and machine-gun fire. From his pinned-down position, Rebstock can fire only in the direction that other Marines gesture to. He can see nothing, and neither can they. They are firing at the roar of the lion, but the lion remains hidden. They fight this way all day and dig in for the night. They lick their wounds and count their casualties, with no enemy bodies in sight.

On February 25, the word comes down to try something else. The usual morning prep fire drives the Japs underground but also signals that an attack is coming. Today there will be no prep fires and no morning attack; instead, they will attack in the afternoon.

The terrain in front of them is as daunting as any in this fractured geological nightmare. From tip to tip, the island is contorted and scarred. It is death valley. A deep indentation crosses their line of advance and then descends a long slope to a level bottom, exiting on the other side by an equally exposed upward slope. There are no illusions that the advance will not be seen by the enemy. The Japanese defenders have stadium seats to watch the whole maneuver. The Americans' only hope is that a late start may turn the rhythm of battle in their favor.

As morning becomes afternoon, Rebstock and his fellow Marines of Company E nervously check, clean, and oil their weapons over and over—as if there is to be a general's inspection. As attack hour approaches, they exchange silent glances, and at exactly 3:00 p.m., they stand up in their lines.

But Rebstock's feet seem rooted to the ground, and he cannot take one step forward. "I guess that's what's called being scared shitless," he says. "I drank almost an entire canteen of water, and only then did my legs move forward."[33]

The hoped-for surprise, though, is no surprise at all. The line advances no more than fifty yards before its world explodes. Marines dive for cover. Rebstock jumps into a hole with three other men. Japanese bullets ping all around; one of the men in the hole is shot straight through his forehead. A second bullet smacks a man, bores a path between his helmet and liner, and miraculously worms its way around his head and out the other side, leaving him unscathed. Such is the randomness of life and death in battle.

Rebstock curls into the fetal position, sandwiched between the bodies of his squad leader and the dead and wounded. Japanese incoming fire then brackets them and thunders in, hurling shrapnel, stones, and dirt in every direction and partially burying them. No one can move in the eye of the artillery and mortar storm.[34]

Above the din, Rebstock hears the clanking of an approaching armored vehicle; almost on top of him, a US tank unleashes a shot with an earsplitting *boom*. That shot goads the squad leader and Rebstock into action as training wins out over fear. The BAR sends a chatter of rapid fire to the front, the stream highlighted with streaking red tracers.

Through the swirling dust, Rebstock glimpses a newly exposed enemy bunker and bangs away at the aperture. Other men creep forward as he changes magazines and targets the narrow slit. To his right he sees his friend Private First Class Leonard Nederveld moving up, clutching a white phosphorous grenade. He moves in low to the right side of the bunker, hoping for a chance to hurl it in and let its thick white smoke blind the gunners, providing cover for the pinned-down Marines.

Nederveld has seen a second opening in the bunker and under cover of Rebstock's constant fire charges the bunker and lobs the grenade in. He races back to his original position as the Marines around the bunker look on. Seconds later, they hear the soft explosion of the grenade. They wait for the choking smoke to pour out of the openings. All weapons are aimed to engage any Japanese who might bolt from the position to escape.

Instead, there is an enormous explosion, as if five hundred pounds of TNT have detonated. A shock wave emanates from the obliterated bunker, and thick smoke hovers over the battlefield. The concussion rips the Browning from Rebstock's hands and flattens him into his hole. Nederveld's grenade has found an ammunition dump; it explodes in rippling echoes.

Gathering his wits, Rebstock crawls out and stands to search for his weapon, but before he can find it, another giant explosion drives him back. The tank, which has taken a direct hit from the Japanese artillery, is engulfed in fire and smoke. The tank and the Japanese bunker detonate in dueling explosions as the ammunition cooks off.

It is over, and a strange silence settles over this tiny part of the battlefield. The ferocity and savagery have peaked and can no longer sustain themselves.

Dazed Marines rise as if from the dead, stagger around in a fog. Rebstock finds his broken weapon and swings it by its barrel, smashing it against a boulder. He replaces it with one from a fallen comrade nearby. Then someone calls out to return to the jump-off point, and the men of Company E stagger back, carrying their latest sixteen casualties.[35]

That night they shiver in the pouring rain, cursing the island and their bad luck of being on it. The next day, D + 7, comes and goes. A resupply of ammunition is brought forward, followed by the arrival of replacement troops.

They are told to stay in their holes, which they gladly do. In the late afternoon, they are alerted to the sight of a Japanese soldier crawling toward their lines. Rebstock trains his weapon on the man, who alternately crawls, stops, raises his hand, and crawls forward again.

As he approaches the line, someone realizes that the pathetic figure is not a Japanese soldier at all but a Marine. Rebstock yells for everyone to hold fire. He goes out and grabs the man under his arms, dragging him into their lines. Almost unrecognizable, his face caked in grime and mud, is Private Nederveld. Knocked senseless by the explosion created by his well-placed grenade, he has been trying for hours to get back to his men.[36]

"We were pulled out of the line because of our depleted numbers, and sent to the rest area in the rear," Rebstock says. "The rest area turned out to be anything but R&R." On the first night, Japanese artillery strikes the 5th Division ammo dump, igniting it in a spectacular series of explosions, not unlike the one Rebstock and the men came from.

The next day, they refurbish their arms and equipment, and each man is given a satchel charge and sent to the mountain. For the next six days, Company E is to clean the Japanese out of the caves of Suribachi or seal them in forever. "R&R," Rebstock says, "was killing more Japs!"[37]

)(

In the center of the island, the 9th Marines prepare to continue the attack initiated by the 21st. Resupply of the front lines continues by all possible means. Harry, Warren, Herman, Charlie, George, and the others trudge forward. After dark, when the Japanese observers cannot see, is the best time. Striking a match will guarantee incoming mortar fire.

Even so, along the Motoyama 2 runway, long after dark, two swinging flashlights appear like beacons in the night. Their beams play along the cratered runway, illuminating a path for a noisy bulldozer pulling a much needed, overloaded trailer of supplies.

A sergeant shakes his head and says with a laugh to those nearby, "In a lotta ways, you gotta be crazy to be in the Marine Corps."[38] The bulldozer and its men carry out their death-defying, heroic night duty.

Even on this desolate island, eventually, mercifully, there is mail call. For some, there might be a dozen letters at a time. At home, fathers, some of whom fought in World War I, encourage their daughters to write to the boys from their high school, knowing how much a letter will mean to them. Parents, aunts, uncles, and neighbors relate news from home, transporting the men, for a few moments, back to the place where things are predictable and sweet. There is no better sound than "Mail call! Colburn! Gray!"

George Colburn: "We all find a spot to open our letters and read them, and then we read them all over again and again. If your buddy didn't get a letter, you'd give him yours to read."[39]

At home in Massachusetts, George's mother, Mary Ellen Colburn, and Anne Gray let each other know every time a V-mail drops through the mail slot. They are searching for clues to where their boys might be. For a time, Harry put a middle initial into his mother's name to let her know: "Anne G. Gray," for Guam, for instance. But for whatever reason, from Iwo Jima he tells it to her straight:

Dear Mom and family,

How is everyone? I'm fine except a slight cold which I should be rid of soon. I suppose you are wondering where I am. Well the place is Iwo. I have been here a week and believe me it is no picnic. I am praying to get off this place and soon; but it looks like another week yet.

I have not been to the front lines yet but it sure has been hot where I am. The first few days I was dodging mortar shells and artillery every minute, but now it seems to be mostly over. Our Marine artillery is firing over our heads continually; right now it is bang and whistling of shells.

Two other fellows and myself are in a hole and you can bet it is very secure. We have worked hard on it by putting bags all around and on the roof. We had one air raid and Mom you can bet I was plenty scared. The living conditions are good and the chow is surprisingly good and plenty of it.

I can only write one letter a day so please tell Dot I'll write her tomorrow. Please don't worry as everything is under control. Well Mom I will go into it about this place later and will write every chance I get. Bob and George [Colburn] are here.

All my love,
Harry.[40]

The next morning is the dawn of another gray day on Iwo Jima. So far, there has been no other kind. The cold sweeps off the deep blue-black water and right inside Harry's uniform, sending a chill up his back as he looks across the crates of ammo and the tarps blowing in the wind on the beach. Another day is spent taking supplies to the front, dodging mortars, eating chow, and counting the days until they can get off this island and onto the next one. The worst duty is carrying the stretchers, taking the dead men to the beach, sorting their equipment, putting their helmets into piles, emptying their ammo, and putting it with the rest. There are hundreds of them, rolled in ponchos lined up on the beach. Then there are the hollers of "Corpsman! Corpsman!" coming from the front lines. Harry picks up one end of a stretcher; the wounded man on it clutches his gushing shiny red wound, trying to hold in what is torn and keep it intact; sometimes he is silent, sometimes he cries out, he wants his mother, he wants his wife, he wants to go home. Harry, too, desperately wants to go home. He's four months shy of nineteen, and he hopes to make it back by his birthday on June 13.

He can see it now: He will step off the train in Boston, and Dorothy will be there. He will be wearing a clean uniform, not this stinking set of herringbone twill utility stiff-caked with sweat and dust that he's had on his back for ten days. He will spin her around and say, "You didn't get married while I was gone, did you?," and she will laugh. "No, Harry, I did not get married. I was waiting for you, silly." They will have tears in their eyes, from smiling so hard. He will love every smell and sight in good ol' Arlington, where everything will look just as it always has, where they will get married and have two kids of their own, a boy and a girl.

He looks out at the beach, at the wreckage and the carnage. How will he ever explain to Mom and Uncle Frank and Nancy what he has done and seen?

He jolts back as a bang and then a whistle signal mortars toward the beach. He tucks in his chin and takes off in a low run to find cover in a crater. He lies flat, pressing his body in as deeply as he can, his rifle over his shoulder, as Herman Graeter, his foxhole buddy from

Ohio, dives in next to him. Harry shakes a bit and looks at the cold sky as shell fragments fly over his head.

That night, after a long afternoon of hauling supplies and men, they climb under the sandbag roof and back into their foxhole. Harry whispers, "Pop, you sleep, I'll watch!" Charlie Gubish closes his eyes, but the truth is that he can't relax. He worries that if he falls asleep, Harry will fall asleep, too, and then all of them in the foxhole will get killed. Charlie rests his eyes and listens to Warren and Harry quiz each other on chemistry questions. He has no idea why they do this, except that Harry is always calling Warren "College Boy" and testing his smarts. Charlie was done with school at age twelve, but he has the wisdom of his twenty-four years. They have lived a lifetime in the past months together. Charlie says they are all "good buddies." George says it's more than that, they are "closer than brothers." On the ship, they played endless rounds of pinochle, but here it's difficult to play cards. Herman Graeter is asleep now. Charlie drifts off. He wakes with a start to a sound. But it is nothing. He hears Harry and Warren quietly talking again; this time it is about home. Charlie squints through one eye under his helmet; Harry has his leather wallet out as he once again shows Warren the pictures of Dot and Nancy and his mom.

※

On February 28, at his desk in Peekskill, New York, Frank Bowes takes out a pen to write a letter to Harry. He has been reading the accounts of Iwo Jima in the *New York Times* and looking at the photographs, captioned "Suribachi Reached in a Fiery Battle," "Wrecked and Abandoned Landing Craft Litter Iwo Beaches," and "Marines in the Final Mop-up Operations on Iwo Island." He scans the photos for a glimpse of his nephew. He puts another clipped-out article into the scrapbook he is keeping for Harry. "Blood Boats Went with Iwo Invaders," it reads. "For the first time in the Pacific war . . . blood has gone along on a special craft on an invasion with the men whose lives it is destined to save."[41]

He writes:

Dear Harry,

You can be sure we are all wondering what the story on you and the 3rd Division is as we are reading the news in the paper. It is hard to believe that you are tossed into one of the worst battles for the first experience. According to the paper it is certainly pretty bad and we are praying that you get through it OK and live to tell the story. We are anxious to hear from you whenever you can write. I had a letter from Grandma yesterday and she said they hadn't heard from you for three weeks. You were no doubt always pretty busy prior to the invasion. I am going over to Arlington Saturday, for a meeting in the office, Mon. Tues. Wed, so I will visit with the folks and have a good talk. You can imagine how your Mom must be worrying, but all Mothers are like that. I am having a hunch you will make it OK. It will be awful rough, but you have the courage kid and we have no doubt about that. Say a prayer when things look bad and we are praying also. Good luck and write when you can.

Uncle Frank

Now the men of the 1st Battalion, 9th Marines, of which Gray, Gubish, Graham, Graeter, and Colburn are a part, stare down the eastern end of Motoyama 2 and prepare to assault the menacing high ground just to the north: Hills 199 Oboe and Peter.

Dominick Grossi, like so many other injured Marines, has made it back from the hospital ship, after insisting to the doctors that he will return to the front lines. A surgeon, Lieutenant Evans, writes about these men:

We had 375 patients through here yesterday, to give you an idea. I've seen all the war surgery I want for a while. . . . They come in with wounds that make you sick to look at, and all they want to do is "Get back at those sons of bitches." You tell them they must be evacuated and they cry.[42]

The attack begins with two battalions abreast. The jump-off point is south of both runways and requires a double crossing of the pavement to advance toward the objectives.[43] Twenty-six tanks of the 3rd Tank Battalion support the assault.

At 9:30 a.m., the tanks crawl onto the southernmost runway and head north with three tanks of Company A in the lead: *Ateball*, *Agony*, and *Angel*. But they don't make it even to the second runway crossing before *Agony* and *Angel* explode in flames. *Ateball* is hit by a high-velocity shell and stopped in its tracks. Japanese gunners fire down the flat runways, unobstructed.

The 9th Marines press forward against murderous fire, but at the end of a five-hour fight, it has little to show for its mounting casualties. The 1st Battalion manages to advance only a hundred yards to the base of Hill Peter, and the 2nd Battalion just makes it across the double runway.[44] Nine tanks are lost.

The next day is more of the same, and after a little progress is

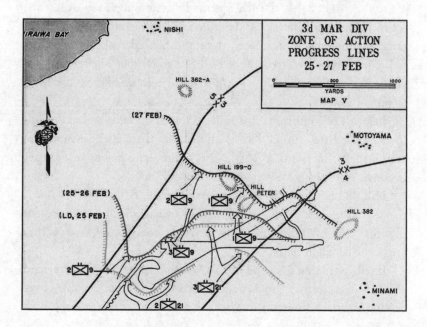

made in the morning, the Marines pause while the artillery fires a ten-minute saturating barrage onto the two hills. As soon as the fire lifts, the 1st Battalion rises and swarms over Hill Peter and then over Hill 199 Oboe to the north while the 2nd Battalion advances a dramatic fifteen hundred yards.[45]

On D + 8, Motoyama 2 is in the Marines' hands, and General Kuribayashi's main line has been completely breached. But the casualties are devastating. Jim Lucas, a veteran Marine correspondent, who witnessed the carnage at Tarawa, writes, "It was bad there, but it was all over in seventy-two hours. This bastardly battle goes on and on from one ridge to another. When will it end? And will anybody be alive when it does?"[46]

Harry Gray's buddy Private George Colburn will later say, "After the flag was raised on Suribachi, it was all a horror from there on out. The Japanese were everywhere in caves below us. We were just picking up bodies all the time. We paid an awful price for that island."[47]

On the right flank, the 4th Marine Division slugs away at its own set of Japanese fortifications, described as a "volcanic area [that] is a tangled conglomeration of torn trees and blasted rocks . . . crevices radiat[ing] from the direction of Hill 382 to fan out like spokes generally in a southeasterly direction providing a series of cross corridors to our advance."[48]

Just east of Motoyama 2 is Hill 382; to the south is a bald prominence called the Turkey Knob; and finally there is the Amphitheater, a rocky, stadiumlike bowl. This triumvirate defensive monster becomes collectively known as "the Meat Grinder."

Hill 382 is the most menacing of them all. After Suribachi, it is the second highest point, and General Kuribayashi's men have spent months toiling within, turning it into an underground fortress that anchors their right flank.[49]

Intelligence describes the hill as "a complicated mass of crevices, 15 to 50 feet deep . . . making it a bastion of defense capable of receiving an attack from any quarter. The crevices are worm-eaten with caves."[50] To guard all natural approaches, the Japanese have buried their tanks up to the turrets.

The three positions are mutually supporting, and defeating them will require simultaneously attacking all. They stand between the Marines and the ocean at the end of the island, and on Iwo Jima, the way to victory is through the Meat Grinder. For two vicious and bloody weeks, from February 25 to March 10, the three regiments of the 4th Division hurl themselves against the bulwarks. On Hill 382, the initial attempt appears to go well, and the 23rd Marines easily gains the summit, but it is a mirage; the men are jammed back to the base of the hill under a shroud of murderous fire and artillery.

The next day sees an act of gallantry almost beyond description. As elements of the 3rd Battalion attempt to seize the summit of Hill 382, a machine-gun burst strikes and kills a bazooka man. Reacting immediately, nineteen-year-old Private First Class Douglas T. Jacobson, a veteran of Saipan, picks up the bazooka and a satchel full of rockets and explosives and races forward. Weaving and zigzagging, he approaches the bunker containing the 20 mm gun and knocks it out with an explosive charge. His Congressional Medal of Honor citation reads:

> [H]e first destroyed two hostile machine-gun positions, then attacked a large blockhouse, completely neutralizing the fortification before dispatching the five-man crew of a second pillbox and exploding the installation with a terrific demolitions blast. Moving steadily forward, he wiped out an earth-covered rifle emplacement and . . . quickly reduced . . . six [more] positions to a shambles, killed 10 of the enemy, and enabled our forces to occupy the strongpoint. Determined to widen the breach thus forced, he volunteered his services to an adjacent assault company, neutralized a pillbox holding up its advance, opened fire on a Japanese tank pouring a steady stream of bullets on one of our supporting tanks, and smashed the enemy tank's gun turret in

a brief but furious action culminating in a singlehanded assault against still another blockhouse and the subsequent neutralization of its firepower. By his dauntless skill and valor, Pfc. Jacobson destroyed a total of 16 enemy positions and annihilated approximately 75 Japanese.[51]

Still, Hill 382 will not succumb, and at 4:30 p.m., the attack is called off, to be resumed the next day. The day has cost the Marines 512 casualties. As the days drag on, the story at the Meat Grinder remains the same: furious Marine attacks against a hail of fire delivered by unyielding, immovable Japanese defenders. Gains are measured in yards; sometimes there are no gains at all. A division officer will later report, "The enemy was determined to deny us Hill 382, and his unusually heavy mortar barrage on it twice forced our troops to retire after having occupied the hill area."[52]

Gradually, though, the Marines' battering ram begins to take a toll: the Japanese wall starts to splinter. On Hill 382, defensive positions are beaten down, incinerated, or exploded. On D + 12, March 3, it, too, is finally in Marine hands.

But six hundred yards to the south, the Turkey Knob and the Amphitheater are still in play. The massive blockhouse near the Turkey Knob is pounded daily, to little avail. The 4th Division is able to sweep forward around the two defensive positions, leaving a huge gap in the Japanese defensive line.[53]

On March 9, the Japanese defenders leave their positions and launch an ill-fated counterattack to break out. In the end, the Marines count 800 enemy dead.

On March 10, the two positions, surrounded and cut off from support, fall. The eastern end of the island is now in sight. The 4th Division's bloody two-week attack has cost 4,000 Marine casualties, including 450 dead.[54]

In the 3rd Division zone on the Motoyama Plateau, the Marines have overrun the incomplete airfield number 3 and at last are advancing toward the end of their long road, the eastern coast. No one knows

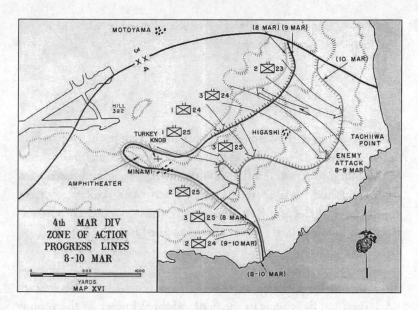

what day it is, but it is Thursday, March 8, and the sun is peeking out for the first time in many days. The Marine line occupies the cliffs overlooking the sea, and a reconnaissance patrol, including Woody Williams, walks the hill down to the edge of the sand and scoops up ocean water in a canteen, proof that they have finally come to the end of the island. It is sent back to the corps commander, Major General Harry Schmidt, with a note: "For inspection, not consumption."[55]

But the heroic Dominick Grossi does not make it to the eastern shore. As he and his men attempt to move down the hill overlooking the beach, his unit comes under heavy flanking fire. The second lieutenant, Navy Cross recipient, and football star from Lockport, New York, is hit in the chest and torso, killed on the hill leading down to the sea.

Days before, he tucked this letter into the outgoing mailbag:

Dearest Mother,

I'm still on Iwo Jima and am well. Our leave from here has been delayed a couple of days. I'll write again as soon as I hit my base.

Give my love to all. Remember I love you all so much. Don't worry
The Lord will see me through.

Your son,
Dom xxx

"By evening of 10 March, except for the enemy pocket which held out for six more days . . . the 3d Division's zone of action up the center of the island was clear."[56] That holdout area, a thousand yards back from the island's east coast, is called "Cushman's Pocket" after the commander of the 2nd Battalion, 9th Marines, Lieutenant Colonel Robert E. Cushman, Jr., whose troops assailed it. It is a hornet's nest.

⚔

The 5th Marine Division smashes its way forward on the western side. The final fighting is in the badlands area known as the Bloody Gorge. The final Japanese defensive line is here, at the northeastern end of the island.

The division's report describes the situation: "The Japs were now cornered in a pocket of resistance approximately 200–500 yards wide and 700 yards long. This was a rocky gorge for the most part with precipitous sides. Scattered through this gorge there was a series of jagged rocky outcrops which were in effect minor gorges."[57]

The men of Company E, 27th Marines, including Private Jay Rebstock, move up onto the final ridgeline and stare down into the canyon below. Rebstock can see the rocky rim on the opposite canyon wall and the Marines there looking back at him. The last Japanese defenders are in between them, in the deep ravine below. Company E no longer resembles the company that landed on D-Day. Most of its men are new.

Rebstock will later count the faces of the men he has known for months. There are only thirty-one of them. There is a thirty-second man who is the only replacement left from the fifty that were sent up to the company.[58]

All the rifle companies are skeletons of what they once were. Company I, 24th Marines, has only 9 left of the 133 that landed. Company D, 26th Marines, has only 17 out of 250. Company B, 28th Marines, has gone through 9 company commanders. Seven hundred Marines have died for every square mile of Iwo Jima[59]—almost 7,000 men, with another 19,000 wounded.

Rebstock is an aberration. He is one of the very few who landed on D-Day and managed to stay on his feet for the entire thirty-six-day bloodbath. As he stands on that final ridgeline, the end is in sight. He makes sure he teams up with another veteran who knows the ropes. He can see the ocean to the northeast, and no one wants to be the last man killed. "The casualty rate among the new men was horrific," he will later say. "Without experience, they fell at an alarming rate. . . . They were cannon fodder."[60]

One of the Marines on the ridgeline slowly descends to the bottom of the gorge while everyone else watches, weapons at the ready. As he reaches the bottom, a sniper's shot rings out, and the man falls dead. A Japanese defender comes out, waving his hands over his head, but the Marines cut him down. A second one comes out, holding something under his arm, and despite a command to hold fire, the Marines pour down fire from above.

"I put my weapon down," Rebstock will later say. "I just couldn't kill anymore."[61]

⋈

In the center, the Japanese stronghold at Cushman's Pocket remains rock solid with tunneled caves and hundreds of spider traps. It bristles with an assortment of weapons, including the tanks dug into their turrets.

In an attempt to batter the stronghold into submission, four 7.2-inch rocket launchers, mounted on sleds, are towed into position by armored dozers. Each launcher has twenty rocket tubes capable of delivering a barrage of twenty rockets at a time into the pocket, equivalent to 640 pounds of TNT.[62]

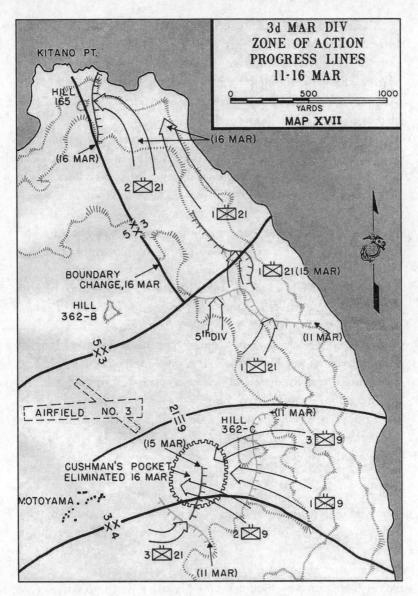

3d MAR DIV
ZONE OF ACTION
PROGRESS LINES
11-16 MAR

0   500   1000
YARDS
MAP XVII

KITANO PT.

HILL
165

(16 MAR)

(16 MAR)

2 [ ] 21

1 [ ] 21

1 [ ] 21 (15 MAR)

5 X 3

BOUNDARY
CHANGE, 16 MAR

HILL
362-B

5 X 3

5th DIV

(11 MAR)

1 [ ] 21

AIRFIELD   NO. 3

2/119

(11 MAR)

HILL
362-C

3 [ ] 9

(15 MAR)

CUSHMAN'S POCKET
ELIMINATED 16 MAR

MOTOYAMA

1 [ ] 9

3 X 4

2 [ ] 9

3 [ ] 21

(11 MAR)

Early on the morning of March 11, these four launchers begin to
hurl a combined, earsplitting ten barrages into Cushman's Pocket—
more than three tons of explosives. When the smoke finally clears, the

three Marine battalions attack from the west and south but make only incremental gains. The Japanese return fire keeps coming, the resistance as deadly as ever.[63]

On the rest of the island, there are pockets of calm in the rhythms of the battle and the routine of supplying the lines allow for small moments of normalcy, even fun. As Charlie, Herman, and Harry walk back from an ammo drop, there is a feeling that the end is near. Harry's steps are light as he runs up a rocky outcrop that has rebar and cement strewn about. "Hey, guys, come here!" With one hand on the top of the abandoned Japanese cave, he pops his head below for a look. "There's a bunch of Jap rifles in there. C'mon! We are going to take these home. We need to bring something back, or even we will never believe we were here."

Charlie warns him that they could be booby-trapped, and tells Harry to back away from the opening. Charlie fires a few rounds to be sure. They all stand looking in for a moment. Nothing in there, nothing alive anyway. Harry laughs and skips down inside. He gathers up the Japanese rifles and hands one to each of the guys. They turn them around, open them up, and inspect them to see what they feel like in their hands. It feels good to hold enemy weapons, inert and powerless, their owners no longer a threat. Harry later writes:

March 12, 1945

Dear Mom,

I suppose you are worried to death over me. Well I am in the best of health and feeling fine with the exception of a few scares. I told you I would write before but I really didn't have a chance. Also, I wrote another letter but couldn't mail it. Tell P.F. I got one for him. Also, tell Joe I have a couple of swell letters for him, but I couldn't mail them yet.

I have received quite a bit of mail from you, Nanc, Gram, Dorothy and Uncle Frank, but I also lost quite a bit of it. Haven't had any for 5 days.

I saw George C[olburn] yesterday and he is fine as far as I know. I haven't seen Bob since we left Guam and I am quite worried about him. The chow is pretty good mom as we eat C-Rations which fill me up pretty well. The weather is quite chilly here and haven't seen an all blue sky all day since I have been here.

Mom will you please buy Dot a nice corsage for Easter and have the tag say "To My Sweetheart with all my love, Harry." I will send five dollars to you.

Hope everyone, and everything is fine.

Love, your son,
Harry

The next morning, Harry, Herman, Warren, Charlie, and George shake off sleep and eat their breakfast, which has been warmed by an ingenious method of burying pots of coffee and eggs in the ground, where the sulfuric steam heats them, making them sort of, almost hot. They grab their rifles and head toward the resupply area up at Motoyama 2 airfield.

There is a bit of a lull, and they lie on their backs, shooting the breeze, waiting for the call. About an hour later they hear "Gubish, Graeter, Gray, Graham! Up to headquarters!" They look at one another and jump up, scrambling out of the crater they've been lounging in. "See ya, George!" Harry says, smiling back at his buddy from Medford, Massachusetts. George will later say, "I'll never forget that."[64]

They head up to the ammo dump at the front line. They will carry ammo and bring stretchers back. They know the drill. There is a line of nineteen men; Gray, Gubish, and Graeter are up front, and Graham is near the end of the line. George ends up joining the back of the line as well.

Charlie says, "We are supposed to go to the relieving outfit, to give them a break. And as we're marching, the mortars are coming from over there to the street. Nobody pays attention. We think they are ours. Then there is one on this side, the same distance, then I know it's coming from the other side. It's enemy fire, and I holler to Gray and Graeter, 'Hit the deck!' and I lay alongside of an engine, and that's when we got it. I see them laying there as sure as Christ, they got us right in the middle.

"Gray is hit direct. When I see him, he's bleeding from his head. He and Herman are both dead."

Nearly seventy-five years later, recalling this, Charlie stops. He's crying. "Graeter, the concussion killed him. I was knocked out, too, but I survived. But I still got shrapnel here. But Graeter, he only had a shrapnel in his leg. He would've lived but for the concussion, because it's that strong, it just kills you. Then I was out, I don't know how long. But then a corpsman passed by me. He was treating some of the others, and then he sees me standing up. He comes running back. He says, 'I thought you were dead!' I couldn't talk, I was in shock, but I saw Graeter and Gray laying there. And then I was crying. Then he saw that I was putting my hand over my left chest and he saw blood coming out of my fingers, so he pushed my hand down, he cut my jacket open, he put a compress on me. I'm still carrying that shrapnel in me today, I still have it in there. But Gray and Graeter, they lost their lives.

"It is a shame. We were great buddies. What are you going to do? War is war."[65]

Three days later, March 16, Cushman's Pocket is eliminated. At 6:00 p.m., after thirty-six days of hell, the volcano island of Iwo Jima is declared secure. By now, thanks to the Seabees, the runways are repaired and redone; B-29s have been landing, being repaired, and taking off again ever since the first one, the *Dinah Might*, came in on March 4. The landing stopped everyone in his tracks that day; the men marveled at the beautiful, lumbering aircraft as it touched down, and then they went back to clearing caves.

Their way of life on the island, to the extent that it exists, is shattered again on March 26. In a final spasm of death, 300 Japanese soldiers silently infiltrate from their defensive positions in the north and fall upon a tent city bivouac of the 5th Pioneer Battalion just off the edge of Motoyama 1. It is occupied by newly arrived Army pilots of the VII Fighter Command, who are to fly air cover for the B-29s flying north. While the men are sleeping, they are brutally attacked with grenades, swords, and automatic weapons in a violent and deadly last gasp. The Marines grab their weapons and engage in an hours-long defense. The only Marines besides the 5th Pioneer Battalion who stand between the attacking Japanese forces and the American airmen are members of the 36th Marine Depot Company and the 8th Marine Ammunition Company, both of 8th Field Depot. These are the African American units, known as the Montford Point Marines. The men served at the supply hub on the beach under Colonel Leland Swindler. The colonel integrated his beach-landing parties. Black and white Marines under Swindler worked side by side. In the last battle on Iwo Jima, as the banzai charge tore through the camp, they fought and died side by side. Two of these brave men received Bronze Stars for their heroism.[66] Corporal Archibald Mosley remembers, "The bullets didn't have color codes on them. I was more proud to have served under Colonel Swindler than if I had been tasked with raising the flag on Suribachi all by myself."[67] When the fighting ends, the 300 men of General Kuribayashi's last combat force are dead. It is said by Japanese survivors that he led the raid. His body is never found.

One hundred pilots and Seabees are killed in the last battle of Iwo Jima; two hundred more are wounded.[68]

The overall toll of Iwo Jima is ghastly: 6,800 Marines are dead, among them Harry Gray of Arlington, Massachusetts, and Herman Graeter of Dayton, Ohio, both eighteen years old; and Dominick Grossi of Lockport, New York, who was twenty-four. Nearly 20,000 are wounded, including Warren Graham and Charlie Gubish, who will spend weeks recovering in Guam. Only George Colburn is left. He remembers waiting in line for chow with the remaining men during the packing up. He hears someone yell, "What day is it?" The

---

date is something none of them had thought of for days and days. But someone else hollers, "March 29!" George looks up and around, at the men on either side of him. "March 29? That's my birthday!" George Colburn has just turned nineteen.

When the ships come to take the last Marines away from Iwo Jima, the men gather at the 5th Marine Division cemetery for a last memorial service. A Jewish chaplain, Lieutenant Roland B. Gittelsohn, says this:

> Here before us lie the bodies of comrades and friends. Men who until yesterday or last week laughed with us, joked with us, trained with us. Men who were on the same ships with us, and went over the sides with us as we prepared to hit the beaches of this island. Men who fought with us and feared with us. . . .
>
> Some of us have buried our closest friends here. We saw these men killed before our very eyes. Any one of us might have died in their places. Indeed, some of us are alive and breathing at this very moment only because the men who lie here beneath us had the courage and strength to give their lives for ours. To speak in memory of such men as these is not easy. Of them too it can be said with utter truth: "The world will little note nor long remember what we say here. It can never forget what they did here."[69]

On March 26, 1945, the day that Iwo Jima is declared secured, the doorbell rings at 17 Linwood Street in Arlington. Anne is at work, and Harry's Grandma Bowes answers the door. She reluctantly takes the envelope. The delivery boy bows his head and turns down the steps. As she opens it, her eyes scan and fall on the only three words that matter: DEEPLY. REGRET. KILLED. She slides down into the hall chair and weeps.

DEEPLY REGRET TO INFORM YOU THAT YOUR SON PRIVATE HARRY E GRAY USMCR WAS KILLED IN ACTION 13 MARCH 1945 AT IWO

JIMA VOLCANO ISLANDS IN THE PERFORMANCE OF HIS DUTY AND
SERVICE OF HIS COUNTRY. WHEN INFORMATION IS RECEIVED RE-
GARDING BURIAL YOU WILL BE NOTIFIED.

TO PREVENT POSSIBLE AID TO OUR ENEMIES DO NOT DIVULGE
THE NAME OF HIS SHIP OR STATION. PLEASE ACCEPT MY HEART-
FELT SYMPATHY. LETTER FOLLOWS=

AA VANDEGRIFT LIEUT GENERAL USMC COMMANDANT OF THE
MARINE CORPS.

Nancy skips up the front steps and opens the door. Her grandmother looks up at her, eyes red and worn. There is a telegram on her
lap. Nancy doesn't know what to say or do. She is fourteen, and she
does not believe the news. It simply cannot be. There is some mistake.
Harry is so alive. He just wrote to them that he would be home soon
and to buy an Easter flower for Dot! But her grandmother is so very
sad. Nancy sits in shock and then falls onto the sofa. Her face pressed
into the cushion, she dissolves into tears. As she cries, she remembers
that the night before, she dreamed this moment. She dreamed that
Harry had been killed.

The neighbors have gone to get Anne at work. How to be the mes-
sengers who tell a mother that her son is gone? How many such mes-
sengers, by the thousands, across the country, are walking up front
steps, finding fathers and mothers at work, knocking on doors?

The priest comes. Anne wrestles the waves of grief; grief is an anvil
on her chest, shock leaves her struggling to breathe, disbelief tries to
poke holes in grief and shock. How can this be? Junior, her light, her
only boy, the one who was going to take care of her one day? He is
so alive. How can he be dead? The priest sits next to her. Bible on his
lap, he reads to her from the Song of Solomon: "Set me as a seal upon
your heart, as a seal upon your arm, for love is as strong as death." She
stares ahead in shock.

In Peekskill, Helen Bowes hangs up the phone and hangs her
head. She seats eleven-year-old Betts at the dinner table. Her little girl
knows that something is very wrong. Frank comes in the front door,

and Helen greets him with a kiss. She takes his black hat and gray coat; she is shaking. She wants him to sit and eat. She cannot bring herself to say the words. They sit at the table, and for a moment, it hangs all over the room. In the dreadful silence, Frank looks into his wife's eyes, which are now filled with tears. He puts his head in his hands. His shoulders begin to shake as he is overcome with sorrow. He pushes away from the table and goes to sit in his chair in the living room. Still no one has spoken a word. What is there to say? Harry is not ever coming home.

Two weeks later, Anne writes this letter:

Dear Frank and Helen,

I received your very lovely letter Helen, and I certainly appreciate all that you folks, your friends and the Nuns and girls have done spiritually for my little boy. I find it extremely difficult to be resigned to what God has permitted to happen to my son, but as life must go on, I will begin again.

I am going back to the office tomorrow and Nancy is starting her weeks vacation so she will be company for Mother another week.

Our friends have all been most kind and thoughtful and sometimes I wonder why I have deserved so much. Junior has received about 200 individual masses, 9 yearly enrollments and 4 perpetual enrollments.

Mother is getting along pretty well considering the terrible shock she has had. Nancy's friends and activities have kept her from thinking too much. We all have a long hard road ahead and I hope that God will help us to keep going.

Hope you all are well.

Love from,
Anne

These letters arrive for Anne Gray and Frank Bowes in the weeks that follow:

April 26, 1945, Central Pacific

Dear Mrs. Gray,

This is about the fifth letter I have started. I can't seem to put into writing just what I want to say. Harry and I were great buddies. It seemed we went every place together. We used to love to talk about home. He told me quite a bit about you, his little sister, and his girl, Dot.

I was with him up on Iwo Jima. I was also with him the day it happened. Harry was hit by a mortar shell, which killed three others. I'm sure he was killed instantly and there was no pain. He was wearing his rosary beads around his neck when it happened, and I'm sure he went to heaven. Harry was a very brave kid.

Well, Mrs. Gray I hope this letter makes you feel better. Oh, one more thing we (some more of Harry's buddies and myself) made a little gravestone and set it on his grave. It read, "Another Marine, from your buddies."

I'd like very much to hear from you, if you'd care to drop me a line. Until I hear from you then I'll say goodbye.

Sincerely,
Harry's buddy George

Friday, May 17, 1945

Dear Mrs. Gray,

My name is probably unfamiliar to you. I doubt Harry ever mentioned me in his letters to you, but I was almost constantly with him ever since Camp Lejeune. I liked Harry from the first day at Lejeune; he was always full of pranks and not afraid of the consequences. He was usually the leader in these undertakings, I tagged along.

I soon learned of his home, his mother and his sweetheart. He used to tell me how he sneaked the car without your knowledge. I remember Dot's name very clearly of the pictures of sweethearts in our group, hers always received the longest admiration. He told of his plans to marry her when he returned.

Harry and I were together in a beach party on Iwo Jima, sleeping in the same foxhole. We didn't have much time for horseplay but at night, we really carried on some intelligent conversations. He was always trying to catch me on questions about chemistry and physics because I was a "Rebel" who had been to college. It was there in the fox hole, just before going to sleep, that he talked of you and Dot. From listening to him, I could almost feel his love and desire to live up to the ideals that you had ingrained in him.

We stayed on the beach until March 7th and then moved up to the second airfield, we stayed there five days, helping to deliver ammo to the dump that was near the front lines, on the morning of March 13th, Harry and I were sent to the dump to carry ammunition and be stretcher-bearers. We arrived there about 8 o'clock and lounged around for about an hour waiting for a call. At 9 o'clock, 19 of us started out single file, each with a case of ammunition for the front lines. We were about a hundred yards from the dump when some Jap mortars landed. The first two shells were off but the third one landed near the lead of the column. I don't remember much after that and I didn't learn that Harry had been killed until I was back on Guam. A friend (Charlie) who was also wounded by the same mortar told me that Harry died almost instantly. I shall always remember Harry for his manliness and courage. I give credit to you, Mrs. Gray, for such a wonderful son, must have had a wonderful and courageous Mother.

Sincerely,
Warren Graham

May 27, 1945

Dear Uncle Frank,

Although, I've never met you, Harry told me much about you. I guess you were sort of like a father to him after his father died.

I met Harry coming overseas on the boat. Bob, Harry and I went swimming together on Eniwetok island in the Marshalls. We were great buddies, it seems we went every place together

Your right it was a job writing to his mother. But it had to be done. Harry was up the front only one day when he got hit. Like I said in my letter to Mrs. Gray, Harry was hit by a mortar shell and was killed instantly.

We left for Iwo together. I guess we were all pretty scared. He's buried in the third division cemetery on Iwo. There's a lot of things I'd like to tell you but I can't say in a letter. Maybe I'll get a chance to see you next time I'm home, and we'll talk it over. Drop me a line anytime you get a chance,

Harry's buddy,
George
PFC George J. Colburn 988282

On June 22, 1945, the Battle of Okinawa ends. It has been the largest amphibious assault ever mounted; Army and Marine forces stormed ashore at the end of March and fought for eighty-three days. With death and defeat at their door, the Japanese have mounted banzai-like attacks from the skies, pilots drilling down to crash their planes into US ships, a final sacrifice to the emperor, who demanded their death before their dishonor. The devastating kamikaze attacks have contributed to the losses of 763 US aircraft; the Navy has lost 36 ships, and another 368 have been damaged. Ten thousand sailors have been killed or wounded and 15,000 Marines. Army casualties have totaled another 25,000.[70]

On August 6, 1945, as the United States plans for the invasion of

Japan, Operation Downfall, the B-29 Superfortress *Enola Gay* drops a uranium atomic bomb, *Little Boy*, on the city of Hiroshima. Three days later, on August 9, the B-29 *Bock's Car* drops a plutonium atomic bomb, *Fat Man*, on the city of Nagasaki. The casualties are approximately 135,000 in Hiroshima and 64,000 in Nagasaki.[71]

Ignoring the Potsdam Declaration, which calls for unconditional surrender, Japan vows to fight on, even to the death of its 100 million people. Through back channels, the Truman administration transmits a glimmer of hope, an extraordinary face-saving measure: "The ultimate form of the government of Japan shall, in accordance with the Potsdam Declaration, be established by the freely expressed will of the Japanese people."[72] There will be no deposing of the emperor. Hirohito will live on, and there will be no war crimes trial for the imperial family. The man who orchestrated Japan's expansionist vision and urged his warriors to fight to the death in his honor fights to the bitter end to preserve himself and his family.

Then on August 15, for the very first time, the emperor deigns to speak to the people of Japan. They have never, until this moment, heard his high-pitched voice. They gather around radios all over Japan, as the death tolls from the two atomic bombs rise, and they hear this: "Our Empire accepts the provisions of their Joint Declaration."

The emperor does not concede defeat in his speech but declares that he is acting to save "human civilization" from "total extinction." He says that the original aim of the war he led was national "existence and self-defense."[73]

He finishes with this message, aimed at securing his place in the eyes of the future:

Having been able to safeguard and maintain the structure of the imperial state, we are always with ye, Our good and loyal subjects, relying upon your sincerity and integrity. Beware most strictly of any outbursts of emotion that can engender needless complications. . . . Let the entire nation continue as one family from generation to generation, ever firm in its faith of the imperishability of its divine land, ever mindful of its heavy burden of responsibilities and of the long road before it.[74]

On September 2, 1945, Hirohito, the only surviving leader of an Axis power, sends his emissaries to sign the Japanese Instrument of Surrender. Some of his men are dressed in formal suits and top hats, others are in their military uniforms. The representatives of the emperor stand in defeat on the deck of the USS *Missouri* in Tokyo Bay. The decks of the ship are packed from top to bottom and bow to stern, every inch and rail standing room only, with US military in crisp uniform craning their necks to witness the historic event. You can hear a pin drop. At a draped table, the men sign the surrender documents as the world listens to the twenty-three-minute ceremony. At 9:08 a.m., General of the Army Douglas MacArthur signs and accepts the document on behalf of the Allied powers. Admiral of the Fleet Chester Nimitz signs at 9:12, followed by the representatives of the Allied powers.

The momentous ceremony over, Frank Bowes, Anne Gray, Patsy and Lena Grossi, Golda and Herman Graeter, Sr., and other families in their homes all across America turn off their radios and sit back in their chairs. They weep for all they have lost. The scars of the war will never leave them. They are grateful for the sacrifice of so many Americans who fought to secure our freedom at such an enormous cost. All the men who make it home carry their own Harrys, Hermans, and Doms in their hearts, always feeling that somehow it is unfair that they themselves got to marry, have children, and have a life when their buddies, who served with valor known only to those with whom they were "closer than brothers," did not.

Epilogue

After the war ended, many of the men were shipped back to San Diego. The trains were packed full of people: soldiers and sailors heading home. Charlie Gubish couldn't get onto any of the first trains out, so he stayed an extra night in San Diego and went out for some chili with some of the guys. On the way back, they got involved in a scuffle with some sailors and some girls. It started with someone whistling at one of the girls and ended with a Marine being carted off by the MPs. But Charlie managed to slip out of the melee and spent the night at a YMCA.

A group of them finally got onto a train to Naval Station Great Lakes, near Chicago. There the men were discharged, and after that they had to find their own way home. Charlie made it to Philadelphia, where some of them put their money together and chipped in on a taxi. Charlie arrived at 4:00 a.m., his duffel bag slung over his shoulder. He rapped on the bedroom window to wake up his wife and tell her he had made it home.

Charlie Gubish went back to work at the fire department at Bethlehem Steel. He and Ethel raised their two boys, Charles and Richard, in their home on Mechanic Street. The family vacationed every summer in Atlantic City, New Jersey. Charlie and his brother-in-law, Stevie, liked to go to the racetrack on the weekends and bet on the horses. In 1981, Charlie retired as a captain. He and Ethel became proud grandparents to seven grandchildren, fourteen great-grandchildren, and twelve great-great-grandkids. They had Sheltie dogs, all named Rebel. After Ethel died, Rebel was Charlie's constant companion.

In 2015, Charles Gubish did an interview with a local reporter. He talked about the two buddies who were with him when he was hit. One was Herman Graeter, and the other was a young pal from Boston. At ninety-six, he couldn't remember his name.

Four years later, I connected with a young man through Shayne Jarosz and Raul "Art" Sifuentes at the Iwo Jima Association of America. Dean Laubach is an excellent researcher of all things World War II, and he became my door to a wealth of information. He knew a man named Charlie Gubish, one hundred years old and sharp as a tack, and he quickly figured out that Charlie was wounded the same day that Harry was killed. Although, in their initial conversation, Charlie didn't remember any other details, Dean asked me to send him a picture of Harry on my phone. Dean showed it to him and it stopped Charlie in his tracks. Tears sprung to his eyes and he stopped. "That's Gray. That's my buddy, Gray. He called me Pop."

Days later, I went to sit down with Charlie and he told me all he could remember about that day. Everything about Charlie's story of what happened on March 13, 1945, on Iwo Jima lined up with the accounts of George and Warren in their letters and the USMC records we used to put them all in that column of nineteen men, bringing ammo to the front lines. My aunt Nancy was shocked when I called her to say that I found someone, alive and living in Pennsylvania, who was with her brother when he was killed. Someone who could answer some of the questions she had carried with her, things unanswered by the telegrams and sketchy details from the War Department.

I brought her to meet Charlie; they hugged and she held his hand and they talked about Harry. Charlie shared the stories of their times together, having beers and grabbing Japanese rifles. Nancy showed Charlie the wallet and ID bracelet that had been sent home. Charlie was so glad to see them, amazed that in the chaos that he saw and worked in, anything had ever been recovered.

Charlie was able to share his firsthand account and a side of the "Marine" Harry that the family never really got to see. He described Harry as a "good buddy and very brave."

I am grateful that Charlie survived the mortar attack that day and came home to have a beautiful family. Several of them came to meet us and were part of that emotional reunion.

Like most of the men I've met from World War II, Charlie is humble and proud to have served, and lives daily with the memory of the sacrifice of so many of his buddies who did not make it home.

During the spring of 1945, the Grossi family went through a time when they didn't know if Dominick was alive or dead. Lena Grossi wrote to a friend whose son had also been on Iwo Jima, pleading for any information he might have. He wrote back that Dom had been wounded and evacuated and had returned to battle and been hit. But the young man said he had gone down to the 3rd Marine Division cemetery and could not find Dom's cross there. "Your hope of life for him may be well to hang on to—one really does sometimes make errors, I'm hoping so myself."

But the Grossis would soon receive the telegram that ended those hopes. An outpouring of letters from fellow Marines and friends followed, all praising Dom's kindness and heroism. Sam Ritz wrote, "This is the hardest letter I have had to write since I have been in the service these three years. I know nothing I say can console you, because your loss is so great. Dom was one of the nicest fellows I have ever known and I was always proud to be a friend of his."

James Quinn wrote, "As your boy's Chaplain, I can assure you that every Catholic was well cared for spiritually. Confessions and Communions before combat were 100 percent. In battle many of the men received four or five times. May our Blessed Mother, whose sorrow at witnessing the death of her Son was very great, aid and comfort you in your sorrow at the loss of your son."

Hundreds of people came to Dominick Grossi's funeral Mass in Saint Patrick's in Lockport, New York, to pay their respects.

That August, Lena and Patsy were notified that Dom would be

one of ten Marines to receive the Navy Cross for his selfless acts of heroism on Iwo Jima.

In May 1948, the path was cleared to return the dead from the cemeteries in the Pacific. They made their last voyage home in funeral fleets of white ships, marked from bow to stern with the purple band of mourning, as mandated by President Harry Truman. Their families were given the option of burying their dead at the National Memorial Cemetery of the Pacific in Hawaii, known as "the Punchbowl," or having them sent home for burial.

The ship that carried Dominick Grossi to New York for arrival on May 14, 1948, had a section that carried thirty-seven bodies, sent home in alphabetical order, according to the records kept by the Office of the Quartermaster General. Next to Grossi were the remains of another beloved young man who was headed to Boston, Massachusetts, Harry E. Gray.

Years later, in 2018, Dominick Grossi's niece Nicolena and Harry Gray's niece, the author of this book, had dinner together with their families in Florida. For all the years of my friendship with the Errico family, it wasn't until that night that I learned the story of their relative Second Lieutenant Dominick Grossi. Months later, while researching this book, my eyes fell upon the list of those transported back together that May, Grossi and Gray, side by side.

In Arlington in 1948, Harry's mother, Anne, had dutifully filled out the forms requesting his return. When the train pulled into South Station in Boston carrying Harry's body, Anne was there to receive it. It was the night of Nancy's high school prom, and Anne wanted her to enjoy it, so she had not mentioned where she was heading that afternoon. On the outside of his casket was a metal tag stamped HARRY E GRAY, 565110, USMC. An envelope also arrived with a list of belongings he had had with him and the items themselves: one brown leather wallet with pictures, one signet ring, one ID bracelet. As Anne took them out carefully and looked at the pictures of herself and then of Nancy and Dot, as well as the prayer her boy had so carefully written inside the small booklet, she saw that the things had been with him until the end. They were stained with his blood.

Dorothy did not come to Harry's memorial service or the funeral three years later. Anne and Nancy never knew why. They never saw her again. It always puzzled Nancy why Dorothy didn't come. Perhaps she was angry that Anne had not wanted them to marry, or maybe, at sixteen, the pain was just too much for her to bear. Many years later, Nancy heard that Dorothy had not had an easy life, that she had married shortly after the war and died young.

Harry was buried in a small military section of Arlington Cemetery. Although Anne and Nancy often could not find the words to talk to each other about their grief, they visited his grave together "all the time."

Years later, when the Gerald B. H. Solomon Saratoga National Cemetery was established in New York, Nancy decided she wanted her brother to have the honor of being buried there. Initially, Arlington Cemetery refused the disinterment, saying that, all these years later, they did not know what would be there. Nancy was adamant, replying that "even if it is a shovelful of dirt, I want him in the national cemetery." After fifty-two years and then five months of negotiations, Harry's casket was exhumed and found to be in perfect condition, the identification tag still attached. On May 18, 2000, a memorial Mass was held at Saint Edward the Confessor in Clifton Park, New York, after which there was a final burial with full military honors. My parents, Betty "Betts" Bowes MacCallum and her husband, Doug, were honored to attend.

The obituary of Herman Graeter, Jr., "Dayton Marine Is Killed on Iwo Jima," read, "The action in which he was killed was his first combat operation." He was the only child of Mr. and Mrs. Herman Graeter, Sr. Golda Graeter took on the sorrowful task of correspondence with the military, requesting information about her son and arranging for his burial. In December 1947, Golda wrote under the section titled "Remarks and Additional Instructions," "Would you please inform me if it is possible to visit the present grave of deceased on Iwo Jima, Mrs. Herman Graeter." She received a letter on December 30, advising her that it would not be possible as disinterment operations on the island had ended several months before. She later requested his burial at the National Memorial Cemetery of the Pacific. At home, Golda and Herman Sr. also received the contents of Herman's pockets: one knife, two keys, and an ID bracelet.

Charlie Gubish remembers that the morning they were all hit, Herman had asked him to carry his pocket watch and return it to his dad. Charlie had said, "What are you talking about, Graeter?" Herman had said, "Every day, somebody gets it." "I took it that he thought he was going to get killed. I didn't want to listen to him."[1] It always bothered Charlie that he hadn't taken Herman's watch that day. Later he tried to find Herman's family, to talk to them about it, but he was never successful. There was no pocket watch on the list of Herman's belongings.

George Colburn was sent to China after Iwo Jima, to round up Japanese prisoners from the Rape of Nanking. He was there a year and then got to go home because his mother was ill. He says that Harry Truman saved all their lives when he ordered the bombs to be dropped.

As George had promised, he went to see Harry's mom when he got back. Uncle Frank went up to talk with him as well. He answered as many of their questions as he could. He told them how close he and Harry had been, "closer than brothers," and how brave Harry was. He told Anne that if Harry had made it back, he would have been so badly wounded, it might have been difficult for them all. He remembers Anne looking at him and saying, "George, if I had to spoon-feed him every day for the rest of his life, I would still want him home."

Early on in the research, we could not find much on George Colburn. But when the book was nearly done, I took one more look at his file. In it, I found a form I had not seen before. It was one that George had filled out years after the war, requesting his military records. He wrote that when he moved from New England to Florida, the records had been lost. At the bottom was an address in Spring Hill, Florida.

I searched for the Florida address and then the name. As always in this research, I tried to find an obituary as a first step but found none. Within twenty-four hours, George, Dean Laubach, and I were on the phone. When I introduced myself to George and told him that I was Harry's "niece," and that Harry's sister, Nancy, was alive and living in New York, he went silent for a moment. He said he had thought of Harry so many times and that he had often thought that "he would've lived a better life than I did." I told him I was so happy to find him and he filled me in on their time together in Massachusetts, playing football against each other, and then connecting on *Rochambeau* on their way to the Pacific. He talked of he and Harry and the others "swimming on Eniwetok" and making an altar for one of the priests out of two barrels and a stretcher. He described the last time he saw Harry, when he ran off to join the column. How clearly he remembered him smiling back at him before he took off.

After Iwo Jima, George and the others went back to Guam, where they got to swim in the ocean again. Then they were off to China. When George came home he got a job with the railroad in Boston and worked on the trains for thirty years. He is father to six children and grandfather to many grandchildren and lives with his second wife in Melbourne Beach, Florida.

Writing this story was like being an archeologist, digging to see where the letters and files led me, to fill in the blanks and connect the dots between these heroes who were such great buddies. I never imagined that we would find so much. After all, there were more than 60,000 Marines on Iwo Jima.

In Japan, after the war, General Tadamichi Kuribayashi's son Taro spoke with Japanese survivors of Iwo Jima (of whom there were about 1,000) to try to put together his father's final hours there. They said he had been killed in the artillery barrage during the final devastating assault on March 26. Taro wrote:

> My father had believed it a shame to have his body discovered by
> his enemy, even after death. So he had previously asked his two

soldiers to come with him. One in front of him, one behind, with shovels in hand. In case of his death, he wanted them to bury his body then and there. It seems shells killed my father and the soldiers, and he was buried at the foot of a tall tree in Chidori Village along the beach near Oskaka mountain. Afterward, General Smith spent a whole day looking for his body to pay his respects accordingly and to perform a burial, but in vain.[2]

On September 27, 1945, Emperor Hirohito posed for a photograph next to the man who would oversee the United States' occupation of his country for the next six years. In the now-famous photo, Hirohito stands stiffly in his formal suit, looking straight ahead. General MacArthur is decidedly nondeferential; towering over the diminutive emperor, he looks casually at the camera, his hands in his back pockets. But together they would rebuild a nonmilitarized Japan. The plan was to avoid the devastation and leadership vacuum that had led to the rise of Hitler in Germany after World War I.

Tojo and five other generals received death sentences at the Tokyo Trial in 1946. They were charged with murder, which covered the attack at Pearl Harbor and the Rape of Nanking.[3] They were all executed by hanging. The bodies were cremated and their ashes dumped into the sea. "A Chamberlain alleges that on hearing the news of Tojo's death, Hirohito went into his office and wept."[4]

Adolf Hitler swallowed cyanide and shot himself in the head in a bunker in Berlin. Benito Mussolini's dead body was strung up on a crane in Milan after being kicked around in the piazza. Hirohito survived them all. He lived to see his country prosper, but like Dickens's Jacob Marley, he walked with the chains he forged in life, the blame he bore for the war that had killed approximately 3 million of his own people.[5] He died of cancer in January 1989 at the age of eighty-seven; by then Japan had the fourth-strongest economy in the world.

In the words of Eugene B. Sledge, who fought on Peleliu and Okinawa:

War is brutish, inglorious, and a terrible waste.

Combat leaves an indelible mark on those who are forced to endure it. The only redeeming factors were my comrades' incredible bravery and their devotion to each other. Marine Corps training taught us to kill efficiently and to try to survive. But it also taught us loyalty to each other—and love. That esprit de corps sustained us.[6]

May the memory of these men sustain us all and remind us of their sacrifice to secure our freedom. May we never forget their bravery and all they gave up so that we might live free. We are forever indebted to these heroes, whose unknown valor we are obligated to know.

Acknowledgments

Two years ago, I met with Eric Nelson at HarperCollins and told him the story of Harry Gray. Of my mother, Betty Bowes MacCallum, sharing his letters with us when we were growing up and of the tears that came to her eyes when she spoke of him. Harry was a smart, caring young man as we see so clearly in his letters. My aunt Anne (Gray) was one of my favorite people growing up. She and Grandpa had a wonderful brother-sister relationship. I had no idea, though, until I wrote this story and had extensive conversations with her daughter, my aunt Nancy (Gray/Shade), how hard her mother's life had been, how brave she was, and how much she had endured. My aunt Nancy is the last of that generation. I am grateful to her for the time we have spent talking about this family history and for her invaluable role in telling this story, and for her never-ending devotion to her brother and his memory. The Bowes-Gray families are an important part of our family legacy, and their strength and faith in God is at the core of what our generation and those to come should admire.

I thank my editor, Eric Nelson, for immediately sensing that this was the book I needed to write and for his steady hand on the tiller in seeing this project through.

It was always my desire to show the heroism of the men who died on the beaches and jagged rocks and ridges for whom no books are written or movies made. Their sacrifice was great, and families all across America have pictures of them in scrapbooks, and an empty space in their family where they should have been. By telling the story of Harry, I want to shine light on all of them as well.

My sincere thanks to my co-author, Ron Drez; his deep military knowledge is the backbone of this book. He tells the story of the origins of the war in the Pacific and the stepping-stones of the battle with clarity and an understanding of the Marines that only a Marine can know. He walked me through Japanese pillboxes in Guam and General Obata's cave. Then to Iwo Jima, where I walked the landing beaches and saw firsthand the airfields and buried tunnels. I climbed Mount Suribachi and looked down just as the flag raisers and Father Suver had on February 23, 1945. Ron took me to the now-grassy area of the Meat Grinder, where Harry was killed. Each year, Ron and the team at Ambrose Military History Tours take veterans of World War II, Korea, and Vietnam back to the battlefields where they fought. It was my honor to travel with some of them to Iwo Jima as well. I thank Ron for his service to our country as a Marine and as a historian.

Dean Laubach, founder and CEO of Corps Connections, has deep ties to the surviving veterans of World War II and is a trusted researcher who provided the links to the men who served alongside Harry Gray. He was always just a text message away as I was writing, often at midnight, and never failed to help me follow up on a lead or track down a detail. Best of all, he was as floored as I was when we found Charlie and then George, and as grateful to them as I was for openly sharing the joyful and painful memories they had locked away for so many years.

My thanks as well to Shayne Jarosz, a Marine, a teacher, and the vice president of Educational Programs for Military Historical Tours. Shayne and his team tirelessly bring our veterans back to the battlefield. On our flight to Iwo Jima were several men in their nineties, many returning for the first time. They came to attend the Reunion of Honor, which brings together Japanese and American veterans and dignitaries to pay tribute to those who lost their lives in that seminal battle. I am grateful for Shayne's guidance, which contributed to the telling of this story as well.

Briana Vota, Fox News producer, and Tommy Chiu, photographer, were with me every step of the way and beyond as they traveled to Saipan and Tinian and then to Hiroshima. Briana conducted some of the interviews, and she and Tommy shared my passion for this story from the beginning. Briana's sensitivity and respect are testaments to her humanity and professionalism. Tommy Chiu is the best, and whether I am in the jungle in Guam or in the crush of a political convention, for all these years, I've felt better at my job when he is by my side.

I am forever grateful to my friend Charlie Gubish for the hours he spent with me and my aunt Nancy. We are proud to know him and grateful for his service and sacrifice for our country, and above all for his friendship to Harry Gray in the final months of his life. I am grateful to the Gubish family, which sent me wonderful pictures of Charlie at Parris Island and in Guam, and recounted their rich family history for generations in Pennsylvania.

My thanks as well to George Colburn. I have had your letters in my files for years, and to hear your voice on the other end of the phone, speaking so warmly about Harry, was beyond words for me and my aunt Nancy. Your description of the friendship the Marines shared on Iwo Jima as being "closer than brothers" could well have been the title of this book. I thank George's daughter, Lisa Mitchell, for sending pictures of her father and of the USS *Rochambeau*, on which Harry, George, Charlie, Warren, and Herman sailed from California to Guam.

My friends Nicki and Bob Errico and Steve and Jennifer Errico led me to Donna Branch, whose mother, Betty, was Dom's sister. Nicki's mother was Dom's sister Rose. Donna opened up the family archives and shared with me wonderful pictures and heartbreaking letters that reveal the tenderness and love of Dom and his family.

I could not have completed this project without the endless hard work of Lori Frye. In addition to assisting in getting *The Story* on the air each day, she also took on the enormous task of coordinating research and edits. Her intelligence, attention to detail, and always-cheerful attitude made her such an asset to the entire process.

My husband, Dan, encouraged this project from the very start, and his understanding through endless nights of typing, as I was buried in documents and files, is just a small part of what makes him the love of my life. Through marriage, raising our three children, and juggling two busy careers, he has been "the wind beneath my wings," as he likes to joke. But the truth is, he is the far better half of our equation and I'm so lucky he's mine.

Our children, Elizabeth, Reed, and Harry, listened every time I gasped at an amazing connection or teared up at a moving letter. They gently nudged me forward and assured me it would turn out well. Someday, when you are parents, you'll know how much you are loved. Harry, I hope this story will stay with you always, as you understand the service to our country and the sacrifice made by your namesake. I have no doubt he would be proud that you are named Harry G. as well.

I'm thankful for the endless support of my dad, Douglas MacCallum. He came with us to meet Charlie Gubish and told me the story that my mom had shared with him about how the Boweses sat silently at dinner the night they learned of Harry's death, unable to speak the words.

Thanks as well to Karyn Shade, my cousin and the niece of Harry Gray, for her wonderful support and encouragement throughout.

To my agent, Olivia Metzger, I thank you for your constant friendship all these years. To David Larabell at CAA, who shared my enthusiasm for this story from the start. My thanks to Hannah Long, whose work with Eric Nelson at HarperCollins was tireless and committed. To my friend Dana Perino, who enthusiastically embraced my request to read my manuscript and offered sage advice. To Suzanne Scott and Jay Wallace and Rupert Murdoch and Lachlan Murdoch, whose support of my work all these years means so much to me.

I thank my executive producer, Brian Tully, and senior producer, Jenna Diaco, and our team at *The Story*. I truly appreciate their dedication to our mission to bring unique stories to our viewers each evening, and their commitment to telling the stories of our World War II heroes. Thanks as well go to Dion Baia, author and audio technician, for sharing the story of what fortunately turned out to be an overproduction of Purple Hearts, in preparation for the invasion of Japan, which mercifully did not happen.

Notes

Introduction: War Plan Orange

1. Matthew Calbraith Perry and Lambert Lilly, *Narrative of the Expedition of an American Squadron to the China Seas and Japan, Performed in the Years 1852, 1853, and 1854, Under the Command of Commodore M. C. Perry, United States Navy* (New York: D. Appleton, 1856), 5.

2. Ronald J. Drez, *Predicting Pearl Harbor: Billy Mitchell and the Path to War* (Gretna, LA: Pelican, 2017), 21.

3. Ibid., 22.

4. Perry and Lilly, *Narrative*, 5, 60.

5. William Elliot Griffis, "Our Navy in Asiatic Waters," *Harper's New Monthly Magazine*, October 1898, 741–42.

6. Perry and Lilly, *Narrative*, 61.

7. Ibid., 261–66.

8. Ibid., 273–76.

9. Ibid., 318.

10. Drez, *Predicting Pearl Harbor*, 35.

11. Ronald H. Spector, *Eagle Against the Sun: The American War with Japan* (New York: Vintage, 1985), 57.

12. Edward S. Miller, *War Plan Orange: The U.S. Strategy to Defeat Japan, 1897–1945* (Annapolis, MD: Naval Institute Press, 1991), 79.

13. Ibid., 79.

14. Ibid., 79.

15. C. V. Glines, "William 'Billy' Mitchell: Air Power Visionary," HistoryNet, quoted from *Aviation History* (September 1997), https://www.history net.com/william-billy-mitchell-an-air-power-visionary.htm.

1: Arlington, Massachusetts, 1938

1. David Darrah, "Chamberlain Rebukes Nazis; They Snub Him," *Chicago Daily Tribune*, December 14, 1938.

2. Edwin Palmer Hoyt, *Warlord: Tojo Against the World* (New York: Cooper Square Press, 2001), 114.

2: Infamy

1. Gray/Bowes family archives.

2. Ronald Drez, interview with Jay Rebstock, March 20, 1999.

3. Diane Diekman, "Battle of Music—USS ARIZONA Band," *Clear Lake Courier*, May 31, 1995, http://dianediekman.com/battle-of-music-uss -arizona-band/.

4. "U.S. Pacific Fleet Band: History," Commander, U.S. Pacific Fleet, https://www.cpf.navy.mil/band/history/.

5. Ibid.

6. Diekman, "Battle of Music."

7. "Brothers Assigned to the USS Arizona," National Park Service, July 2, 2019, https://www.nps.gov/valr/learn/historyculture/brothersassigned arizona.htm.

8. Gray/Bowes family archive.

9. Franklin D. Roosevelt, speech, December 8, 1941, Library of Congress, https://www.loc.gov/resource/afc1986022.afc1986022_ms2201/?st=text.

3: Outrage

1. Blanchard would enlist in the Army in 1943 and be stationed in New Mexico with a chemical warfare unit until he enrolled in the United States Military Academy at West Point in 1944. His three-year career led to three national championships, a 27–0–1 record, and a Heisman Trophy. See "Felix 'Doc' Blanchard, 1945," Heisman Trophy, http:// www.heisman.com/heisman-winners/felix-doc-blanchard/.

2. Ronald Drez, interview with Jay Rebstock, March 20, 1999.

3. Stephen Bower Young, "God, Please Get Us Out of This," *American Heritage*, April 1966, https://www.americanheritage.com/god-please-get -us-out.

4. Ibid.

5. Ibid.

6. Ibid.

7. Ibid.

8. Ibid.

9. Ibid.

10. Ibid.

11. Ibid. In all, 429 sailors from *Oklahoma* died in the attack. Stephen Young and 31 other men were rescued from entombment in the capsized hull of the ship. Many other men were trapped farther below. Tapping sounds were heard for many days, but the men could not be saved.

12. "Attack on Pearl Harbor—1941," Atomic Heritage Foundation, June 18, 2014, https://www.atomicheritage.org/history/attack-pearl-harbor-1941.

13. Herbert P. Bix, *Hirohito and the Making of Modern Japan* (New York: Harper, 2000), 445.

14. Ronald J. Drez, *The War of 1812: Conflict and Deception* (Baton Rouge: Louisiana State University Press, 2014), 183.

15. Bix, *Hirohito*, 188.

16. Ibid.

17. Ibid., 193.

18. Cesare Salmaggi and Alfredo Pallavisini, *2194 Days of War: An Illustrated Chronology of the Second World War* (New York: Milano Gallery Books, 1977), 179, 239.

19. Jack McClure, "Besieged on the Rock," *Military History Quarterly* 14, no. 4 (Summer 2002): 16.

20. Ronald J. Drez, *Predicting Pearl Harbor: Billy Mitchell and the Path to War* (Gretna, LA: Pelican, 2017), 229–30.

21. Edwin P. Hoyt, *Japan's War: The Great Pacific Conflict* (New York: Da Capo, 1986), 198.

4: The Changing Tide

1. Robert Leckie, *Strong Men Armed: The United States Marines Against Japan* (New York: Ballantine, 1962), 3.

2. Quoted in Meredith Hindley, "Christmas at the White House with Winston Churchill," *Humanities* 37, no. 4 (Fall 2016), https://www.neh.gov/humanities/2016/fall/feature/christmas-the-white-house-winston-churchill.

3. Ibid.

4. Henry H. Arnold, *Global Mission* (New York: Harper & Brothers, 1949), 274.

5. Ibid., 289.

6. Carroll V. Glines, *Doolittle's Tokyo Raiders* (New York: D. Van Nostrand, 1964), 12–19.

7. Thirteen of the crews successfully bombed their targets and then crash-landed in China. One crew had to land in Russia and was interned for the rest of the war, and two crews crashed, killing two members, with the remaining eight captured by the Japanese. The Japanese executed three, and a fourth died from harsh treatment.

8. Ronald J. Drez, *Twenty-five Yards of War: The Extraordinary Courage of Ordinary Men in World War II* (New York: Hyperion, 2001), 15.

9. "Yanks Bomb Tokyo," *Santa Ana Register*, April 18, 1942.

10. Ben Wolfgang, "News of Doolittle Raid Leaks Slowly as Roosevelt Keeps Silence," *Washington Times*, April 12, 2012, https://www.washingtontimes.com/news/2012/apr/12/news-doolittle-raid-leaks-slowly-roosevelt-silence/.

11. Ibid.

12. Gray/Bowes family archives.

13. Naval Analysis Division, *The Campaigns of the Pacific War: United States Strategic Bombing Survey (Pacific)* (Washington, DC: U.S. Government Printing Office, 1946), 52.

14. Ibid., 57.

15. Ibid., 52–53.

16. Ibid., 55.

17. "15 Jap Ships Sunk, Lexington Is Lost, in Coral Sea Fight," *The Sun*, June 12, 1942.

18. "13 to 15 Jap Ships Sunk or Damaged; Great Victory in Making, Says Nimitz," *Sunday Telegram*, June 7, 1942.

19. E. B. Potter and Chester W. Nimitz, *The Great Sea War: The Story of Naval Action in World War II* (New York: Bramhall House, 1960), 221–23.

20. "Battle of Midway: Timeline of Significant Events," Navy Live, June 2, 2013, https://navylive.dodlive.mil/2013/06/02/battle-of-midway-timeline-of-significant-events/.

21. Gray/Bowes archives.

5: What Hirohito Knew

1. Quoted in Herbert P. Bix, *Hirohito and the Making of Modern Japan* (New York: Harper, 2000), 450.

2. Edwin P. Hoyt, *Japan's War: The Great Pacific Conflict* (New York: Da Capo, 1986), 35.

3. Lionel Giles, trans., *The Art of War: Sun Tzu* (London: Luzac, 1910), 8.

4. Ibid.

5. Susan Chira, "Hirohito, 124th Emperor of Japan, Is Dead at 87," *New York Times*, January 7, 1989.

6. Hoyt, *Japan's War*, 59.

7. Ibid., 60.

8. Bix, *Hirohito*.

9. Hoyt, *Japan's War*, 66.

10. Ibid.

11. Ibid., 69.

12. Ibid., 74–75.

13. Ibid., 87.

14. Ibid., 111.

15. Ibid., 112–13.

Notes

16. Ibid., 112–30.

17. Ibid., 144.

18. Ibid., 173.

19. Quoted in Hua-ling Hu, *American Goddess at the Rape of Nanking: The Courage of Minnie Vautrin* (Carbondale: Southern Illinois University Press, 2000), 97.

20. Quoted in Iris Chang, *The Rape of Nanking: The Forgotten Holocaust of World War II* (New York: Perseus, 1997), 154.

21. Quoted in Hoyt, *Japan's War*, 172.

22. "Contest to Cut Down a Hundred! Two Second Lieutenants Already Up to Eighty," *Tokyo Nichinichi Shimbun*, November 30, 1937.

23. Masato Kajimoto, "Nanking War Crimes Tribunal," The Nanking Massacre; December 1937, https://thenankingmassacre.org/2015/07/04/nanking-war-crimes-tribunal/.

24. Honda Katsuichi, *The Nanjing Massacre: A Japanese Journalist Confronts Japan's National Shame* (Armonk, NY: M. E. Sharpe, 1999), 123–27.

25. Quoted in ibid., 125–27.

26. Ibid.

27. Quoted in Fei Fei Li, Robert Sabella, and David Liu, eds., *Nanking 1937: Memory and Healing* (Armonk, NY: M. E. Sharpe, 2002), 56.

28. John Gittings, "Japanese Rewrite Guardian History," *The Guardian*, October 4, 2002, https://www.theguardian.com/world/2002/oct/04/artsandhumanities.japan; Harold John Timperley, telegram, intercepted and deciphered by US intelligence on February 1, 1938, published by US National Archives and Records Administration (NARA) in September 1994, https://commons.wikimedia.org/wiki/File:Nanking_telegram_Harold_John_Timperley.gif.

29. Iris Chang, *The Rape of Nanking: The Forgotten Holocaust of World War II* (New York: Penguin, 1997), 40.

30. Bob Tadashi Wakabayashi, "Emperor Hirohito on Localized Aggression in China," *Sino-Japanese Studies* 4, no. 1 (October 1991): http://chinajapan.org/articles/04.1/04.1wakabayashi4-27.pdf, 7.

31. Bix, *Hirohito*, 448.

6: The First Step: Say a Prayer for Your Pal on Guadalcanal

1. Gubish family archives.

2. Cesare Salmaggi and Alfredo Pallavisini, *2194 Days of War: An Illustrated Chronology of the Second World War* (New York: Milano Gallery Books, 1977), 263–67.

3. Ken Burns and Lynn Novick, directors, *The War*, Public Broadcasting System, 2007, episode 2.

4. Quoted in George McMillan, *The Old Breed: A History of the First Marine Division in World War II* (Washington, DC: Infantry Journal Press, 1949), 3.

5. Quoted in ibid., 7.

6. Quoted in ibid., 10.

7. Ibid., 4.

8. "Enlisted Pay Chart 1941–1942," Navy CyberSpace, https://www.navy cs.com/charts/1941-military-pay-chart.html.

9. Quoted in McMillan, *The Old Breed*, 15.

10. John L. Zimmerman, *The Guadalcanal Campaign* (Washington, DC: Historical Section, Headquarters, United States Marine Corps, 1949), 1.

11. Ronald J. Drez, *Twenty-five Yards of War: The Extraordinary Courage of Ordinary Men in World War II* (New York: Hyperion, 2001), 217.

12. Ronald Drez, interview with James Russell, April 21, 1999, Drez archive; Drez, *Twenty-five Yards of War*, 89.

13. "US Forces in New Zealand," New Zealand History, https://nzhistory .govt.nz/war/us-forces-in-new-zealand.

14. McMillan, *The Old Breed*, 16.

15. Quoted in ibid., 18.

16. Ibid.

17. Clemens had left his government post at Aola on the northern coast of Guadalcanal on May 18 when the Japanese occupied the nearby island of Tulagi. Instead of evacuating, he chose to engage in the very dangerous duties of a Coastwatcher hiding in Japanese-occupied territory.

18. Zimmerman, *The Guadalcanal Campaign*, 10.

19. Ibid., 11.

20. James Bowen, "The Battle for Guadalcanal, 7 August 1942–7 February 1943," Pacific War Historical Society, http://www.pacificwar.org.au/Guadalcanal.html.

21. Ibid.

22. Zimmerman, *The Guadalcanal Campaign*, 24.

23. Naval Analysis Division, *The Campaigns of the Pacific War: United States Strategic Bombing Survey (Pacific)* (Washington, DC: U.S. Government Printing Office, 1946), 106.

24. Ibid., 107–9.

25. "Clark Gable in Army as Private," *Boston Post*, August 12, 1942.

26. Scott Harrison, "From the Archives: Clark Gable Joins the Army," *Los Angeles Times*, January 2, 2019, https://www.latimes.com/visuals/photography/la-me-fw-archives-clark-gable-joins-the-army-20190102-htmlstory.html.

27. "Famous Veteran: Clark Gable," Military.com, 2019, https://www.military.com/veteran-jobs/career-advice/military-transition/famous-veteran-clark-gable.html.

28. John Miller, Jr., *Guadalcanal: The First Offensive* (Washington, DC: Center of Military History, United States Army, 1995), 105.

29. Ibid., 109.

30. Ibid.

31. Ibid., 110.

32. Ibid., 149.

33. "Marines Repulse Japs 3 Times; Guadalcanal Troops Plug Hole Cut in Line," *Boston Globe*, October 30, 1942.

34. "Battle of Guadalcanal," Encyclopaedia Britannica, https://www.britannica.com/event/Battle-of-Guadalcanal.

35. David Alan Johnson, "Withdrawal from Guadalcanal: Abandoning the Island of Death," Warfare History Network, November 27, 2018, https://warfarehistorynetwork.com/daily/wwii/abandoning-the-island-of-death/.

36. Ibid.

37. Quoted in ibid.

38. Ken Burns and Lynn Novick, directors, *The War*, Public Broadcasting System, 2007, episode 1.

39. Quoted in Johnson, "Withdrawal from Guadalcanal."

40. Gray family archives; author's interview with Nancy Shade, October 18, 2018.

41. Gray/Bowes family archives.

7: 1943

1. Richard N. Armstrong, "1943: World War II's Forgotten Year of Victory," HistoryNet (originally published January 2013 in *Armchair General*), https://www.historynet.com/1943-world-war-iis-forgotten-year-victory.htm.

2. Robert F. Dorr, "Killing Yamamoto: How America Killed the Japanese Admiral Who Masterminded the Pearl Harbor Attack," *The National Interest*, August 4, 2018, https://nationalinterest.org/blog/buzz/killing-yamamoto-how-america-killed-japanese-admiral-who-masterminded-pearl-harbor-attack.

3. Armstrong, "1943."

4. Quoted in John L. Zimmerman, *The Guadalcanal Campaign* (Washington, DC: Historical Section, Headquarters, United States Marine Corps, 1949), 6–7.

5. Ronald H. Spector, *Eagle Against the Sun: The American War with Japan* (New York: Vintage, 1985), 223–24.

6. Ibid.

7. United States Department of State, *Foreign Relations of the United States: The Conferences at Washington, 1941–1942, and Casablanca, 1943* (Washington, DC: U.S. Government Printing Office, 1968), 781.

8. James R. Stockman, *The Battle for Tarawa* (Washington, DC: Historical Section, Headquarters, United States Marine Corps, 1947), 1.

9. Spector, *Eagle Against the Sun*, 253.

10. Quoted in ibid., 255.

11. Quoted in Robert Leckie, *Strong Men Armed: The United States Marines Against Japan* (New York: Ballantine, 1962), 186.

12. Ibid.

13. Ibid., 185.

14. Quoted in Stockman, *The Battle for Tarawa*, 7.

15. Quoted in Leckie, *Strong Men Armed*, 191.

16. Ronald Drez, interview with James Russell, April 21, 1999.

17. Ronald J. Drez, *Twenty-five Yards of War: The Extraordinary Courage of Ordinary Men in World War II* (New York: Hyperion, 2001), 90–91.

18. Ibid.

19. Ronald Drez, interview with James Russell, April 21, 1999.

20. Quoted in Rafael Steinberg, *Island Fighting* (Alexandria, VA: Time-Life Books, 1978), 106.

21. Drez, *Twenty-five Yards of War*, 100.

22. Stockman, *The Battle for Tarawa*, 15–16.

23. Ronald Drez, interview with James Russell, April 21, 1999.

24. Drez, *Twenty-five Yards of War*, 100.

25. Ibid.

26. Ibid., 101.

27. Stockman, *The Battle for Tarawa*, 16.

28. Quoted in ibid., 16.

29. Quoted in ibid., 17.

30. Drez, *Twenty-five Yards of War*, 102.

31. Michael P. Ryan, "Tarawa," *Marine Corps Gazette* 68, no. 11 (November 1984): 122.

32. "Tarawa: The USMC's First Use of M4 Medium Tanks," The Sherman Tank Site, November 22, 2015, http://www.theshermantank.com/tag/tarawa/.

33. Drez, *Twenty-five Yards of War*, 104.

34. Quoted in Ryan, "Tarawa."

35. Quoted in ibid.

36. Quoted in Joseph H. Alexander, "Tarawa: The Ultimate Opposed Landing," *Marine Corps Gazette* 77, no. 11 (November 1993): 28.

37. Stockman, *The Battle for Tarawa*, 33.

38. Drez, *Twenty-five Yards of War*, 106.

39. Ibid., 107–8.

40. Joseph H. Alexander, "Issue in Doubt," *Marine Corps Gazette* 86, no. 11 (November 2003).

41. Robert Sherrod, "Kerr Eby: Combat Artist," *Leatherneck*, November 1992, 67.

42. Tom Bowman, "WWII Combat Cameraman: 'The Public Had to Know,'" NPR, March 21, 2010, https://www.npr.org/templates/story/story.php?storyId=124631492.

43. Grossi family archives.

8: Cracking the Inner Ring

1. Colburn archives.

2. Edwin P. Hoyt, *Japan's War: The Great Pacific Conflict* (New York: Da Capo, 1986), 335–38.

3. Ronald J. Drez, *Twenty-five Yards of War: The Extraordinary Courage of Ordinary Men in World War II* (New York: Hyperion, 2001), 54.

4. Hoyt, *Japan's War*, 301.

5. Quoted in ibid., 336.

6. Quoted in ibid., 336.

7. Bob Tadashi Wakabayashi, "Emperor Hirohito on Localized Aggression in China" *Sino-Japanese Studies* 4, no. 1 (October 1991), 5, http://chinajapan.org/articles/04.1/04.1wakabayashi4-27.pdf.

8. Ibid., 17.

9. Ibid., 17.

10. Ibid., 17–18.

11. Ronald H. Spector, *Eagle Against the Sun: The American War with Japan* (New York: Vintage, 1985), 269; Naval Analysis Division, *The Campaigns of the Pacific War: United States Strategic Bombing Survey (Pacific)* (Washington, DC: U.S. Government Printing Office, 1946), 193.

12. Quoted in John C. Chapin, *Breaking the Outer Ring: Marine Landings in the Marshall Islands* (Washington, DC: Marine Corps Historical Center, 1994), 4.

13. Ibid., 28.

14. Quoted in ibid., 29.

15. Robert Leckie, *Strong Men Armed: The United States Marines Against Japan* (New York: Ballantine, 1962), 286.

16. Quoted in Chapin, *Breaking the Outer Ring*, 9.

17. Quoted in ibid., 9.

18. Quoted in ibid., 9.

19. Movietone News, "Marshalls Invasion!," 1944; Movietone News, "U.S. Troops Capture Roi-Namur Island in Kwajalein Atoll," 1944, uploaded by CriticalPast, May 23, 2014, https://www.youtube.com/watch?v=mMoNh4wrEtY.

9: Willing to Fight

1. John Stuart Mill, "The Contest in America," *Harper's New Monthly Magazine*, April 1862, 683–84.

2. Ibid., 682.

3. Ibid.

4. Ibid., 683–84.

5. Joseph Warren, "Account of the Battle of Lexington," April 26, 1775, http://www.west-windsor-plainsboro.k12.nj.us/UserFiles/Servers/Server_10640642/File/bugge/Chapter%206/Account%20of%20the%20Battle%20of%20Lexington%201775.pdf.

6. Joseph B. Mitchell, *Decisive Battles of the American Revolution* (n.p., GA: Mockingbird Books, 1962), 27.

7. Gray/Bowes family archives.

8. Sally Rogers, "The Battle of Menotomy," Arlington Historical Society, https://arlingtonhistorical.org/learn/articles/the-battle-of-menotomy/.

9. Gray/Bowes family archives.

10. Ibid.

11. John C. Chapin, *Breaching the Marianas: The Battle for Saipan* (Washington, DC: Marine Corps Historical Center, 1994), 5.

12. Quoted in ibid., 6–7.

13. Robert Leckie, *Strong Men Armed: The United States Marines Against Japan* (New York: Ballantine, 1962), 315.

14. Ronald H. Spector, *Eagle Against the Sun: The American War with Japan* (New York: Vintage, 1985), 277.

15. Ronald J. Drez, *Twenty-five Yards of War: The Extraordinary Courage of Ordinary Men in World War II* (New York: Hyperion, 2001), 218.

16. Ibid., 219.

17. Ronald Drez, interview with Jay Rebstock, March 20, 1999.

18. Ibid.

19. Ibid.

20. Gray/Bowes family archives.

21. Gray/Bowes family archives.

22. Dwight D. Eisenhower, radio address, June 6, 1944, recording at Southwick House, Portsmouth, England, Imperial War Museum.

23. Franklin D. Roosevelt, "Franklin Roosevelt's D-Day Prayer," June 6, 1944, Franklin D. Roosevelt Presidential Library and Museum, http://docs.fdrlibrary.marist.edu/odddayp.html.

24. "Hitler's Sea Wall Breached; Invaders Fighting Way Inland; New Allied Landings Made," *New York Times*, June 7, 1944.

10: D-Day: From Normandy to Saipan

1. A. A. Vandegrift, speech, 1944, Marine Corps Combat Recordings, Library of Congress, Washington, DC.

2. Ibid.

3. Quoted in Edwin P. Hoyt, *Japan's War: The Great Pacific Conflict* (New York: Da Capo, 1986), 333.

4. Quoted in Carl W. Hoffman, *Saipan: The Beginning of the End* (Washington, DC: Historical Branch, Headquarters, United States Marine Corps, 1954), 36.

5. Ronald Drez, interview with James Russell, April 21, 1999.

6. Hoffman, *Saipan*, 60.

7. Ibid., 50.

8. Gordon L. Rottman, *Saipan & Tinian 1944: Piercing the Japanese Empire* (Oxford, UK: Osprey Publishing, 2004), 51.

9. Hoffman, *Saipan*, 54.

10. Rottman, *Saipan & Tinian*, 50.

11. John C. Chapin, *Breaching the Marianas: The Battle for Saipan* (Washington, DC: Marine Corps Historical Center, 1994), 3.

12. Hoffman, *Saipan*, 69.

13. Robert Leckie, *Strong Men Armed: The United States Marines Against Japan* (New York: Ballantine, 1962), 325.

14. Quoted in ibid., 326.

15. Quoted in Naval Analysis Division, *The Campaigns of the Pacific War: United States Strategic Bombing Survey (Pacific)* (Washington, DC: U.S. Government Printing Office, 1946), 233.

16. Quoted in ibid., 233.

17. Leckie, *Strong Men Armed*, 327.

18. Ronald Drez, interview with James Russell, April 21, 1999.

19. Leckie, *Strong Men Armed*, 327.

20. Quoted in ibid., 328; Ronald H. Spector, *Eagle Against the Sun: The American War with Japan* (New York: Vintage, 1985), 304–5.

21. Herbert P. Bix, *Hirohito and the Making of Modern Japan* (New York: Harper, 2000), 476.

22. Ibid., 330.

23. Ibid.

24. Rottman, *Saipan & Tinian*, 58.

25. Leckie, *Strong Men Armed*, 331.

26. Quoted in Chapin, *Breaching the Marianas*, 13.

27. Ibid.; Leckie, *Strong Men Armed*, 331–32.

28. Leckie, *Strong Men Armed*, 332.

29. Chapin, *Breaching the Marianas*, 16.

30. Leckie, *Strong Men Armed*, 328.

31. Naval Analysis Division, *The Campaigns of the Pacific War*, 234.

32. Chapin, *Breaching the Marianas*, 16.

33. Naval Analysis Division, *The Campaigns of the Pacific War*, 214.

34. Ibid.

35. Barrett Tillman, "Coaching the Fighters," *U.S. Naval Institute Proceedings*, January 1980, 41–43.

36. Spector, *Eagle Against the Sun*, 309.

37. Naval Analysis Division, *The Campaigns of the Pacific War*, 214.

38. Spector, *Eagle Against the Sun*, 309–10.

39. Leckie, *Strong Men Armed*, 336–37.

40. Ronald J. Drez, *Twenty-five Yards of War: The Extraordinary Courage of Ordinary Men in World War II* (New York: Hyperion, 2001), 153–54.

41. Naval Analysis Division, *The Campaigns of the Pacific War*, 215.

42. Ibid.

43. Author's interview with Charles Gubish, April 14, 2019.

44. "MCRD Parris Island: About," https://www.mcrdpi.marines.mil/About/; Elmore A. Champie, *A Brief History of the Marine Corps Recruit Depot, Parris Island, South Carolina* (Washington, DC: Department of the Navy, 1962), 10.

45. Author's interview with Charles Gubish, April 14, 2019.

46. Ibid.

47. Gray/Bowes archive.

11: Japan's Doorstep

1. "Historical Snapshot: B-29 Superfortress," Boeing, https://www.boeing.com/history/products/b-29-superfortress.page.

2. Bryan R. Swopes, "18 February 1943," This Day in Aviation, February 18, 2019, https://www.thisdayinaviation.com/18-february-1943/.

3. D. M. Giangreco, *Hell to Pay: Operation Downfall and the Invasion of Japan, 1945–1947* (Annapolis, MD: Naval Institute Press, 2009), 340.

4. Herbert P. Bix, *Hirohito and the Making of Modern Japan* (New York: Harper, 2000), 470.

5. Eric Hammel, *Iwo Jima: Portrait of a Battle: United States Marines at War in the Pacific* (St. Paul, MN: Zenith Press, 2006), 23.

6. Naval Analysis Division, *The Campaigns of the Pacific War: United States Strategic Bombing Survey (Pacific)* (Washington, DC: U.S. Government Printing Office, 1946), 212.

7. Quoted in Edwin P. Hoyt, *Japan's War: The Great Pacific Conflict* (New York: Da Capo, 1986), 428.

8. Quoted in ibid., 428.

9. Shannon J. Murphy, "WWII: Oral War Histories of the Chamoru People," Guampedia, October 13, 2019, https://www.guampedia.com /wwii-oral-war-histories-of-the-chamorro-people/.

10. Cyril J. O'Brien, *Liberation: Marines in the Recapture of Guam* (Washington, DC: History and Museums Division, Headquarters, United States Marine Corps, 1994), 1.

11. Quoted in ibid., 8.

12. Ronald H. Spector, *Eagle Against the Sun: The American War with Japan* (New York: Vintage, 1985), 320.

13. O'Brien, *Liberation*, 42–43.

14. Memorial standing in the South Pacific Memorial Park in Yigo, Guam.

15. Richard Harwood, *A Close Encounter: The Marine Landing at Tinian* (Washington, DC: History and Museums Division, Headquarters, United States Marine Corps, 1994), 5.

16. Ronald Drez, interview with James Russell, April 21, 1999.

17. Quoted in Carl W. Hoffman, *The Seizure of Tinian* (Washington, DC: Historical Division, Headquarters, United States Marine Corps, 1951), https://www.usmcu.edu/Portals/218/Hoffman_The%20Seizure%20 of%20Tinian.pdf, 20.

18. Ibid., 3.

19. Spector, *Eagle Against the Sun*, 318.

20. Quoted in Hoffman, *The Seizure of Tinian*, 20.

21. Norman V. Cooper, "The Military Career of Lieutenant General Holland M. Smith," PhD dissertation, University of Alabama, 1974, 365–66.

22. Hoffman, *The Seizure of Tinian*, 23–24.

23. Quoted in ibid., 12.

24. Ibid., 15.

25. Commander in Chief, U.S. Pacific Fleet and Pacific Ocean Areas, "Operations in the Pacific Ocean Areas During the Month of July 1944," National Archives and Records Administration, EO 13526, declassified December 31, 2012.

26. Ibid., 43–44.

27. Ibid., 59.

28. Harwood, *A Close Encounter*, 6.

29. Ibid., 6–7.

30. Ibid., 13–14.

31. Hoffman, *The Seizure of Tinian*, 63.

32. Ibid.

33. Ibid., 64.

34. Quoted in ibid., 65.

35. Robert Sherrod, "The Nature of the Enemy," *Time*, August 7, 1944.

36. Quoted in "Turning Women into Weapons: Japan's Women, the Battle of Saipan, and the 'Nature of the Pacific War,'" in *Women and War in the 20th Century, Enlisted with or without Consent*, ed. Nicole A. Dombrowski (New York: Garland Press, 1999), 240–61.

37. Hoffman, *The Seizure of Tinian*, iii.

38. "Tinian," GlobalSecurity.org, https://www.globalsecurity.org/military/facility/tinian.htm.

39. Gray/Bowes family archives.

40. *Lockport Union-Sun & Journal*, May 4, 1999.

41. Grossi family archives.

12: "A Ghastly Relentlessness"

1. Ernie Pyle, *Ernie's War: The Best of Ernie Pyle's World War II Dispatches* (New York: Touchstone, 1986), 332.

2. Quoted in Ronald J. Drez, *Predicting Pearl Harbor: Billy Mitchell and the Path to War* (Gretna, LA: Pelican, 2017), 233.

3. Quoted in ibid., 56.

4. Quoted in ibid., 57.

5. Edward S. Miller, *War Plan Orange: The U.S. Strategy to Defeat Japan, 1897–1945* (Annapolis, MD: Naval Institute Press, 1991), 364.

6. Ibid.

7. Robert Leckie, *Strong Men Armed: The United States Marines Against Japan* (New York: Ballantine, 1962), 399–400.

8. Quoted in William Manchester, *American Caesar: Douglas MacArthur* (Boston: Little, Brown, 1978), 369.

9. Quoted in George McMillan, *The Old Breed: A History of the First Marine Division in World War II* (Washington, DC: Infantry Journal Press, 1949), 269.

10. Quoted in ibid., 270.

11. Frank Hough, *The Assault on Peleliu* (Nashville: Battery Press, 1990), 16–17.

12. Leckie, *Strong Men Armed*, 398.

13. Quoted in Hough, *Assault on Peleliu*, 192–93.

14. Quoted in ibid., 192–93.

15. Quoted in ibid., 192–93.

16. Leckie, *Strong Men Armed*, 396.

17. Hough, *Assault on Peleliu*, 17.

18. Gordon D. Gayle, *Bloody Beaches: The Marines at Peleliu* (Washington, DC: Marine Corps Historical Center, 1996), 8.

19. Ibid., 9.

20. Ibid.

21. Ibid., 10.

22. Leckie, *Strong Men Armed*, 401.

23. Hough, *Assault on Peleliu*, chapter 3, note 6.

24. Ibid., chapter 3, note 5.

25. Leckie, *Strong Men Armed*, 405.

26. Hough, *Assault on Peleliu*, 51.

27. Gayle, *Bloody Beaches*, 18; Hough, *Assault on Peleliu*, 57.

28. Quoted in Hough, *Assault on Peleliu*, 77.

29. Ibid., 78.

30. Quoted in Leckie, *Strong Men Armed*, 412.

31. Quoted in Hough, *Assault on Peleliu*, chapter 4, note 45.

32. Ibid., 88.

33. Ibid., 103.

34. Bill O'Reilly and Martin Dugard, *Killing the Rising Sun: How America Vanquished World War II Japan* (New York: Henry Holt, 2016), 33.

35. Hough, *Assault on Peleliu*, chapter 8, note 13.

36. Ibid., 183; "Battle of Peleliu," Howling Pixel, https://howlingpixel.com /i-en/Battle_of_Peleliu.

37. Leckie, *Strong Men Armed*, 427.

13: "An Island of Sulphur: No Water, No Sparrow, and No Swallow"

1. Yoshitaka Horie, "Explanation of Japanese Defense Plan and Battle of Iwo Jima," 1946, quoted in Whitman S. Bartley, *Iwo Jima: Amphibious Epic* (Washington, DC: Historical Branch, G-3 Division, Headquarters, United States Marine Corps, 1954), https://upload.wikimedia.org /wikipedia/commons/2/2e/Iwo_Jima-_Amphibious_Epic.pdf, 5.

2. Quoted in Bartley, *Iwo Jima*, 6.

3. Quoted in Yoshitaka Horie, "Fighting Spirit—Iwo Jima" (memoir, manuscript copy, 1965, Rebstock/Drez archives), 34.

4. Quoted in Bartley, *Iwo Jima*, 16.

5. Horie, "Fighting Spirit," 37.

6. Naval Analysis Division, *The Campaigns of the Pacific War: United States Strategic Bombing Survey (Pacific)* (Washington, DC: U.S. Government Printing Office, 1946), 315.

7. Quoted in ibid., 281.

8. Ibid., 317.

9. Horie, "Fighting Spirit," 39.

10. Viktor Suvorov, *The Chief Culprit: Stalin's Grand Design to Start World War II* (Annapolis, MD: Naval Institute Press, 2008); "Summary and Lessons," *Military History*, http://militera.lib.ru/h/kondratyev_v/09.html.

11. Horie, "Fighting Spirit," 40.

12. Joseph H. Alexander, *Closing In: Marines in the Seizure of Iwo Jima* (Washington, DC: History and Museums Division, Headquarters, United States Marine Corps, 1994), 3.

13. Quoted in Robert Leckie, *The Battle for Iwo Jima* (New York: Simon & Schuster, 2004), 11.

14. Tadamichi Kuribayashi, *"Gyokusai Sōshikikan" no etegami* (Picture Letters from Commander in Chief) (in Japanese), ed. Taro Kuribayashi (Tokyo: Shogakukan, 2002), quoted in Leckie, *The Battle for Iwo Jima*, 36.

15. Horie, "Fighting Spirit," 47.

16. Ibid., 63.

17. Ibid., 75.

18. Ibid., 77.

19. Ibid.

20. Quoted in ibid., 83.

21. Quoted in ibid., 83.

22. Ronald H. Spector, *Eagle Against the Sun: The American War with Japan* (New York: Vintage, 1985), 495.

23. Alexander, *Closing In*, 5.

24. Horie, "Fighting Spirit," 76.

25. Alexander, *Closing In*, 5.

26. Ibid., 3.

27. Bartley, *Iwo Jima*, 30.

28. Author's interview with George Colburn, October 10, 2019.

29. Gray/Bowes archives.

30. Author's interview with Charles Gubish, April 17, 2019.

31. Ibid.

32. Ibid.

33. Richard F. Newcomb, *Iwo Jima: The Dramatic Account of the Epic Battle That Turned the Tide of World War II* (New York: Signet Books, 1965), 40.

34. Ronald J. Drez, *Twenty-five Yards of War: The Extraordinary Courage of Ordinary Men in World War II* (New York: Hyperion, 2001), 228.

35. Ronald Drez, interview with Jay Rebstock, March 20, 1999.

36. Ibid.

37. John C. Chapin, *The 4th Marine Division in World War II* (Washington, DC: History and Museums Division, Headquarters, United States Marine Corps, 1974), 43–44.

38. G. B. Erskine, "3d Marine Division Reinforced, Iwo Jima Action Report, 31 October 1944–16 March 1945," April 30, 1945, https://www.scribd.com/document/110606038/Iwo-Jima-Campaign-1945, 1.

39. Newcomb, *Iwo Jima*, 41.

40. Erskine, "3d Marine Division Reinforced, Iwo Jima Action Report," 3.

14: "Hell with the Fire Out"

1. Richard F. Newcomb, *Iwo Jima: The Dramatic Account of the Epic Battle That Turned the Tide of World War II* (New York: Signet Books, 1965), 63.

2. Whitman S. Bartley, *Iwo Jima: Amphibious Epic* (Washington, DC: Historical Branch, G-3 Division, Headquarters, U.S. Marine Corps, 1954), https://upload.wikimedia.org/wikipedia/commons/2/2e/Iwo_Jima-_Amphibious_Epic.pdf, 39.

3. Quoted in Newcomb, *Iwo Jima*, 57.

4. Ibid., 58.

5. Bartley, *Iwo Jima*, 40.

6. Newcomb, *Iwo Jima*, 70.

7. Quoted in Robert Leckie, *Strong Men Armed: The United States Marines Against Japan* (New York: Ballantine, 1962), 441.

8. Bartley, *Iwo Jima*, 35.

9. Newcomb, *Iwo Jima*, 68.

10. Bartley, *Iwo Jima*, 44.

11. Newcomb, *Iwo Jima*, 68.

12. "World War II Medal of Honor Recipients (F–J): Herring, Rufus G.," https://ibiblio.org/hyperwar/MoH_F-J.html#herring.

13. Bartley, *Iwo Jima*, 45, n. 113.

14. Ibid., 47.

15. "Iwo Jima," SFR Productions, Freund Enterprises, 2012, https://www.youtube.com/watch?time_continue=2&v=fwmFBQZq9Z0.

16. Quoted in Newcomb, *Iwo Jima*, 29.

17. Author's interview with Dean Laubach, nephew of Colonel Swindler, Corps Connections, April 2019.

18. Newcomb, *Iwo Jima*, 37.

19. Ronald J. Drez, *Twenty-five Yards of War: The Extraordinary Courage of Ordinary Men in World War II* (New York: Hyperion, 2001), 230.

20. Ibid., 230–31.

21. Ibid., 231.

22. Bartley, *Iwo Jima*, 51.

23. Quoted in Drez, *Twenty-five Yards of War*, 232.

24. Ibid.

25. Ibid.

26. Ibid., 232–33.

27. Bartley, *Iwo Jima*, 53.

28. Ronald Drez, interview with Jay Rebstock, March 20, 1999.

29. Bartley, *Iwo Jima*, 53.

30. Quoted in Bill D. Ross, *Iwo Jima: Legacy of Valor* (New York: Vintage Books, 1986), 67.

31. Quoted in Newcomb, *Iwo Jima*, 103–4.

32. Drez, *Twenty-five Yards of War*, 236.

33. Charles W. Tatum, *Iwo Jima: Red Blood, Black Sand: Pacific Apocalypse* (Stockton, CA: Charles W. Tatum Publications, 2002), 156–57; Ronald Drez, interview with Charles Tatum, 2006.

34. Tatum, *Iwo Jima*, 157–58.

35. Ibid., 159.

36. J. D. Simkins, "Valor Friday: The Legend of John Basilone," *Marine Corps Times*, June 29, 2018, https://www.marinecorpstimes.com/news/your-army/2018/06/29/valor-friday-the-legend-of-john-basilone/.

Notes

37. Larry Smith, *Iwo Jima: World War II Veterans Remember the Greatest Battle of the Pacific* (New York: W. W. Norton, 2009), 4.

38. Carl W. Proehl, *The Fourth Marine Division in World War II* (Washington, DC: Infantry Journal Press, 1946), 152–53.

39. Ibid., 152.

40. Ibid., 152.

41. Quoted in Raymond Henri, *Iwo Jima: Springboard to Final Victory* (New York: U.S. Camera Publishing Corporation, 1945), 30.

42. G. B. Erskine, "3d Marine Division Reinforced, Iwo Jima Action Report, 31 October 1944–16 March 1945," April 30, 1945, https://www.scribd.com/document/110606038/Iwo-Jima-Campaign-1945, 1.

43. Ibid., 2.

44. Ibid.

45. Ibid., 3.

46. Joseph H. Alexander, "Iwo Jima: Hell with the Fire Out," *Leatherneck* 78, no. 2 (February 1995): 17–18.

47. Tatum, *Iwo Jima*, 79.

48. Ross, *Iwo Jima*, 140.

49. Author's interview with Hershel Williams, August 14, 2019.

50. Ibid.

51. Ibid.

52. "Williams, Hershel Woodrow," Congressional Medal of Honor Society, http://www.cmohs.org/recipient-detail/3066/williams-hershel-woodrow.php.

53. Erskine, "3d Marine Division Reinforced, Iwo Jima Action Report," 5–6.

54. Newcomb, *Iwo Jima*, 119.

55. Quoted in Joseph H. Alexander, *Closing In: Marines in the Seizure of Iwo Jima* (Washington, DC: History and Museums Division, Headquarters, United States Marine Corps, 1994), 24.

56. Quoted in Yoshitaka Horie, "Fighting Spirit—Iwo Jima" (memoir, manuscript copy, 1965, Rebstock/Drez archives), 93.

57. Quoted in ibid., 93.

58. Newcomb, *Iwo Jima*, 122.

59. Donald R. McClarey, "February 23, 1945: The Mass on Suribachi," The American Catholic, February 23, 2015, https://www.the-american -catholic.com/2015/02/23/the-mass-on-mount-suribachi-2/.

60. Tatum, *Iwo Jima*, 200.

61. Drez, *Twenty-five Yards of War*, 240.

62. Newcomb, *Iwo Jima*, 123.

63. Ibid.

64. Quoted in ibid., 124.

65. Quoted in Alexander, *Closing In*, 26.

66. Ibid., 27.

67. The Marine in the Rosenthal photo previously thought to be Private First Class Rene Gagnon was determined to be Corporal Harold "Pie" Keller. Confirmed by the U.S. Marine Corps on October 16, 2019.

68. For more than seventy years, Navy Corpsman John Bradley was misidentified as one of the famous flag raisers on Iwo Jima. In 2014, two amateur history buffs, Eric Krelle and Stephen Foley, forensically examined all the photos taken atop Mount Suribachi that day and proved that although Bradley was in the first flag raising, he was not in the second. Private Harold Schultz was the sixth Marine in Joe Rosenthal's famous photograph. See Matthew Hansen, "New Mystery Arises from Iconic Iwo Jima Image," *Omaha World Herald*, November 23, 2014, https://dataomaha.com/media/news/2014/iwo -jima/.

69. Winston Churchill, speech at the Lord Mayor's Luncheon, Mansion House, London, November 10, 1942, The Churchill Society, http:// www.churchill-society-london.org.uk/EndoBegn.html.

70. McClarey, "February 23, 1945: The Mass on Suribachi."

15: The Badlands

1. Author's interview with George Colburn, September 25, 2019.

2. G. B. Erskine, "3d Marine Division Reinforced, Iwo Jima Action Report, 31 October 1944–16 March 1945," April 30, 1945, https://www .scribd.com/document/110606038/Iwo-Jima-Campaign-1945, 3.

Notes

3. Whitman S. Bartley, *Iwo Jima: Amphibious Epic* (Washington, DC: Historical Branch, G-3 Division, Headquarters, U.S. Marine Corps, 1954), https://upload.wikimedia.org/wikipedia/commons/2/2e/Iwo_Jima-_Amphibious_Epic.pdf, 94.

4. Bill D. Ross, *Iwo Jima: Legacy of Valor* (New York: Vintage Books, 1986), 163.

5. Quoted in Raymond Henri, *Iwo Jima: Springboard to Final Victory* (New York: U.S. Camera Publishing Corporation, 1945), 78.

6. Erskine, "3d Marine Division Reinforced, Iwo Jima Action Report," 5.

7. Quoted in Ross, *Iwo Jima*, 161.

8. Ibid., 164.

9. Erskine, "3d Marine Division Reinforced, Iwo Jima Action Report," 3.

10. Ibid.

11. Ibid., 33.

12. Quoted in Richard F. Newcomb, *Iwo Jima: The Dramatic Account of the Epic Battle That Turned the Tide of World War II* (New York: Signet Books, 1965), 132.

13. Ibid., 132.

14. Erskine, "3d Marine Division Reinforced, Iwo Jima Action Report," 4.

15. Ross, *Iwo Jima*, 165.

16. Quoted in ibid., 165.

17. Erskine, "3d Marine Division Reinforced, Iwo Jima Action Report," 4.

18. Quoted in Ross, *Iwo Jima*, 166.

19. "Grossi, Dominick J.," Traces of War, https://www.tracesofwar.com/persons/31649/Grossi-Dominick-J.htm?c=aw.

20. Ross, *Iwo Jima*, 168.

21. U.S. Marine Corps, *Third Marine Division's Two Score and Ten History* (Paducah, KY: Turner Publishing Company, 1992), 133.

22. Quoted in Ross, *Iwo Jima*, 165.

23. Ibid., 98.

24. "Archambault, Raoul J.," Traces of War, https://www.tracesofwar.com/persons/30409/Archambault-Raoul-J.htm.

25. Erskine, "3d Marine Division Reinforced, Iwo Jima Action Report," 6–7.

26. Ross, *Iwo Jima*, 169.

27. Ibid.

28. Author's interview with Charles Gubish, April 17, 2019.

29. Quoted in Joseph H. Alexander, *Closing In: Marines in the Seizure of Iwo Jima* (Washington, DC: History and Museums Division, Headquarters, United States Marine Corps, 1994), 31.

30. Quoted in ibid., 31.

31. Quoted in Ronald J. Drez, *Twenty-five Yards of War: The Extraordinary Courage of Ordinary Men in World War II* (New York: Hyperion, 2001), 240.

32. Quoted in ibid., 240.

33. Ibid., 242.

34. Ibid.

35. Ibid.

36. Ibid., 244.

37. Ronald Drez, interview with Jay Rebstock, March 20, 1999.

38. Ross, *Iwo Jima*, 169.

39. Author's interview with George Colburn, September 25, 2019.

40. Author's archives.

41. Warren Moscow, "Blood Boats Went with Iwo Invaders," *New York Times*, February 24, 1945.

42. Quoted in Newcomb, *Iwo Jima*, 226.

43. Bartley, *Iwo Jima*, Map V.

44. See blue line of advance on ibid.

45. See green line of advance of February 27 on ibid.

46. Quoted in Ross, *Iwo Jima*, 219.

47. Author's interview with George Colburn, September 25, 2019.

48. Division intelligence report, quoted in Bartley, *Iwo Jima*, 150.

49. Bartley, *Iwo Jima*, Map V.

50. Quoted in Carl W. Proehl, *The Fourth Marine Division in World War II* (Washington, DC: Infantry Journal Press, 1946), 156.

51. "Jacobson, Douglas," Congressional Medal of Honor Recipients, https://themedalofhonor.com/medal-of-honor-recipients/recipients/jacobson-douglas-world-war-two.

52. Quoted in Bartley, *Iwo Jima*, 154.

53. Bartley, *Iwo Jima*, Map XVI.

54. Ibid., 177.

55. Quoted in ibid., 122.

56. Ibid.

57. John C. Chapin, *The Fifth Marine Division in World War II* (Washington, DC: Historical Division, Headquarters, United States Marine Corps, 1945), https://archive.org/details/fifthmarinedivis00chap/page/14, 15.

58. Drez, *Twenty-five Yards of War*, 248.

59. Alexander, *Closing In*, 47.

60. Ronald Drez, interview with Jay Rebstock, March 20, 1999.

61. Ibid.

62. Bartley, *Iwo Jima*, 178.

63. Ibid.; see also Map XVII.

64. Author's interview with George Colburn, September 25, 2019.

65. Author's interview with Charlie Gubish, April 17, 2019.

66. John J. Foster, *History of the Eighth Field Depot and Eighth Service Regiment, 1944–1946* (Lebanon, PA: 1989), 39.

67. Archibald Mosley, interview with Dean Laubach, Corps Connections, October 2015.

68. Alexander, *Closing In*, 46–47.

69. Quoted in Larry Smith, *Iwo Jima: World War II Veterans Remember the Greatest Battle of the Pacific* (New York: W. W. Norton, 2009), 316.

70. H. Avery Chenoweth, *Semper Fi: The Definitive Illustrated History of the U.S. Marines* (New York: Main Street, 2005), 368.

71. "The Atomic Bombings of Hiroshima and Nagasaki: Total Casualties," Atomic Archive, http://www.atomicarchive.com/Docs/MED/med_chp10.shtml.

72. Edwin P. Hoyt, *Japan's War: The Great Pacific Conflict* (New York: Da Capo, 1986), 407.

73. Quoted in Herbert P. Bix, *Hirohito and the Making of Modern Japan* (New York: Harper, 2000), 526.

74. Quoted in ibid., 527.

Epilogue

1. Quoted in David Venditta, "70 Years Later, Marine Veteran, 96, Recalls Battle for Iwo Jima," *The Morning Call*, February 21, 2015, https://www.mcall.com/news/local/mc-iwo-jima-anniversary-gubish -20150221-story.html.

2. Derrick Wright, *The Battle for Iwo Jima, 1945* (Stroud, Gloucestershire, UK: Sutton Publishing, 2007), 45.

3. Herbert P. Bix, *Hirohito and the Making of Modern Japan* (New York: Harper, 2000), 608.

4. Quoted in ibid., 610.

5. "2019 World Population by Country," World Population Review, http:// worldpopulationreview.com/.

6. Quoted in Donald R. McClarey, "February 23, 1945: The Mass on Suribachi," The American Catholic, February 23, 2015, https://www .the-american-catholic.com/2015/02/23/the-mass-on-mount-suri bachi-2/.

About the Author

MARTHA MACCALLUM is anchor and executive editor of *The Story with Martha MacCallum*, seen Monday through Friday on the Fox News Channel. She is also coanchor of Fox News election coverage, moderating town halls and debates with the presidential candidates alongside Bret Baier and Chris Wallace. Prior to *The Story*, MacCallum anchored *The First 100 Days*, reporting nightly on the first months of the Trump administration and interviewing the president on his hundredth day in office. She has covered presidential and midterm elections for Fox News since 2004 and has done extensive reporting from the field on primary races across the country. MacCallum has reported from Normandy, France, during the 75th Anniversary of D-Day commemoration and from Iwo Jima's Reunion of Honor ceremony. Prior to working at Fox News, MacCallum was an award-winning reporter for CNBC and NBC News, covering homeland security and the US economy, and a reporter/producer for Wall Street Journal Television.

RONALD J. DREZ is an award-winning and bestselling author of ten books, among them his most recent works *The War of 1812* and *Predicting Pearl Harbor: Billy Mitchell and the Path to War*. He is a former Captain of Marines and a decorated combat veteran of the Vietnam War.